I0646404

Granta

new series: volume one, number two

Editors Bill Buford and Pete de Bolla
Assistant Editor Cathryn Gwynn
Contributing Editor Michael Hoffman
EditorialCorrespondence Box 666, King's College
Cambridge CB2 1ST.
All manuscripts are welcome
but must be accompanied by a
stamped addressed envelope or they
cannot be returned.
Subscriptions For individuals, £5.50 for one year; for
institutions, £7.00 for one year. For
foreign subscriptions add £2.00 per
year for postage. Individual issues:
£1.50.
Granta is typeset by A.G.P.
Typesetting Ltd., P.O.81 London S.W.6
Tel: 01-731 3570

American Subscriptions
and Business
Communications Jonathan Levi, 25 Claremont Ave.,
New York, N.Y. 10029. Single
copies: $4.00. Subscriptions: $13.00
and $16.50.
Special thanks to Eric Burns, Elaine Feinstein, and Tony
Tanner.
Advertising assistance Leslie Taylor Rushworth

TONY TANNER
A Preface to A.H.

George Steiner has long been preoccupied with two basic paradoxes or problems. How could one of the high moments of European culture (particularly turn-of-the-century Vienna) produce, or allow to develop, the utter barbarism of Nazism? And the other problem is simply the uncontrollable ambiguity of language itself. As Jane Austen put it with characteristic economy, it is rather worrying to realize that people can use words to say a thing is white when in fact it is black. An awareness of the ambiguous uses to which language may be put is as old as literature—Clytemnestra's 'welcome' to Agamemnon, for instance. And no-one was more aware of the possible abuses of rhetoric of all kinds than Plato. But with Hitler the problem took on a new dimension, as it were. The problem, we may simply say, is that speech is in some sense a divine gift—the gift of tongues. Yet it can be transformed into the diabolical eloquence of a Hitler. Thus to take two statements uttered by characters in Steiner's novella, the first by Lieber:

> As it is written in the learned Nathaniel of Mainz: there shall come upon the earth in the time of night a man surpassing eloquent. All that is God's, hallowed be His name, must have its counterpart, its backside of evil and negation. So it is with the Word, with the gift of speech that is the glory of man and distinguishes him everlastingly from the silence or animal noises of creation. When he made the Word, God made possible also its contrary. Silence is not the contrary of the Word but its guardian. No, He created on the night-side a lan-

guage a speech for hell. Whose words mean hatred and
vomit of life....There shall come a man whose mouth
shall be as a furnace and whose tongue as a sword
laying waste. He will know the grammar of hell
and teach it to others.

Another character, Gideon, in a feverish delirium, voices a kind of dis-
trust of language which must go along with the feeling that—as a Jew—
he is one of the people of the Word:

We are the people of the word. That's what they call us
isn't it? Well, listen to me....He [Hitler] is the master of
the word....Why there is nothing he could not do with
words. They danced for him. They set fire to stone.
They made men drunk or battered them to death. We
talk too much, Elie. For five thousand years we've
talked too much. Talked ourselves and the world half to
death. That's why he turned on us, that's why he could
tear the guts out of us. Because he too is a man who
made words louder than life. He and us. He and Lieber.
O such a need of each other. A dog and his puke.

This is not to say that the novella endorses any one particular statement about language, but it opens up the problems of the languages of
politics, racism, genocide, religious intensity, law, retribution, ethics,
and aesthetics in a vivid and often disturbing way.
    The novella itself is based fairly obviously—and no doubt deli-
berately—on Conrad's *The Heart of Darkness*, and it both is, and explores,
what might be said to be an ultimate Jewish fantasy—the capturing alive
of Adolph Hitler. It is also an attempt to explore how and why a civilization can collapse into savagery. It goes into the ultimately unexplorable
problem of 'the camps', not only the evil that they represent but also what
surviving Jews—indeed all the survivors—may make, have to make, cannot make, of that unbearable, unforgettable memory. In the novella, a
small band of Jews have dedicated themselves to the single cause of a
perhaps monomaniacal man, Emmanual Lieber. This is to track down
Hitler. Marlow finds his Kurtz, and, after a somewhat Conradian search
into the impenetrable depths of South America, this little band of Jews
ultimately find Adolf Hitler—the figure who in himself was the heart of
the heart of the darkness. He is indeed brought back to face 'justice'—
one of the many problematical areas touched on in the novella. Are there
bits of history, countries, individuals, which are somehow outside the
law? As one character argues—either justice, the law, is an 'ontological

totality' or it is an 'ephemeral fiat in this or that corner of history....If there is a law for the drunken homicide down the street there must be one for Attila.'

And Hitler. Though—and Steiner is well aware of this—confronted with the figure of Hitler, the law, like language itself, seems tempted to give up. And in many ways the most extraordinary section of the novella is the final speech by Hitler in his own defence. As it happens, I am not particularly taken by Steiner's suggestion—made elsewhere—that anti-Semitism may in part be explained by the fact that the Jews invented conscience, with its attendant travails. On this point I find Sartre, for example, more convincing. However, in this novella he gives the theory in an extreme form to Hitler. It is in fact hard to assess that amazing last speech—which in some ways is mad yet in other ways seems to come close to some very provocative and disturbing ideas. I am not saying that Steiner has given the devil all the best lines, but they are certainly not the worst ones—any more than some of the opinions of the Jewish hunters are far from unequivocal. From that point of view the novella maintains a really quite disturbing ambiguity. And Hitler's last words—'The *Reich* begat Israel'—resonate beyond the framework of this fiction.

However, we should remember that it is a work of fiction and in no sense a disguised tract or polemic. As such it does not load the dice, though the very nature of the material is, inevitably heavily loaded. It is the load which had to be taken on by the mid-twentieth century conscience, and Steiner's obsessed figures—most of them are obsessed in one way or another—make us aware of many of the difficulties involved in taking on that load, along with the very understandable temptation to junk such an unspeakable load altogether. But finally it is, I think, a fiction centering on the ambiguity of the word. Words can move mountains, but also Nuremberg rallies. To the extent that the Jews feel themselves to be in some special way the people of the Word, these ambiguities of the word may be felt by them with special force. But they are ambiguities which involve us all—as do the many problems raised by George Steiner's compact and powerful novella.

Note

In its entirety, George Steiner's *The Portage to San Cristobal of A.H.* is about one third longer than the text we present here. The novella has seventeen chapters of varying lengths; we do not print six of those chapters (in the original, numbers 2, 4, 5, 8, 11 and 12), and take only part from three others (in the original, numbers 9, 13 and 16).

What we have retained could easily be described as the central sustaining narrative of the novella. With the author, we have administered the cuts with care to make sure that the reader's understanding of the text is not hampered at any point. Partly because the text we present will seem to stand by itself, however, we must stress that significant passages *have been* cut — passages which serve, in many ways, to refract the essential experience depicted in the central narrative. *The Portage to San Cristobal of A.H.* is quite properly and effectively a fiction, a 'story' in a very conventional sense, about Adolf Hitler. It is also quite properly and effectively about the 'experience' of Hitler, the world *created* by his madness: the novella presents a multiplicity of vantage places — English, German, French, American, Jewish, gentile, and that of the third world — from which to view the consequences of Hitler's determination to exterminate the Jews. The main narrative, then, is really only a centre from which several other complementing lines of thought — fan-like — open out. We are, we regret, able to print only this 'centre' and able only to suggest the other lines of thought.

The Portage to San Cristobal of A.H. was first printed in the United States by the *Kenyon Review*.

GEORGE STEINER
The Portage to San Cristobal of A. H.

— You.

The very old man chewed his lip.

— You. Is it really? Shema. In God's name. Look at you. Look at you now. You. The one out of hell.

And saying it the young man, almost a boy, tightened his calves and tried to drive his worn boots into the ground. To be implacable. But the voice shook inside him.

— It is you. Isn't it. We have you. We have you. Simeon is sending the signal. Everyone will know. The whole world. But not yet. We have to get you out of here. Ours. You are ours. You know that don't you. The living God. Into our hands. He delivered you into our hands. And it came to pass. You.

And the boy forced himself to laugh, but couldn't hear the echo. The still air lay between them, the rain shaking out of its hot, still folds.

— Silent now? Whose voice. They say your voice could.

The boy had never heard it.

— Burn cities. They say that when you spoke. Leaves turning to ash and men weeping. They say that women, just to hear your voice, that women.

He stopped. The last woman they had seen was on the river bank at Jiaro. Endless marches back. With no teeth. Squatting by the green pool and not waving to them.

— Would tear their clothes off, just to hear your voice.

And now the rage came. At last.

— Why don't you speak? Why don't you answer me? They'll make you speak. They'll tear it out of you. Ours. We have you. Thirty years hunting. Kaplan dead. And Weiss and Amsel. Oh you'll talk. Till we have the skin off you. The soulskin.

The boy was shouting now. Sucking at the air and shouting. The very old man looked up and blinked.

— Ich?

●

Simeon bit at his broken nail and tasted oil. The anatomy of transistors and close threaded wires lay before him intricately hurt. The delicate beast corroded by the incessant damp, until its voice had dimmed to an unsteady croak under the larger voice of the rain. He braided the wire around the bent screw, but where the insulation was gone the metal itself seemed to sweat under a fine web of decay. Bending close over the set he could see the spreading life of the fungus. He had cleaned the circuit-boards a dozen times over. Now the soldering came apart in his sweating fingers. He turned his shoulders slightly to get out of Benasseraf's near shadow.

— Did you get through?

— I think so. I'm not sure. There's almost no juice. Look at the wiring here. Rotten all the way through.

— But you think they picked up the signal?

— I hope so. I can't be certain. Look for yourself. Turn the crank

Simeon bent close listening for the voice of the broken thing.

— and nothing happens. Dead. I don't think I can patch it again. But something did get through. It must have. Part of it at least.

— If I forget thee O Jerusalem.

The words sang under Benasseraf's breath.

— They *must* have heard us. If we're to get him out alive. If they didn't get your signal, there'll be no one to get us out. They've heard us, Simeon. The plane will be in San Cristobal. To fly us home. To fly. After the years of walking. Lieber will be there to meet us. He knows now. That we've found him. My God, Simeon, we've found him.

But Simeon wasn't listening. Not after the word Lieber. It brought back to him, with a pressure sudden and more blurring than the rawness of his sweating face, the notion of a world beyond the clearing, beyond the barbed, dripping wall of trees. Emmanuel Lieber, whose fingers they were, often fumbling and ten thousand miles from his arm's length, but his as surely as if he were now standing with them, dreaming the web, spinning and tightening it over the grid of the jungle, directing their racked, unbelieving bodies to the quarry, as he had for thirty years from London, then from Turin (where they had first, in worlds past it seemed, picked up the scent) and now from the small, unmarked office in Lavra Street in Tel Aviv. They were his creatures, the animate embers of his calm, just madness. Of a will so single, so inviolate to any other claim of life, that its thread went through Lieber's sleep producing one incessant dream. That of this capture. Emmanuel Lieber in San Cristobal, waiting at the landing strip which they had hacked out of the lianas and then covered over with brush and vine leaves. Waiting to fly them out, the lost hunters and their game. An image almost absurd, because of the silence, the necessary absence of Lieber's person and the loud waste of the jungle. There was next to nothing left of Emmanuel Lieber when he crawled out from under the burnt flesh in the death pit of Bialka. And he had never taken the time to mend, so that his will raged visible beneath the gray, splotched skin, and behind the thick glasses. Yet he was beautiful. Simeon remembered that now and was startled. His eyes. Marked by the things seen. As if the fires at Bialka, the children hung alive, the bird droppings glistening on the shorn heads of the dying, had filled Lieber's eyes with a secret light. No, that was kitsch. Not a secret light. But a perception so outside the focus of man's customary vision had given Lieber's broken features and low voice, and the shy rigour of his motions, a piercing strangeness. The stench went from Lazarus but even long after no one could take their eyes from him.

Beyond Lieber and San Cristobal waited the great tumult of voices, of those who would soon hear the news and not believe.

— Found him, Simeon. Found him.

Now he looked at Benasseraf and the dead weight of the radio transmitter came back into his shoulders. Yes, they had found him. But the shock of the last hours was too new. And the memory of the near abandonments. First when Stroessner's hooligans had drawn Amsel into a death trap at Paraña. Then when a whole squad of hunters (my dervishes, said Lieber) had disappeared, almost without human trace, in the swamp lands south of the Cordilla Nera. Was his the last party left? Simeon was no longer certain. And what of their own surrenders, of the innumerable times they had resolved to turn back, doubting, deriding the quiet mania of Lieber's conviction? Only a year ago, not five hundred miles in from the coast, when Father Giron had explained to them, speaking out of the knowledge of his own skin, parchment yellow and bruised by countless journeys, that no man, be he devil's spawn, could live in the unmapped quicksand and green bogs beyond the falls. And a hundred times after that. Nearly every day. When Benasseraf fell ill in the encampment at the headwaters of the Bororo and danced in the heat of his fever. When the rains, black stampedes of water, swept away their supplies, split their boots open as with rat's teeth and all but lashed the clothing off their backs. When the maps went mute.

As they did about two hundred miles south south-west of Jiaro. Where cartographers had marked, with pale blue strokes and wavelets, a blank of uncharted swamp land. No man could live beyond the falls, in the quaking marsh and sulphurous air. So said Father Giron, and the Chava Indians who had watched them pass with hungry derision. But had lent them a guide, a hollow-ribbed heron of a creature who could throw slivers of bark on to the green scum of the morass and tell where there was footing.

Perhaps that had been the nearest point to rout. When, only ten days ago, yet it seemed to Simeon much much longer, the Indian had melted away from them, refusing to wade a step further into the stinking water, his mouth set with panic. And the five of them had stood, up to the armpits in the green heat of the living mud, the swamp sucking at their blistered skins like the pale-bellied leeches. They had stood single file, trying to hold their packs above their heads, the midges swarming at their swollen eyelids. And Simeon knew that if he faced about, if he turned his shoulders under the suffocating canvas of dead, poisoned air, they would turn back, to Jiaro, and the crossing of the Cordillera and the wonder of cold beer and open sky that waited at San Cristobal. The next step had been everything. Hosannah, though he had almost fallen into the shifting ooze and his bones had frozen at the sudden slither of the snake. He had taken that step because Lieber was at his back. Whose voice, as they read the cipher, insisted, with an insistence deeper, more binding than even the swamp, that the man was in there, that this was his lair and desolation, that another thirty miles.

They had crawled those thirty miles. Inchwise. On their knees and with loosening bowels. Until the clearing, and the point of light. The insect-swarming oil lamp in his window.

— Yes. We've found him. Praise be to God and peace on our souls.

But as he said it and reached out to touch Benasseraf's hand, Simeon knew that he was deceiving himself. About the exhaustions and physical barriers that had so nearly made them turn back. It had not been Amsel's death, or the disappearance of Kaplan, or the hideousness of jungle and swamp. These things had made them maniacs and browned skeletons. But the true obstacle, each of them carrying it inside himself like hidden leprosy, was far greater. Indifference. Common sense with its fine sharp bite. A boredom with vengeance so acute that it rose in them, during the fever marches or stinging nights, like the taste of vomit. So what? Even if he is alive. Why drag the aged swine out of this stretch of hell? Who cares, now, thirty years after, or is it more? We're doing his bidding here, emptying our lives in this stinking jungle when we could be building, when we could be knitting ourselves new and forgetting. No one cares any more. Even if we find him alive, if we get him out, who'll want the stinking carcass? And what will they do to him? He's no more than a poisonous ghost now, and we're mad to hunt him down. Mad as he is. Exactly what is it he did to man? What is it they say he did? Who will be left alive to remember?

They had not spoken these sentences aloud. Not since they had taken the oath just before their ship sailed from Genoa, Lieber touching each one of them on the forehead and then lost in the crowd at the bottom of the gangplank. To find him, be it at the cost of their lives. Not to return until they had found him or had absolute proof that he was dead. Simeon remembered the plangent tumult of Italian partings. And John Asher, next to him at the railing, saying: Immigrants, like ourselves. We're immigrants out of life.

So they had not said any of these things out loud. But had thought them so intensely, with such deepening bitterness, that Simeon could make out each question, doubt, crisis of self-mockery or forgetting, in their sleeping faces, in their rebellious stumbling, in the rages that had all but torn them apart during the final year of the chase.

— It was time we did. High time.

Benasseraf eased the strap on his sweat-blackened shirt and nodded. It seemed to Simeon that they had spoken very little of late. All of them. As if they were afraid of the poisoned gnats that might enter their mouths. But he was trying to get the thing clear, those last hours and the capture. As Lieber had dreamt it. It was in his dream that they had moved, in the insane, unwavering certitude of Lieber's dream. Right to the edge of the clearing.

They had stumbled on it at twilight, the sudden break of sky over the circle of charred stumps. And crouched at the rim, in the insect-loud grass, like men overwhelmed. They had crouched the whole night through, their bones knotted by the cold breath of the swamp. Not saying a word. Their thoughts numb at the fantastic nearness of the end. Believing Lieber now, yet unable to believe that he had actually mapped this minute rent in the forest, that he had drawn this last small circle around the man, unravelling the sinuous logic of his successive flights, deeper and deeper into the interior, from one foul cover to the next. They had crouched there till the sour note of a tucca bird signalled the dim, wet rise of day. Two men had come out of the hut. An old man, one-armed and in a gray tunic, and a much younger, dark-faced guard, carrying a fowling-piece, which he pointed vaguely at the sky before sitting down.

Isaac Amsel, to whom the enterprise had become a vengeance too narrow, too selfish, and whom they had tried to send back since first he hung around them in the marshalling yard at São Paolo, rushed forward, against Simeon's order. And fired. So that the sound of the shot rebounded in an absurd, thunderous echo from the green wall of the forest. The guard had risen, spun histrionically and fallen dead. What had killed the other man as he scratched at the thin bed of lettuce was not clear. Fright, perhaps, or the end of the long wait.

They had raced across the open ground, each momentarily lost to the others. Mindless of Lieber's warnings, of the curare-tipped staves which they found outside the abode in the Sangra cañon, of the trip wires and anti-personnel mines sown around the first bunker, his opulent lair in the hills above Paraña.

There had in fact been a wire, and Asher tripped over it. But it ended in a pit of sodden leaves, the firing pin long since rotten.

Beyond Benasseraf's heavy breathing, the fever was often at him, Simeon could hear the click of the spade. Striking the patch of gravel which was the lone bit of solid ground in the waterlogged clearing. They were burying the old gardener and the man with the gun. There was no ammunition. They knew that now. He had spent the last shot, long ago perhaps, on the marmots and rubber-bellied lizards whose blueish bones they had found behind the stove.

Simeon and Benasseraf walked over to the grave. Asher was smoothing down the broken grass and gray mud. The grave was shallow and Simeon could make out the contour of the guard's foot. It was slightly deformed and where the spade had struck the toes had come wide apart. He could not take his eyes off the vague shape and it filled his mind with ugly, tattered images. They cut across the film of sweat which seemed to close around him at every motion and the raw edge of the transmitter pressing on the small of his back. Asher looked up.

— Did you get through, Capitano?

— I think so. Not the whole of it. But enough to let them know.

He wanted to explain about the transmitter and the corroded generator coils. But Elie Barach had begun his prayers for the dead. Had stepped back from the hurried pit and begun the rise and fall of his prayer. Over the months of heat and jungle drippings, the forest sticking to them like resin, Barach's cap had become a blacker patch in the tangled blackness of his hair. The morning shone through his threadbare shawl and his body swayed gently with the words. His eyes were closed and he appeared to move outward with the tide of his prayer, easily, being so light a guest in his own flesh.

— And may You take their souls into Your keeping. And give rest unto those who had none upon earth. May they find peace who brought none. And forgiveness who so need it. Amen.

But the prayer began anew.

— For Thou alone art judge. Thine is the vengeance and Thine the pardon. It behooves not us. It is not ours. Guard us, O Lord, from the temptations of righteousness. Guard us from certitude. From dealing in Thy name when that name, hallowed be it, is a secret beyond secrets. Selah. From doing Thy will when we know it not. Or only, O God, such small part of it. Make us Thine instrument but not Thy replacers. For we stand in exceeding peril. We who have striven so long that we have become our single purpose. Who are less than we were because Thou hast given us beyond our deserving. Do not ask of us, O Lord, that we do vengeance or show mercy. The task is greater than we are. It passes understanding. And whom Thou hast now delivered into our hands, may he be Thine utterly. Amen.

— Yes, said Simeon,

— they must have picked up our call. Can you imagine Lieber. In this hour, when he knows.

— If we manage to get him out. To bring him out alive.

And Asher repeated it, giving a last tug at his spade.

If he did it a little less well, thought Benasseraf, if the words were a little less round. Like the gold coins when we dug up the jar in Caesarea.

Elie passed his hands over his moist forehead and smiled, still in the wake of his prayer.

— We'll get him out. If we have to carry him. Every stinking mile.

Benasseraf spoke loudly.

— Just as we said in our oath. With our lives if need be. We'll hand him over to Lieber. If he has to ride on our backs to get there.

— That might be the only way.

Asher said it brushing the rust gray hair out of his eyes.

— Because I don't see him walking. Not far. He's an old man now. I thought of that last night, when we were in the grass, freezing our balls off. Born in 1889. That's it, isn't it? It says so on Lieber's warrant. I remembered that last night. Walk through the swamp, at his age?

— And over the moraine, said Elie.

— And how strong do you think he is? I mean, look at what they've been eating. Mice and raw beans and lots of muck scratched off the trees. We'll be lucky if we can *carry* him out alive. He shakes, even out here in the sun.

He said it without looking back at the hut.

— Ninety years old. That's as old as he is. Men and women ninety years old. The crippled and the blind and the ones spitting blood. They made them walk barefoot, over the cobbles. And whoever fell behind, they threw water over their feet. So that they would freeze to the stones. And stand there till they died. Burning alive in their skins. At

Chelmno, there was a rabbi, a man of wonders. A hundred years old. And they tore out his tongue

Benasseraf brought his hands to his mouth.

— and made him hold it before him, and walk. A mile. More than that. Till he came to the fire pit. And they told him: Sing. Sing you man of wonder.

He went on picturing the device in his own mind.

— When he can't walk, we'll carry him. In a litter. We can use one of the hammocks and tie it between two poles. We'll put a poncho on top to keep his carcass dry. We'll take turns carrying him. Like the ark.

— And dance before it, said Asher.

— Are you being serious, Ben? Carry a man through the swamp, when we can barely keep our heads above the filth? And Elie is right. What of the rock-fall? Most of our ropes are gone. Swept down the bloody falls or torn to shreds. It can take hours to go a hundred yards in that stinging hell. Imagine trying to get a hammock through. He isn't all that light. There's a paunch on the bleeding old ghost. No. We need help. And fast.

Simeon looked up at Asher, entranced, as so often, by his sober fantasies.

— They've got to get supplies to us. Blankets, guy-ropes, benzedrine, iodine, crampons, a new transmitter, we could do with two more sleeping bags, batteries are rotten in two of the flashlights, quinine. The lot. We need cocoa and fishing lines. I've got one decent lure left. And we could do with more fuel for the primus. I say we wait here, until they drop some of the stuff. And skirt the swamp. I don't know that we can get ourselves back through that ordure, let alone carry the old devil. Track along the western edge, until we find open ground. I don't think we can make San Cristobal. Not in a month of Sundays. It's all very well on Lieber's map. Red arrow in and blue arrow out. He hasn't been here. He hasn't seen the poisonous muck. Or the Chavas. If we try to slog out there won't be enough left of our bones to fill a matchbox. Look here, Capo, you try and get a supply drop, and then we can make it to the scrub. And wait till they lift us out. Or ferry him at least. Look at the rabbi's boots. I can see his bleeding corns.

Elie smiled and shifted his foot.

— We'd be mad to try. Stark raving mad. And he'd die on us inside a week. Turn over and die like a bloated water rat. They owe us that much. I mean we've found him, haven't we? Found him alive at the bottom of nowhere. The four of us and that nit. Why shouldn't they get us out? Helicopters, medics, the whole shooting match. To drown in that hell bog? After all this. After we've gone and dug him up alive. Or freeze to death on the bloody col? I won't do it.

— Even if I can get the transmitter working

Elie leaned forward and interrupted Simeon.

— they won't come for us. No one will. Perhap Emmanuel will be waiting in San Cristobal. Perhaps he won't even be there. We don't know that he's still alive. That his life has outlasted our news. There was only one thing left of him: his waiting. That was his soul and nerve and bone. Just like this man. Waiting. He too must have known that we would find him, some day, when he closed his eyes for an instant at the bottom of his warren. Two men will know that Simeon was not lying when he sent his message. He and Lieber. Who else will believe us? Even if they remember, why should they believe that the dead come to life, and in a hammock yet, carried out of the jungle. Even before we left they thought Emmanuel was sick in the head, that he had death and ashes in his brain. They wouldn't give him any help. Our own people. "Stop it, Lieber. Stop telling ghost stories. The beast is dead. Those rumours from the Chaco, those spoors in Paraguay, the telephoto bought from Major Gomez—and at what a staggering price, dear Lieber—all journalist's gossip. Trash. Someone trying to make a fool of us or start a diplomatic incident. Look what it's got us. Amsel murdered. The best agent we had. A professional, Lieber, and no offense meant. Murdered in a mousetrap. And for what? A wild whisper, a map which is probably a fake. Stop haunting us. Stop waiting outside our offices. We won't back you another inch. Not a penny. No more false papers and consular immunities. *Genug*, Emmanuel. If you find any men left *meschugge* enough to believe you, to go out there on a fool's errand, we don't want to know about it. If they die, their blood be on your head." That's what they said to Lieber. In the Ministry, at Military Intelligence, wherever he turned. "You're crazy, Lieber. Get out of the sun." If Emmanuel got our message, if he's still alive, he will meet us. His boots may be shabbier than mine. But he'll meet us. The others. May God wake them.

Asher caught the note of invocation: — and flay them alive.

Simeon marked the words pouring out after the long quiet. Gideon Benasseraf, John Asher, Elie Barach. Taking on their own shapes again in the better light of late morning. He spoke slowly, making them draw near.

— It isn't that. Or it wouldn't be now. There *would* be help. And a helicopter coming in as far as Jiaro. If the news could be released. O if everyone knew, there'd be an airfield dug here, bigger than Lod. And roads bulldozed. And a million television cameras. And a Hilton. They wouldn't believe us, not at first, and not all of them. But if they heard his voice and we described just what he looks like, they'd come like locusts. And take him from us. That's the whole point. They'd take him to New York or Moscow or Nuremberg. And we'd be lucky if they allowed us to stand in the anteroom peering over a million heads. That's how it is in the museum, at Auschwitz. "Here perished the heroic Polish combatants against Fascism. Here the vanguard of the heroic Communist partisans were executed." And then in the corner: "Eighty Jewish women from the Warsaw Postal Service were deported here and died." *Eighty*. No. He'd be theirs to try, or parade around the world, or pension off. They wouldn't let us near him. We'd have waded up to our eyes in the filth and death of this place, so that *they* could take him out. That's what Lieber fears most. And he's right. That story about the man and the large fish. The largest ever. But the sharks hammering at it, stripping it to the bone before he could reach the dock. If we call for help, if Lieber went to the Ministry and they were to send planes to get us out, or drop supplies, everyone would know. From São Paolo to Lima. And swarm at us. To take him away, to kick us onto the garbage heap. "Now we take over. This is too big for you to handle. Much too big. Mr. Hurok will handle it. And the International Court. We might call you to say your piece. Or we might not. Off with you now. No loitering." Eighty women. Subtract eighty from six million, and what do you get? Zero. The mathematics of the goy. *This* is the time when we must move fast, and keep most silent, and be secret to all. Don't you see? Until we have him home. Then go to the four corners of the city and blow your trumpets. But not now. If they knew we had him, if they could follow us in here, they wouldn't leave us his shadow.

Simeon looked up, with sudden comfort, at the steaming mist.

— The way we came? There must be another way. We won't get out alive. Not any of us.

— I haven't had time to think about it, Gideon. There may be another route. At least for part of the way.

He unfolded the map from its waterproof case.

— But not at the start. The swamp is everywhere around us. That's why he came here. Because no man could follow. Except through the black water and the quicksand. He crouched in the dead centre, on this mud bank, and we've got to wade through the thing if we want to get out.

— Bleeding Jesus. I'd rather rot here.

Asher's terminology, and the rich variants on it, always brought an elfin, secret expression to Elie Barach's face.

— Look for yourself. There's no other way. And after that we've got to reach Jiaro and see what we can dig up of our stores. I've left some spare circuit-boards there, and wiring.

— Supper for termites, said Asher.

Simeon was bending over the map.

— But after Jiaro there *might* be an easier way. If we could turn the falls on the north side and avoid that portage. Here. About half a degree south of the Querracho. Do you remember what Giron said? That there was some kind of very large ruin in the valley. A lost city. Known to the Indians, and bits of it seen from the air. There was thought to be a road leading from it, stone slabs laid down by the Mayanos and leading to the quarries, to the blue stone quarries here, just above Orosso. If there's any kind of paving, it'll be easier to get through. And if we have to carry him—

— Isn't there a landing strip at Orosso?

Benasseraf pointed at the faintly-drawn propeller in the middle of the green hatchings.

— I think so. Probably used by surveyors. But Lieber warned us not to use it. We'd be seen there. And we wouldn't have the range to fly out. It's got to be San Cristobal.

— That means the mountains, and as he said it, Barach swayed on his heels.

— The rock-fall, and the two pitches below the col. Without crampons or axes. And carrying the old swine on our backs. You're mad.

Simeon nodded, puzzled by his own gaiety, by the delight he took in Asher's rebellious good sense.

— We'll rest up somewhere outside Orosso. Perhaps there's another track. To the right of the glacier. Perhaps we don't need to go as high. And once we're over that

His finger straightened out to touch San Cristobal. Though the easy unbending was a lie. The breadth of his oil-blackened nail covered ten thousand steps. The shadow of his finger spanned interminable hours hacking through jungle, thick as leather, and marching through the razor grass of the uplands. The map was an ambush, set to catch dreams. Extended eastward from the swamp his hand reached well into the blue void of the South Pacific, into safety and the long flight home. It should not be so easy to place a hand across a map where our feet must follow. An hour of sweat and fear to a thousandth of an inch.

— We're almost in reach. One or two of us can go ahead to contact Lieber. You and the boy. We'll see. Once we're off the mountains

— the soulskin.

The word was so loud and ludicrous that the four men started up from the map and turned to look at the hut Isaac Amsel saw them staring at him, flushed, and stepped back from his prisoner.

Simeon folded the map carefully, cradled the transmitter against his back and walked slowly toward the door of the hut. The others followed. He had not yet looked at the man. Not directly. He knew he would have to now. In his throat the air seemed to close like a fist. The sweat lay cold and prickly at the corners of his mouth. He was near to gagging, but bound himself tight lest he make some stupid, irremediable gesture.

The old man had been looking at the boy. Seeing Simeon's shadow lengthen toward him he turned. And raised his head. Simeon choked. The caged air hammered at his ribs. He saw the man's eyes. For the first time. He saw the gray-green pupils under the puffed lids and the vein which rimmed them like a livid thread. The eyes were dead. But suddenly, in the cold ash, a minute, sharp crystal of light blazed. Then the gray smoke passed again over the man's glance. But in that instant Simeon found breath. The voice sprang out of him harsh and pent-up. The words spoke him and he trembled.

— AUFSTEHN. LOS. I have a warrant here. Born April 20, 1889. In the name of man. For crimes herewith listed. In the face of God. AUFSTEHN. We're starting out. We're starting now. To take you home, Herr Hitler.

●

Ajalon to Nimrud. Message received. Can you hear me? Ajalon
to Nimrud. Glory to God. In the highest. And for ever. The sun stood still
over Ajalon so that we could prevail. But then the night stood still. For
twelve years. Darkness unmoving. Over us and our children. Can you
hear me? Over. But now there is light again, at Gilead and in Hebron,
and to the ends of the earth. I tell you there is light as never before. And
tonight the stars will dance over Arad. And the world stand still to draw
breath, and the dew be like cymbals in the grass. Because he is ours.
Because he is in the hands of the living. In your hands. Ajalon to
Nimrud. Listen to me. You must not let him speak, or only few words.
To say his needs, to say that which will keep him alive. But no more. Gag
him if necessary, or stop your ears as did the sailor. If he is allowed
speech he will trick you and escape. Or find easy death. His tongue is like
no other. It is the tongue of the basilisk, a hundred-forked and quick as
flame. As it is written in the learned Nathaniel of Mainz: there shall
come upon the earth in the time of night a man surpassing eloquent. All
that is God's, hallowed be His name, must have its counterpart, its
backside of evil and negation. So it is with the Word, with the gift of
speech that is the glory of man and distinguishes him everlastingly from
the silence or animal noises of creation. When He made the Word, God
made possible also its contrary. Silence is not the contrary of the Word
but its guardian. No, He created on the night-side of language a speech
for hell. Whose words mean hatred and vomit of life. Few men can iearn
that speech or speak it for long. It burns their mouths. It draws them into
death. But there shall come a man whose mouth shall be as a furnace and
whose tongue as a sword laying waste. He will know the grammar of hell
and teach it to others. He will know the sounds of madness and loathing
and make them seem music. Where God said, let there be, he will unsay.
And there is *one* word—so taught the blessed Rabbi Menasseh of
Leyden—*one* word amid the million sounds that make the secret sum of
all language, which if spoken in hatred, may end creation, as there was
one that brought creation into being. Ajalon to Nimrud. Are you getting
me? Perhaps *he* knows that word, he who very nearly did us to death,
who deafened God so that the covenant seemed broken and our children
given to ash. Do not let him speak freely. You will hear the crack of age
in his voice. He is old. Old as the loathing which dogs us since Abraham.
Let him speak to you and you will think of him as a man. With sores on
his skin and need in his bowels, sweating and hungering like yourselves,

short of sleep. If he asks for water fill the cup. If he asked twice he would
no longer be a stranger. Give him fresh linen before he needs it. Those
who speak to us of their dirt and the itch in the groin are no longer
enemies. Do not listen to his sleep. Over. If you think of him as a man,
sodden when the rains come, shaking to the bone when you reach the
Cordilla, you will grow uncertain. You will not forget. O I know you will
never forget. Rememberers for Jacob. But the memory will turn alien
and cold. A man's smell can break the heart. You will be so close now, so
terribly close. You will think him a man and no longer believe what he
did. That he almost drove us from the face of the earth. That his words
tore up our lives by the root. Listen to me. Ajalon calling. Can you hear
me? This is an order. Gag him if you must. Words are warmer than fresh
bread; share them with him and your hate will grow to a burden. Do not
look too much at him. He wears a human mask. Let him sit apart and
move at the end of a long rope. Do not stare at his nakedness lest it be
like yours. Over to you. Are your receiving me, Simeon? I am not mad.
There are thousands of miles to go before he is safely in Jerusalem. You
will come to know him as you do your own stench. Look away from his
eyes. They say that his eyes have a strange light. Do not leave the boy
alone with him. The boy knows but does not remember, not in his own
flesh. What this man did. Ajalon calling. Come in, Nimrud. Tell me that
you remember. The garden in Salonika, where Mordechai Zathsmar, the
cantor's youngest child, ate excrement, the Hoofstraat in Arnheim where
they took Leah Burstein and made her watch while her father, the two
lime trees where the road to Montrouge turns south, 8th November 1942,
on which they hung the meathooks, the pantry on the third floor, Nowy
Swiat xi, where Jakov Kaplan, author of the *History of Algebraic
Thought in Eastern Europe 1280-1655,* had to dance over the body of, in
White Springs, Ohio, Rahel Nadelmann who wakes each night, sweat in
her mouth because thirty-one years earlier in the Mauerallee in Hanover
three louts drifting home from an SS recruitment spree had tied her legs
and with a truncheon, the latrine in the police station in Wörgel which
Doktor Ruth Levin and her niece had to clean with their hair, the fire-
raid on Engstaad and the Jakobsons made to kneel outside the shelter
until the incendiaries, Sternowitz caught in the woods near Sibor talking
to Ludmilla, an aryan woman, and filled with water and a piano-wire
wound tight around his, Branka seeing them burn the dolls near the ramp
and when she sought to hide hers being taken to the fire and, Elias
Kornfeld, Sarah Ellbogen, Robert Heimann in front of the biology class,
Neuwald Gymnasium lower Saxony, stripped to the waist, mouths wide
open so that Professor Horst Küntzer could demonstrate to his pupils the
obvious racial, an hour of school which Heimann remembered when at

Matthausen naked again, Lilian Gourevitch given two work-passes for her three children in Tver Street and ordered to choose which of the children was to go on the next transport, Lilian Gourevitch given two work-passes, yellow-coloured, serial numbers BJ7732781 and 2, for her three children in Tver Street and ordered to choose, Lilian Gourevitch, the marsh six kilometers from Noverra where the dogs found Aldo Mattei and his family in hiding, only a week before the Waffen-SS retreated northward, thus completing the register of fugitives, five Jews, one Gypsy, one hydrocephalic, drawn up at the *prefettura* in Rovigo, the last Purim in Vilna and the man who played Haman cutting his throat, remember him, Moritz the caretaker whose beard they had torn out almost hair by hair, pasting on a false beard and after the play taking the razor in the boiler-room, Dorfmann, George Benjamin Dorfmann, collector of prints of the late seventeenth century, doctor and player on the viola, lying, no kneeling, no squatting in the punishment cell at Buchenwald, six feet by four and one half, the concrete cracked with ice, watching the pus break from his torn nails and whispering the catalogue numbers of the Hobbemas in the Albertina, so far as he could remember them in the raw pain of his shaven skull, until the guard took a whip, Ann Casanova, 21 rue du Chapon, Liège, called to the door, asking the two men to wait outside so that her mother would not know and the old woman falling on to the bonnet of the starting car, from the fourth floor window, her dentures scattered in the road, Hannah, the silken-haired bitch dying of hunger in the locked apartment after the Küllmans had been taken, sinking her teeth into the master's houseshoes, custom-made to the measure of his handsome foot by Samuel Rossbach, Hagadio, who in the shoe-factory at Treblinka was caught splitting leather, sabotage, and made to crawl alive into the quicklime while at the edge Reuben Cohen, aged eleven, had to proclaim "so shall all saboteurs and subverters of the united front," Hagadio, Hagadio, until the neighbors, Ebert and Ilse Schmidt, today Ebert Schmidt City Engineer, broke down the door, found the dog almost dead, dropped it in the garbage pit and rifled Küllman's closets, his wife's dressing-table, the children's attic with its rocking horse, jack-in-the-box and chemistry set, while on the railway siding near Dornbach, Hagadio, the child, thrown from the train by its parents, with money sewn to its jacket and a note begging for water and help was found by two men coming home from seeding and laid on the tracks, a hundred yards from the north switch, gagged, feet tied, till the next train, which it heard a long way off in the still of the summer evening, the two men watching and eating and then voiding their bowels, Hagadio, the Küllmans knowing that the smell of gas was the smell of gas but thinking the child safe, which, as the thundering air blew nearer

spoke into its gag, twice, the name of the silken-haired bitch Hannah,
and then could not close its eyes against the rushing shadow; at Maidanek
ten thousand a day, I am not mad, Ajalon calling, can you hear me,
unimaginable because innumerable, in one corner of Treblinka seven
hundred thousand bodies, I will count them now, Aaron, Aaronowitch,
Aaronson, Abilech, Abraham, I will count seven hundred thousand
names and you must listen, and watch Asher, I do not know him as well
as I do you, Simeon, and Eli Barach and the boy, I will say Kaddish to
the end of time and when time ceases shall not have reached the
millionth name, at Belzec three hundred thousand, Friedberg, Friedman,
Friedmann, Friedstein, the names gone in fire and gas, ash in the wind at
Chelmno, the long black wind at Chelmno, Israel Meyer, Ida Meyer, the
four children in the pit at Sobivor, four hundred and eleven thousand
three hundred and eighty one in section three at Belsen, the one being
Salomon Rheinfeld who left on his desk in Mainz the uncorrected proofs
of the grammar of Hittite which Egon Schleicher, his assistant newly
promoted Ordinarius, claimed for his own but cannot complete, the one
being Belin the tanner whose face they sprinkled with acid from the vat
and who was dragged through the streets of Kershon behind a dung-cart
but sang, the one being Georges Walter who when they called him from
supper in the rue Marot, from the blanquette de veau finely seasoned,
could not understand and spoke to his family of an administrative error
and refused to pack more than one shirt and asked still why why through
his smashed teeth when the shower doors closed and the whisper started
in the ceiling, the one being David Pollachek whose fingers they broke in
the quarry at Leutach when they heard that he had been first violin and
who in the loud burning of each blow could think only of the elder-bush
in his yard at Slanič, each leaf of which he had tried to touch once more
on the last evening in his house after the summons came, the one not
being Nathaniel Steiner who was taken to America in time but goes
maimed nevertheless for not having been at the roll call, the one being all
because unnumbered hence unrememberable, because buried alive at
Grodne, because hung by the feet at Bialistok like Nathansohn, nine
hours fourteen minutes under the whip (timed by *Wachtmeister* Ottmar
Prantl now hotelier in Steyerbrück), the blood, Prantl, reporting,
splashing out of his hair and mouth like new wine; two million at, unspeakable because beyond imagining, two million suffocated at, outside
Cracow of the gracious towers, the sign-post on the airport road pointing
to it still, Oszwiecin in sight of the low hills, because we can imagine the
cry of one, the hunger of two, the burning of ten, but past a hundred
there is no clear imagining; he understood that, take a million and belief
will not follow nor the mind contain, and if each and every one of us,

Ajalon calling, were to rise before morning and speak out ten names that day, ten from the ninety-six thousand graven on the wall in Prague, ten from the thirty-one thousand in the crypt at Rome, ten from those at Matthausen Drancy Birkenau Buchenwald Theresienstadt or Babi-Yar, ten out of six million, we should never finish the task, not if we spoke the night through, not till the close of time, nor bring back a single breath, not that of Isaac Löwy, Berlin, Isaac Löwy, Danzig (with the birthmark on his left shoulder), Isaac Löwy, Zagreb, Isaac Löwy, Vilna, the baker who cried of yeast when the door closed, Isaac Löwy, Toulouse, almost safe, the visa almost granted, I am not mad but the Kaddish which is like a shadow of lilac after the dust of the day is withered now, empty of remembrance, he has made ash of prayer, AND UNTIL EACH NAME is recalled and spoken again, EACH, the names of the nameless in the orphan's house at Szeged, the name of the mute in the sewer at Katowic, the names of the unborn in the women ripped at Matthausen, the name of the girl with the yellow star seen hammering on the door of the shelter at Hamburg and of whom there is no record but a brown shadow burnt into the pavement, until each name is remembered and spoken to the LAST SYLLABLE, man will have no peace on earth, do you hear me Simeon, no place, no liberation from hatred, not until every name, for when spoken each after the other, with not a single letter omitted, do you hear me, the syllables will make up the hidden name of GOD.

He did it.

The man next to you now. Whose thirst and sour breath are exactly like yours.

O they helped. Nearly all of them. Who would not give visas and put barbed wire on their borders. Who threw stones through the window and spat. Who when six hundred escaped from Treblinka hunted down and killed all but thirty-nine—Polish farmers, irregulars, partisans, charcoal burners in the forest—saying Jews belong in Treblinka. He could not have done it alone. I know that. Not without the helpers and the indifferent, not without the hooligans who laughed and the soft men who took over the shops and moved into the houses. Not without those who said in Belgravia and Marly, in Stresa and in Shaker Heights that the news was exaggerated, that the Jews were whining again and ped-dling horrors. Not without D. initialling a memo to B-W. at Printing House Square: *no more atrocity stories. Probably overplayed.* Or Foggy Bottom offering seventy-five visas above the quota when one hundred thousand children could have been saved. Not alone.

But it was he who made real the old dream of murder. Everyman's itch to clear his throat of us. Because we have lasted too long. Because we foisted Christ on them. Because we smell other.

It was he who turned the dream into day. Read what he said to his familiars, what he spoke in his dancing hours. He never alludes to the barracks or the gas, to the lime-pits or the whipping blocks. Never. As if the will to murder and the knowledge were so deep inside him, so much the core of his being that he had no more need to point to them. Our ruin was the air he moved in. We do not stop to count our breaths.

It was he. With his scourge of speech and divining rod. His wrist breaking each time he passed over other men's weakness. With his nose for the bestial and the boredom in men's bones. His words made the venom spill. Over to you, Simeon. Can you hear me?

Do you remember the photograph in the archive in Humboldtstrasse? Munich, August 1914, the crowd listening to the declaration of war. The faces surging around the plinth. Among them, partially obscured by a waving arm, but, unmistakable, his. The eyes upturned, shining. Within twenty-four months nearly every man in the photograph was dead. Had a shell found him out, a bullet, a grenade splinter, one of millions, the night would not have stood still over us. We would have grown old in our houses, there would be children to know our graves.

It was he. The sweating carcass by your side. The man picking his nose as you listen to me or dropping his trousers.

None of the others could have done it. Not the fat bully or the adder. He took garbage and made it into wolves. Where his words fell lives petty or broken grew tall as hate. He.

Do not listen to him now. Guard him better than eyesight. We must have him alive. Knit the skin to his bones. Carry him if you must. Let him lie in the sun and in dry places. Force his mouth open if he won't eat. Search his teeth for poison and smear ointment on his boils. Tend him more dearly than if he were the last child of Jacob.

Skirt Orosso if you can. The ground is not sure. And keep from men's sight. If it was known that we had him they would snatch him from us. And mock us again.

I shall wait for you in San Cristobal. Send me news of your position. Each day at the agreed hour. I shall leave here in good time. Life is new in me now. I shall wait for you at the edge of the forest. Ajalon calling. Come in Nimrud. Come in. Can you hear me?

Simeon, answer me. Over to you. Over. This is Lieber calling
this is Lieber
this is

●

Trapped, the black tick had stung Simeon's ear. The lobe had swollen. Now a warm cotton hum lay between him and the world.

His attention, moreover, strained to interpret the new rhythms of the march. For months there had been at his back, grown familiar to him as the wince of his own muscles, a four-stress motion. By ear, by the antennae sharper than hearing which seemed to pulse from the nape of his neck, Simeon had learned to register the forward progress, the falterings, of Elie Barach, John Asher, the boy, and Gideon Benasseraf who usually held the rear. After bending a liana he could distinguish, without having to turn around, the four-fold interval during which each man bent the vine in turn for the next to grasp until Gideon let it lash away behind him into the thorny weave of the forest. In the sucking stench of the bog he had been able to mark the position of his four companions as sharply as if he had eyes in his spine.

Now the beat had totally altered.

His thin arms tugging at their shoulders, the right hand jabbing in a constant palsy, Hitler, after his fall from the hammock, had been half-carried and half-drawn through the steaming water by Asher and Benasseraf. At moments Hitler's head brushed against Gideon's cheek like a clump of wet leaves. Where footing was steadier—snake-grass plaited to spongy mats, vines cut and wound to a spiral around sub-merged branches, humps of packed mud iridescent with the sheen of sulphur, formed brief shoals and dykes even in the heart of the swamp—Hitler's grip loosened and he came forward on his own.

But whether borne, dragged or labouring at his own pace, the old man had broken the habitual pattern of heavy breathing and snapped branch which Simeon had come to locate in the wake of his every motion. Nearly at each step he wanted to turn around to make out the meaning of unfamiliar shufflings and sudden leaps of water. His back prickled with the sense of a new presence. Behind the slither and frequent pauses in Hitler's progress he could not locate the lighter gait of Isaac Amsel. Who now came last and had added a part of Benasseraf's gear, and the carbine, to his own pack. Yet Simeon knew he must not turn his head.

The yards ahead, more often it was a matter of a few feet, exacted his total attention. He could hardly think of reality any more except as dark green. To exist was to guard one's sweating mouth and hands against an unbroken rush of spiked and thrashing shapes, against blotting creepers that left filaments and small burning shards in one's skin and hair. To Simeon breathing had become a smell musky and heavy as dead water. Unknowing, he had grown new feelers. The scent of rot had only to thicken a little, to steam more densely from the moss, for Simeon to know that rain was near and from which quarter in the green cage of the world it would hammer down. A leathery slide in the barbed grass, an abrupt whorl of stillness in the saw of the swamp-cicadas, and he would keep his foot poised waiting for the adder to whip away. A dimpled swelling of the bark told Simeon of the tree-scorpion. He could hear the woodpecker in the unseen thicket. That there might be another order of life, where one step followed unheeding on the other, where breath passed cool through open lips, seemed knowledge as distant, as irrelevant to his present being as was Simeon's remembrance —was it still within his reach?—of the last Sabbath of peace in Lemberg, when the end of summer air lay blue around the candles and the grain of cinnamon shone on the white cloth.

The new, often alarming shapes of sound at his back, the lure of Hitler's feet ten yards behind him and the utter watchfulness demanded of him by the swamp, made Simeon insensible to the wisps of noise from the transmitter. He carried the thing with him still, gutted as it was, its delicate skein of wires dishevelled. If the damp had not eaten through the canvas wrappings, there spare coils and circuit-boards waiting at Jiaro. Now it was only a weight, a hot rub across his left shoulder and a frequent jab in the small of his back.

Nevertheless, some part of his brain, inexplicably idling or numb to the pressure of the swamp, *had* registered the bursts of static. He understood that the set was alive and picking up a signal though it could no longer amplify or sort it out. When they had taken a break after the collapse of the hammock to let Hitler wring the water out of his trousers, Simeon had swung the receiver nearer to his good ear and listened.

The fret and whine had come through in staccato fusillades. Simeon remembered the double rasp of shotguns in the arcade in October, when he was a small boy. He strained to hear. And imagined Lieber's voice saying urgent words, giving precise indications of help, instructing the party of the planes under way, of the supply-drops being marshalled on the edge of the swamp. But instead of being in a frenzy over the failure of the set, over the betrayal of rubber and metal which cut him off from Lieber's guiding genius and assurance of relief, Simeon found himself drifting. The needling at his ear was not being produced by Emmanuel Lieber. The rhythm was wrong. It was not Lieber speaking at the other end of the transmitter, or if these pricks of sound were indeed Lieber's they had been emitted a long time ago. They were reaching

Simeon like light waves from a burnt-out star. Lieber was dead. Or had given them up for lost. He had left the airless room in Lavra Street locked, gathering dirt. The mice were at the maps and a large fly lay dead on the silicone mouthpiece. There would be no one at San Cristobal, no sulfa tablets at Jiaro. Lieber had not been there to receive his call. Who was trying to reach him now?

The thought must have shown. Asher had stopped laughing and was staring at him across the dripping poncho. Simeon pulled himself up, swung the transmitter back over his shoulder and stopped listening.

Or almost. Now, in sight of the day's goal, he could still make out below the shrilling of the bugs the obstinate pulse of static. Simeon let the strap slide down his arm as he lurched the last few yards toward the sand-spit.

He had marked the place on the way in but was too preoccupied to celebrate the precision of his bearings. Here the basket-weave of water and shifting ooze had widened to a large pool. Though the drag of swamp continued in the deeps and everywhere around, the water in the pool had a clear black stillness. Forming an almost regular circle it mirrored a round patch of sky unbroken by the sway of vines and the close knit of tree tops. The high sun skimmed over the pool like a gold sovereign. Though the winds did not reach them, the waters reflected, in a strange fixity, the tearing of rain-clouds and the green and copper of dawn as it streamed across the Cordillera. On one side the pool was rimmed by a crescent of fine sand. From it a spit of ground extended a few hundred yards into the dark funnel of water. Neither the salt stench of strangled vegetation nor the vapour of insects intruded on this small peninsula. Simeon had seen only one sign of life when they passed the sand-spit on the march in, a tree-toad no larger than the flat of his hand, its horns and sharp ridge of its spine glinting like pale silver.

Though he had been in the rear, Isaac Amsel splashed past Simeon at a run and was the first to dump his pack and blanket-roll at the edge of the pool. In the dimming light the figures jostled and appeared to move without aim. Hitler's presence, he stood on the verge of the jungle almost invisible against the soft stuff of leaf and nightfall, had splintered the order of march and the close-hammered drill of encampment.

Asher's question woke Simeon from his trance.

— Shall we tie him up? Not that he'd get very far.

Simeon panicked momentarily. Hitler had vanished. Then he saw him, a few feet inside the undergrowth, urinating. A final streak of daylight had caught the old man's face as he bent forward. It lay like a white moth against the flatness of the leaves.

— Yes. Tie him up.

Elie Barach began laying out the primus stove. He blew on the wick and brushed the grid with his sleeve. The sounds, coming in their right sequence as they did with each sunset, braced Simeon.

— Tie him securely. Use one of the guy-ropes.

— Use a long rope, said Ellie,

— tie one end to his leg and the other to one of us or the hammock-pole. We can hammer it into the ground. That way he can move a bit and be on his own. I don't suppose he sleeps much. And Nebuchadnezzar shall graze, yea like a tethered goat.

— He won't run away, said Benasseraf,

— I'll guard him. I couldn't sleep. I'll stand watch.

And Isaac Amsel flourished the carbine above his head. He had seen the gesture on a poster advertising an American film of espionage and liberation in São Paolo.

— He wouldn't last the night in that bog. He'd die alone not knowing who he was. In a thousand square miles we're the only ones to know. He needs us.

And Benasseraf unrolled the canvas sheets and staked out the pegs for the lean-to.

When Asher knelt before him and tied the rope to his ankle, Hitler moved his lips. He made a hoarse sound but said nothing. Asher knotted the other end to a peg and drove it into the ground between his and Simeon's bedding. Then he dipped his hands in the water and said to no one in particular

— Cold. The water's really quite cold.

Blackness had fallen from the sky at a single stroke. Meeting the blackness of the pool it formed an opaque pillar. It muted the beat of Benasseraf's mallet and the crinkle of the stove. Simeon had noticed before how the sudden night took sounds with it. Only smells stayed distinct. He inhaled the rust sweetness of the tea even before Elie came out of the shadows to hand him the mug. The boy lit the hurricane-lamp but its light seemed to recoil from the pressure of darkness. It was only in the shelter that a stain of red showed against the ground and the taut canvas.

The rope had moved a little when Elie carried a mug of tea into the outer darkness. Now it lay still, coiling away from the faint sheen of light. Isaac Amsel crouched next to Elie and opened the tins of meat and noodles. Simeon could see the points of light on the opener but heard no crack of metal. At that instant, from far in the jungle, the cry of a parakeet came high and piercing. The rope quivered, then slackened again.

— I'll take the food to him, said Benasseraf,

— he'll want more salt than that. He's sweating his bones away.

Each man ate inside his own cone of blackness. The line between earth and black water had vanished. Though there was no motion in the air a soft booming, as from some quarry many marches away, reverberated now and again in the deeps of the pool. Benasseraf came back into the patch of light. He drank avidly. Simeon stopped chewing and listened. Now the transmitter was really mute. He tried to recapture the inflection of Lieber's voice, the exact shade of his skin. He couldn't. The darkness sucked everything from him except the sour odour and chill of his own body. He saw Asher look toward the water and pucker his lips. Asher could whistle like a yellow finch, liquid obligatos that woke the forest to a chatter. But he kept silent and turned back to the shelter testing the rope with his foot.

— I'll get his plate, said Elie.

The boy felt for the water's edge and rinsed the mugs and spoons. His bowels were churning and he farted. Quickly he rattled the tin plates, but they made hardly any noise. He was breathing fast. The night closed on his eyes and mouth like a blotter. When Elie Barach's shadow cut across the lamp, Amsel couldn't even see his own hands. He put down the canteens and hurried to the bushes sweating. The depths of the pool sounded again, a muffled stroke, long drawn out. It went through him like a cramp.

When he returned to the bivouac, stepping wide over the rope, Isaac Amsel saw that Asher and Simeon had rolled themselves inside their sleeping-bags. Next to Simeon, seeming to form an enclosure against the reaching chaos of the jungle, lay his revolver, the holster strap unfastened, the short-wave transmitter, the zinc box of snake-serum and novocaine, and Simeon's large flashlight. The mosquito netting was so near Asher's face that it followed the contour of his nose and cheek-bone like a cob-web on the effigy of an armoured personage, tensed to spring from repose. An egg-shaped hump of shadow, barely distinguishable from the surrounding dark, told Isaac that Barach was at prayers, wrapped in his shawl, his knees close-pressed under his bowed chin. By the outermost lamp, at the point of the sand-spit, a red ember brightened and dipped in abrupt arcs. Benasseraf had lit one of his coarse-leaved cigarillos. The ashes flaked into the pool. The boy went to him and sat down in the sand. He saw the stock of the carbine resting against Benasseraf's knee. Gideon's face was turned away from him staring at the night air which dragged on the water like black felt.

— I can't sleep either. Not with him out there.

Benasseraf didn't answer. He didn't want the boy near him. It was a cliché, part of the scenario Lieber had contrived and whose pages

they were now turning probably at the cost of their souls. It was part of
every bad novel. There had been a time for bad novels. Paper escarp-
ments of them guarding his unmade bed in the Rue de Rennes. The drug
of pulp, drowsier than mandragola. Bad novels that packed his brain like
sawdust in an art-gallery crate and kept the jagged, twisted objects of his
memory from crashing about, from piercing the walls of his skull. It was
he who resented Amsel most. Who had tried hardest to get rid of him,
first in São Paolo, then at Orosso where the boy should have stayed to
watch over the stores of the botanical expedition. It was Benasseraf who
found Isaac's flouishes and turns of heroic phrase—confetti out of old
war-films—most aggravating. Nevertheless, or because of this, the
boy would seek him out on the march and when they made camp. He
could have entered into Elie's tabernacle, into that complicity of prayer
and parable which seemed to advance so fluently even through the
jungle. Or learned from Asher how to drink life through a straw, barely
cutting the rind of the orange. Instead he came to him in patient blackmail. Setting traps for recognition. Precisely as a banal fiction would
have it. The son choosing the father.
    — You can't sleep either, can you, Gideon? Is it loaded?
    — No. Why should it be?
    — You don't think he'll try to escape?
    — Where to? The bog is alive almost everywhere around us. If he
didn't drown there are the ants. Did you see the mud move back there?
Simeon saw it. As if a cloud of red pepper was blowing along the ground.
They'd scour his bones.
    — If I was he I'd try to escape. No matter what. I'd saw the rope
with my teeth. Because he must know what we'll do to him. Or be
thinking about it all the time.
    It was easier to talk than to say nothing. The words blew away
with the ash of the cigar.
    — And what will we do to him?
    — Ah, said the boy throwing back his head. The night soot was
in his hair.
    — Ah, that's up to Lieber isn't it? And all the others. They must
be running wild with excitement. Getting everything ready. They'll try
him in the high court. In the highest. And hang him. After breakfast.
That's not what I would do. I've thought about it. I wouldn't do it that
way at all. Quiet and clean. You don't feel anything. I've read about it.
Just a hammer blow, with the hammer in a rag. I'd do it so that he knew
it was being done. Every thousandth of a second. And done many times.
Not all at once. Snap and it's all over. So he'd wonder about the next
time, that's how I'd do it, and hear himself howl. I'd chain him to a

stake on top of a pile of wood. So high that he could see beyond the city. And lay a trail of powder or a wick a hundred miles long, winding through every street and coiling around the square. And light it. He'd see the flame travelling nearer. He'd have to watch if for hours. Closer and closer. Just before it reached the faggots I'd jump in front of the crowd and stamp it out. I'd stamp it out with my own heel. And have them light the fuse all over again, at the far end. Or hang him on a pulley just above a vat of acid. Each day someone would come, there'd be tickets or numbers drawn, and turn the crank so that some bit of him would dip in the acid. One turn if you've lost a wife, two for each child. I'd jam a prop in his mouth so that he couldn't scream. Till his eyes burst. Or set his balls in a carpenter's vice. For a few minutes each day. Until he fainted. Putting a time-table on his wall so that he would know exactly when the next session came. And skin his leg to make the lamp-shade in his cell. How does a man live with the smell of his own skin outside him? Or have a jar with rats, starved rats behind a grate.

— You've got that out of a book. You're not talking about *him*. You're emptying your own mind. Of garbage.

— No, said Isaac Amsel,

— I'd do all those things. I'd do all those things. And keep him alive. And start all over again. What would you do Gideon, what would you do?

— I haven't thought about it. I'd let him go.

The boy's images were like the sour breath of the pool.

— I'd let him go wherever he wanted inside Israel. With only the clothing on his back. Every single time he wanted food or water or shelter he'd have to ask for it and say who he was. Everyone would know, of course. But I would make him repeat it each time, very loud. "I am Adolf Hitler. I am Adolf Hitler. I beg bread off you, a cup of water. Give me shelter in your house." I'd make him say it loud.

— What would be the good of that? If that's what you want why not let him die in the jungle? Why not turn him loose?

— Why not? I don't know. Imagine it. He'd die a very old man. Well fed. A fat old tourist in the land of Israel.

Amsel slid his knuckles over the butt of the carbine.

— If you feel that way Gideon, why are you here? You're not telling me the truth. You want him, just like the rest of us.

— You're stupid. No one wants him like anyone else. Each in his own little way. You because. Because you'll pretend you're making good your father's death. Because you've seen too many movies. Brave boy. Sunset. Father avenged.

He tried to flick the ash far into the water. But it seemed to catch in the net of the dark and fell on his boot.

— How do you want him?

— I don't know. Not now. Not like Lieber and Simeon. I don't think it was that way for me even at the start. To me he isn't Elie's Beast of the Seven Fiery Heads. I never wanted him that way.

The boy leaned back, content. Night talk, closer than he had ever had with Gideon. Whom he worshipped. Who was the strongest of the lot. Stronger even than Simeon, or different. Whom they would never have drawn into that cheap death-trap at Paraña.

— Not to get even. For what? You wouldn't understand. But when I hear about vengeance, about his eye for an eye, I want to vomit. There can be no vengeance, no making good. Why should history apologize, just to the Jews? Don't stare at me Amsel as if you knew what I was trying to say. You don't. You think it's a game, ten points to each side. Because we've got Hitler and can tear his nails out and wait for them to grow again the dead will sit up and give themselves a dusting. They won't. Not one of them. Not if you parade him over every grave, over every ash-pit, not if you dip him in boiling oil six million times. Do you really believe a man can get even for the murder of his children? For what a six-year-old girl saw before she died, for the fear which was so great that she dirtied herself, that she was driven down to the street in her—

He had been told, years after. By Moritz Levenfisch who, inexplicably, survived. Who had sniffed him out in Paris and was a liar and *schnorrer*. It might not be true. Or perhaps it was. Benasseraf had locked out memory and come to Lieber empty. He had brought only himself. Why remember now? The three children were not clear in his mind. How old would they be this night? Shlomo had been eight when. What was the colour of Rebecca's hair? A burnt brown. Even before the fire. He felt frightened and nauseated. As if his foot had missed two steps in a black staircase. He almost turned on Isaac Amsel.

— own dirt. You think that can be made good? You can't be that much of a fool. It doesn't matter. The rest of us aren't any wiser. There are two kinds of Jews left, the dead and those who are a bit crazy.

This time the ash flicked away but went out long before it reached the surface of the pool.

— That's why I don't want anyone to touch him. To torment him, to hang him would be to pretend that something of what he has done can be made good, that even a millionth of it can be cancelled. If we hang him history will draw a line. Accounts settled. And forget even faster. That's just what they want. They want us to do the job for them and put the whole guilt on him. Like a great crown. *He*'s the one to blame. Let the Jews hang him high. *He* did it all. They must be the ones who know. We're acquitted now. First they nailed up Christ and now Hitler. God has chosen the Jew. For his hangman. Let them carry the blood. We're in the clear. You don't understand, do you? I'm talking mad talk. The leeches have sucked my brain. At the first town we come to we should leave him. Go to the hotel, put him in an arm-chair and leave him. Then we should scatter, turning away from each other on the run. Not looking back. Let them try him and do what they will. He's *theirs*!

Gideon thought he had shouted the word. Perhaps he had. In his first drift of sleep Asher felt the rope move momentarily. He had looped it across his waist.

— He's theirs.

Saying it once more he almost touched the boy. Isaac Amsel smiled in the dark.

— Gideon,

He didn't have to hurry now.

— Where will you go? I mean afterwards. After we hand him over.

— Afterwards? I'll go look for Adolf Hitler.

Isaac tried to choose the right laugh.

— You don't think that's him? You think we've got the wrong man? Are you serious?

He wanted to take the lamp and swing it close to Gideon's face.

— I don't know whether that's Hitler. Have you smelt him? He smelt too much like a man. He's got diarrhoea. The scourge of God shouldn't smell that way. The real Hitler is inside the mountain. You haven't ever seen the *Riesengebirge*, like the mouth of an old leopard, white and gray teeth curving into the sky. The cold breath of those mountains hits you miles away. Listen to the pool, Amsel, listen.

The muffled booming of the gong passed just below them and drummed away into the unechoing forest.

— It's much louder than that in the mountains. That's where he's hiding, in the mouth of the black winds with the Redbeard and his ar-moured men. They were Jew-killers too. You can draw gold out of a Jew's bladder if you squeeze hard enough. I read that, carved on the wall in the prison tower at Schwarzberg. I don't think he'd let himself be caught and done to death, not by a few scarecrows wading through a swamp. When a grenade bursts the sharp bits scatter. This is one of his splinters. Perhaps there are many flying about. The thousand-year *Reich* has hardly begun, count for yourself. I know when Hitler will die. I know the day. When the last Jew is dead. Then he'll shout once more, one last bellow, so loud that the mountains will crack, and he'll smile and fall dead on the stone table. But not until then. To be a Jew is to keep Hitler alive.

They heard Elie Barach's steps scuffing the sand as he went to the shelter, still mantled in his shawl.

— Why do you listen to me? Go to sleep. Check the paraffin and go to sleep.

— I want to go with you. Afterwards.

— Where?

— To Paris.

Isaac felt such lightness in himself, piercing through the weight of sleep and the churn of his bowels that he fluttered his hands before the hurricane-lamp, a moth beating against the glass.

— To Paris. Where I'll study to become a film director. O I know it takes a long time. You've got to know languages; they make you spend six months in the cutting room just watching. But I'll become a director and write my own scripts. Like Jean Renoir. He's the greatest. I've seen everything he's done. I've seen *The River* five times. You remember when the flute stops sounding and you know that the snake has come? I'm going to make a picture about us, how Lieber's men went into the jungle and found Hitler. *Journey Into the Green Hell.* Wide screen. No one has learned how to use a wide screen yet, not really. Antonioni faked it. I think he's really a still photographer. No film sense. I'll show how the Chavas surround us and won't let us go until we leave a hostage. Or until one of us fights against their best warrior using a spear set with piranha teeth. Long panning shot of the fight and the circle of spectators. I think I'll cast you in the part of the fighter. You'll win, of course, but we'll have to show a great scar. At the end we'll be seen staggering out of the jungle, bearded, limping, almost delirious, and a great crowd will surge toward us. I'll use a zooming lens to show a sea of faces, ecstatic, unbelieving. We'll hand Hitler over to the waiting guards. Press helicopters overhead, painted bright yellow, cameras looking at my camera. But I'll never show Hitler's face, not full-on. Only from the side or in a shadow. In the last frame there'll be the back of his head and Lieber moving towards him.

— And the two heads will become as one.

— Yes. As one. Do you remember *Umberto D.?* Made years ago. I saw it at a Festival of Old Films. There was an old man in that. I don't remember his name. I want him to play Lieber, if he's still alive.

— And use the back of his head for Hitler?

— Yes. No. I don't know why you say that.

Gideon's voice was almost too near.

— I want that old man to play Lieber. There was a marvellous close-up, the light glinting off the rim of his glasses. I'll never forget that. The camera must have been angled from below.

Benasseraf tapped the ash. His cigar was nearly out.

— Why should I go to Paris?

— Because you said you would. I heard you say it to John, in the train. That it was the only place where you could forgive. No. Not forgive. Not exactly. I don't remember the word. But something like that.

Isaac Amsel rocked gently on his heels. It warmed him and made him feel strangely housed to try and remember. They were old friends now labouring to get things right.

— And during the fever you said

Too many things. He carried the still in his mind, perfectly framed, ready for the long touch of his senses. A table fifty yards from the corner of the Place Fürstenberg, the trefoil silhouette of the street-lamps almost touching the red and white table-cloth. A little while earlier he had walked past the Librairie des Saint-Pères and seen his monograph newly displayed in the window. G. Benasseraf, agrégé, *Le Silence et le poète*, Editions de Minuit, the characteristic font, tight and a little forbidding, on the off-white jacket. Now, at the restaurant, he had ordered lunch: pâté de campagne, brochette de fruits de mer sauce béarnaise with pommes pailles, to be followed by the Boursin with its shade of garlic and a pear, speckled gold and burnt to the touch as was the sunlight of early afternoon. Before him the early edition of *Le Monde* with a feuilleton on his book. "*M. Benasseraf, dont la plume vive et érudite . . . . cette page admirable de probité et d'intelligence sur Valéry . . . . qui quoique de souche étrangère maîtrise la sensibilité française comme ne le font que trop peu de nos critiques en vogue. . . . dont la lecture de René Char est témoignage philosophique non moins poétique . . . .*" The cold earth savour of pâté was in his nostrils, the sunlight shivered into small eddies and crystals of red fire as it passed through the glass of Gigondas, the bread was new as morning, the chimes of St. Etienne were striking half past one their dry ivory note still clear behind the splash of the fountain. *Werd ich zum Augenblicke sagen.* This perfect moment outweighing eternity, richer than damnation. And she was sitting across the table from him, waiting for Gideon to take the first bite, her hair smoke-brown as September grass, hooded in the soft dartings and quivering of the sun, her hand laid next to his, the cuff of her blouse closed with a charm, an ancient hammered thing of silver which, only an hour hence, in the sudden dark of their room, he would fumble at and unclasp. Her eyes were on the newspaper article mirroring his name but changing it, as her mouth changed his mouth, as the silent weight of her breasts changed his hand when he held them. In a moment he would bring the bread to his teeth and set the reel in motion again. But so long as his being dwelt on that image, on that convergence of all dreams, the chimes marked one-thirty and the sun danced untiring in the burning of the wine.

It was a glossy post-card, tourist-bait. Made up of all the miracles and re-awakenings of his three years in Paris after his release from the sanatorium in Lündfjord. *Silence and the Poet* was unwritten though tenaciously projected. He had been to that restaurant once, but only to watch a friend eat, a shallow friend. He no longer knew his name. The breasts in his hand had been light, tired after short sleep. There had been no one to transmute him. He had not wanted to give that much of himself lest some ineradicable message in the blood carry over to a child his own memories, lest a child be born and grow up carrying with it his knowledge of pain or the monstrous shapes of fear and the inhuman which filled him. The cuff-links were real. He had broken a nail toying with their intricate clasp. Who had worn them? A man or a woman? Gideon was no longer certain.

Yet the snapshot glittered inside him with a weird pressure of life. It arrested in a waking dream the otherness of the world, the illusion of total possibility without which the soul falls to a dusty heap. To sit at that particular table and smell the summer in the wine, to write that book and hear the rustle of paper and fireman's fanfare of literary acclaim— *gloire* has the shape of a fireman's helmet—to lie with such a woman in the sea-noises of a Paris afternoon, these were indispensable longings. That post-card, sharp in every line, was Gideon's remembrance of the life to come.

He hated its banality, the fact that so many other men had taken the same view. It was a'bright chromo, common as tinsel. It belonged to every young man in Paris who had read Balzac, who had seen Sartre pause to wipe his glasses in the Rue Jacob. Hope as cliché, as the uplifted finger of the street photographer. Why did these common wonders possess him? Who had been housed in hell. Why had his fantasies not been ennobled and made immune? Benasseraf loathed the quick sensuality of his day-dreams. A piece of cheese and its garlic tang sat more solid in his memory than the long hunger in the forest south of Grodny. When he turned imagination on his wife and the three children the focus was blurred and the light too naked. The montage of his unwritten book and of a woman's hand poised over the table-cloth had a wondrous precision. A man whose child has been burnt alive and who has eaten dung in a sewer should know rarer, more exigent temptations.

— No. Not forgive. Not exactly. I don't remember the word. And during the fever you said

Amsel was near enough the truth. Not "forgive." He had never said that word to Asher on the journey from São Paulo. He had said "become spurious like a child's tantrum." That was the trap of his life in Paris. His hatred and the memories which made up the substance of his life were being nudged away. One by one the words in his mouth were beginning to drift into the future tense. A man whose child has been burnt alive, whose wife has led another of his children into the gas, should use the future tense sparingly. Only to harry time, to make it ripen into vengeance. In Paris it had ripened into books and garlic cheese and the silver skein of cuff-link. That was why Benasseraf decamped and sought out Lieber.

— Back to Paris? Why should I? I'm not going back anywhere. I'm setting up a trading post at Jiaro. Kosher meats and shrunken heads.

Isaac could make out that Gideon had turned to him, that he was speaking to him more directly than ever before. But he knew he was losing him. Gideon cracked stupid jokes whenever his thoughts were distant.

— Look, said Isaac,

— look what I've been hiding. Even Simeon doesn't know.

He had got to his knees and was rummaging furiously in his pack.

— Look, Gideon.

He was on his feet, swaying and coiling like a wisp of smoke. He was clutching something, a small oblong. He gyrated, teasing and triumphant, beating a tattoo in the muffling sand. Suddenly, it was the first glint of light, Benasseraf caught a flash of metal. Still arching to and fro, Isaac Amsel began pulling out a thin, bending stalk.

— Look, Gideon, look. A transistor. A Japanese one. Nakima. I bought it in São Paulo. It picks up short-wave. Sometimes. When the nights are clear.

— Why have you been hiding it?

— Mine, said the boy,

— mine. Not yours, not even Simeon's.

He was laughing, darting out of reach.

— No one would steal it from you. And stop dancing. Why are you dancing? You're a fool, Isaac.

— I bought it with the money father left me. Before he went. It took nearly all I had.

— What good will it do you? You won't pick up anything. Not out here.

The boy was still laughing and shushing and putting his finger to his lips. He turned the little radio around and around, now above his head, now at arm's length, whipping the antenna through the heavy air.

— Listen. Can't you hear?

His whisper was startling. It carried. Sounds were beginning to lift and take shape. The pool had stopped booming. Somewhere, quite near, a bubble broke and the rings glinted in the water.

The whisper had turned to a burst of static, needles showering a distant forest in the Cordillera. Isaac stood frozen. Only his wrists moved, banking the transistor now to the side, now upward, the antenna tracing delicate loops like a fly-rod.

— Listen, Gideon. Can't you hear it now?

And in the same moment in which he looked up, at the break of light, Benasseraf heard it.

— *hombre hombre hombre mío*

Light tided in a sudden bright stain from the centre of the pool. The dark spilled along the edge of the jungle. Gideon was on his feet watching the canvas flap, the banana trees and the bodies of the sleeping men surface, their black forms edged with a silver contour. In the light of the sudden moon the air cleared and sounds quickened. A sandcrab scuttled past his foot leaving a braided spoor.

— I've got something. Listen.

From one of the senders on the vast perimeter of the Amazon Basin.

— *hombre hombre hombre mío*

A woman singing, and behind her the oily slide of the tango. Late night music. Incessant, always the same and inescapable up and down the entire continent, from Guyana to the Cape. Greasy as the cantina floor.

— Now you can hear it.

From San Martin. Or Orosso. No, there was no station in Orosso, only the wireless in the shack by the air-strip. But the new radio tower at Villa Blanca might reach. It seemed almost impossible. Across the desolation of the grass-lands, the web of the falls, the Cordillera, the muffling rag of the swamp.

— *bésame bésame hombre mío*

The boy stood rigid, the transistor away from his body. His eyes were on Gideon's; they had gathered the new light and were dancing.

— *mioooooii*

Her trill lifted and flexed like a monkey's tail before vanishing in the hot thump of the saxophone. Then, at once, the voice started again.

— *salida del sol salida d'amor*

The rope was moving.

Asher jerked up out of his first sleep feeling it slide across his wrist. Simeon lifted his head. In the moonlight the hurricane lamps had dimmed to a candle-flame. The rope was moving on the sand.

— *flores del mío cor flores flores.*

The voice reached them. Asher remembered the butter gone rancid on the march to Jiaro. Simeon sat up. A slow shadow passed across the tent-cloth. Benasseraf saw him, his face like a plaster mask, the hair glued to it. He was shuffling toward Amsel, his hand cupped to his ear. The top button on his fly was undone.

— Music. Music, said Hitler.

The boy turned and sprang back. He swung the radio away from Hitler in a wild toss. It dangled from his wrist and the strap twisted.

— Let me hear the music. I haven't heard music. O in a long time. Many years perhaps. *Blumen.* It is a long time since I have heard a woman sing.

— No. No.

Amsel was yelling. Yelling so the forest rang.

— No!

Hitler stood, staring at him.

— I won't harm the radio. I want to hear the music. Only the music.

The box had gone silent but the minute sphere at the tip of the antenna continued to vibrate.

— Stop shouting, said Benasseraf.

— stop it.

He was shivering and threw his cold cigar into the pool.

●

When to Rabbi Jehudah Ben Levi God, hallowed be His Name, dictated the Torah, greatly against His instincts, for the Word had been until then living, seed burning in the flesh because unwritten, might there have been an error made? Because the stylus slipped or the wax of the tablet flaked in the bronze heat of the Babylonian day. Because a gnat had lodged in Jehudah's ear. Because, for a millionth of a second, the Master had drowsed. Because God, may He forgive the libel of my thought, chose to plant one tare in the harvest of His giving, one false accent, one letter wrong, one word out of place, out of which speck has grown till it smothers man the black tree of our hurts. Out of which has sprouted the knife between my toes and the pus hammering at my heel, out of which rises the acid in my baked mouth and the red cry of my neck where the pack rubs. Out of which have swarmed the green flies that hang on the wet sore in my crotch. The black tree of life whose shadows are like nets around my feet and sicken the brain. Whose roots rear out of the swamp to trip me, whose vines will slap my face at the next step, now, O God, hallowed be Thy Name I am falling, whose droppings are the slime in my hair and the stench the stench the stench. I have not fallen.

But *which* word? Which letter or vowel sign or number? It may be only one digit in the numbering of the people or of the cubits of terebinth prescribed for the outward pillars of the tabernacle. Which *iod* has been omitted, which *gimel* misplaced in the three million and eleven characters of Torah. Which being thus imperfect has brought to man not peace not love not clean water but the stench the razor under my sole the needles in my shoulders where the strap burns. Not linen to lie in at evening but the rubber sheet stinking in my hand. Not the child's step in the lit house but *his,* just behind me now, at the root where I fell. Almost fell. Praised be Thou that hast led us.

Which word, which word?

The most learned Isaac of Saragossa declared that the error was in Genesis 22, i. God would command an old man to slay his child but not *tempt* him to do so. Temptation is vile, like a memory of blue air and open sea here in the cauldron of the swamp. Nathaniel Ben Nathaniel of Gdansk had, in 1709, conjectured that Rabbi Jehudah had misheard, O ugly mystery of misprision, Exodus 15, xx, for though it be right to dance before the eyes of Pharaoh's drowning host it is wrong to *strike timbrels.* That dance must have been a heavy and silent thing like the hover of the honey-wasp in the jungle.

I can't go on much further,
thought Elie,
the sweat blinds me and draws the flies. They cover my mouth.

In Mainz, Ephraim the Cabbalist had taught his disciples that the mistake was to be found in the seventy-eighth letter of the thirty-third verse of the 26th chapter of Numbers, seventy-eight being the cipher of Tammuz the hanged one, thirty-three that of the degree of Mercury when it is in the house of the crab and twenty-six

O God let me take twenty-six steps more before I fall and take the knife from under my feet and let cold water

But Ephraim had been burnt and Gamaliel of Messina, the learned of the learned had written, in a hand disguised and in a midrash found only after his death, that the Name of God in the Torah, be it sanctified for ever and evermore, was a false name, that even that Name which no man may pronounce was, as compared with the true Name, no more than the dust of dung when set beside rubies. Each time we call upon Him we call in error and cough like toads in the green scum. Lance the boil under my arm whatever be Thy name. Bring me to firm ground. Simeon is falling. Simeon. And the boy is shouting. The flies are in my breath. My breath is like a stink. My own master, Shelomoh Bartov, said to us that the unfathomable error, the breach through which evil has rushed on man was the word *and* in Leviticus 10, v. He said it with such sadness that none of us dared question him. We pored over the text in feverish wonder. A word without shadow, a word lighter than a mote in a sunbeam.

Why *that* word? So I asked. Whereupon the Master called me a dunce, one who understands less than a goy, and answered, as in a song to himself, why that *and*? For the reason deeper than reason that it could be any other. And had begun to sing louder and driven us out of *cheder*, like mice, before the song would lift him from the ground. Shelomoh Bartov who was a just man and who danced in the fire-pit at Grodny.

Where I ought to have been with him. It would have been quicker. Than this red scratch in my neck. Quicker than this march which is like many deaths. Death up to the groin, death where the pus hammers, where the buckle scrapes across the blistered skin. Blasphemy. The flies are on my tongue. If Simeon doesn't call a halt. But *he* is keeping up. I heard his step behind me. Stronger than yesterday. He takes small hops like an old frightened man. He *is* frightened of the swamp and the fright pricks him. Like an old puppet of a man in little hops. The thorns have scratched his cheek. Now I know which word it is. 2 Deuteronomy xxv: and shall *tremble*.

Benasseraf's trembling had not stopped. The shakes began as he turned from the pool that morning, a slow pounding out of some broken, feverish place beneath the skin. It jerked at the corners of his mouth and made the sweat cold between his fingers. Elie Barach had watched Gideon's back as they set out. Under the blackened shirt, under the carbine strap and the lanyard on which he carried two water-flasks, Gideon's ribs and back-bone quivered. At every few steps a drum-roll beat under Gideon's skin from the neck down and the flasks tinkled. Elie could smell the sweat in Gideon's hair. And sourer than sweat the smell of the fever. It made his own heart race. Simeon knew. Elie could tell by the frequent short halts. By Simeon's decision that Asher bring up the rear.

The fever had passed to the forest. The ooze shook under their feet. Daylight vibrated in sharp jabs, out of reach above the dank shivering vines. Benasseraf had his teeth set and walked in a hunch as if carrying through the mist of the bog a fragile, knife-edged burden. Now and again he would bend low and emit a choked cry.

They stopped where a hummock of swamp-grass, its thorny blades high as a man, protruded from the morass. Isaac Amsel sat down in the green cage and picked at a bleeding scab. Simeon had his hand on Benasseraf's left shoulder. He felt the tremors pass through his own arm. Their faces were close in the thick air.

— Gideon. *Mensch.*

The electric eel was loose in Gideon. He clenched his teeth against the next jolt.

— Have you taken?

Early that morning Asher had tapped the powder into his unsteady palm.

— You've got to take more. You'll break in pieces. Do you want us to carry you? *He* can walk. He's been nimble as a goat. Stop it. You'll break if we go on.

The low cry and Gideon's teeth unlocked.

— I've had worse attacks. I. I. Don't stop. Not here. It's the swamp. It makes the fever

A spasm shot through him. Simeon tightened his grip. He smelled Gideon's sick breath.

— makes the fever worse. I can make it. If we reach dry ground. I

They swayed and argued, close as wrestlers.

— We're getting you out of here alive. If we have to camp a week.

— Let me be, Simeon. I'm better when I keep going.

He fumbled for the quinine and the chain of the flask tinkled loud.

— I am better. Let me. We have to move.

Gideon tensed his body and swallowed the drug. As he straightened a cold current passed down his spine. He dropped the water bottle. Simeon bent down and their cheeks brushed.

— We're stopping here until you're better.

— If we stop here I'll. Get us to dry ground. We can't be too far. I'm better already. Not here.

A bird's egg lay in the mud near Asher's foot. He looked closely. It was teeming with red dots, miniscule, devouring swamp-lice. He bent lower still. He thought he heard a sound, like the scratch of a nail far off. A smell of sulphur rose at him.

They hacked their way through the dripping net. For the first time Amsel was front man. Simeon had dropped back to be with Benasseraf.

When he swung the machete Isaac pivoted on his hips and forced his shoulders down as Gideon had taught him. His wrists were swollen. When the blade tore through nothing but dead vines or tree-moss it wrenched him off his feet. At other strokes it cut clean and the white sap spurted. At every few yards Isaac wiped the edge. Sodden fibres and thorns stuck to his fingers. Once, absently, he touched his muddied knuckles to his mouth and spat violently. Something jellied had moved across his lips. The vegetation arched above his head.

The six men slogged knee-deep through the swamp. In the fitful light the water gave off an oily sheen. The cutlass slashed a windless tunnel through the lianas. Rats slid away their eyes blind and blood-rimmed. Between strokes the boy spoke to himself.

We are in the sewers. They run west south-west under the ghetto wall and come up in Novy Swiat. But we've missed the right grate. If I lift the cover now there'll be a boot standing on my face.

He hacked faster. Too fast. Wasting motion and slicing too high so that the spikes whipped back and tore their legs. His lungs hurt. There was no touch of life in the air. As if the bog had drawn and exhaled the same dead breath over a million years. The harder he breathed the more he seemed to choke. A rubber mask pressing down.

Isaac Amsel lashed out with his free arm but the leaves lay heavy on his face. He bent double, panting. Behind him Simeon waited. The boy felt a drilling inside his head. The sound rose to a white screech and filled his ears. He swung his head groping for air. The machete dragged him down. He was going to faint. But the sound was too loud. It spiralled above him and behind. It drowned the chattering of Gideon's teeth and the slither of the rats. Hitler was jabbering and pointing upward.

— Like Stukas. Rrrrrrr. Blitzing.

The fever had opened the sores on Gideon's legs. High in the massaranduba tree a brown cluster, lice-ridden and mantled in sleep, had caught the odour of blood. The brown furry grape burst. The bats plummeted, their wings flaring. They found a rent in the canopy of leaves. They careened in the hot shadows shrilling. Their brown leather wings slapped the cane-grass and crazy for flight they wheeled from the thrashing men. But the thorn-brakes and hollow of vines held them caged. They dived at the hot smell in the trodden grass and screeched.

— Rrrrrr

said Hitler, ducking. The bat veered away a strand of gray hair in its crooked thumb. A brown shape tore at Asher's knee. He kicked wildly and for a moment the bat lay on its back, its belly the colour of smoke. Then it flew straight up, inches from his face, its screech like a file across his teeth.

— *Die Vampiren*

cried Hitler

— the drinkers of blood

and fluttered his hands in front of his face. A bat skimmed Isaac's hair. The sound whipped like wire across his skull. Now the leech came in again. He could see its eyes, green as mould, and the skin pinched around its wet nostrils. Its foxes' ears were taut in flight. He stood paralyzed, his throat muscles pounding. The bat was drivelling. As it swerved its spittle flecked the boy's cheek. Amsel cried loud. The air rushed out of him as from a man drowning. He swung the machete in a crazy arc and cried again.

A small bat writhed in the leaves its wing pinned under Simeon's foot. Its other wing slashed the air. A wild piping came through its teeth. Simeon bent down. He wanted to touch the raging thing, to pass his finger over the quivering stays. The bat watched him its eyes bursting at the rim. For a second it lay motionless its claw open. Simeon wondered at the delicate curve of the nails. Hands of a blind child. Then the biter exploded under his foot. The animal foamed at the muzzle and Simeon felt the wing raking his leg. He brought down the butt of his carbine. He heard the bat's skull splinter. The wing leaped up and fell broken. Simeon drew back his shoe. Where the bat lay the ground sprang alive. In a moment the white maggots were at its belly and a dung-beetle had its scissors in the dead wing.

Then he heard Amsel's cry and flinched from the wheeling blade.

— Stop that. Stop swinging that thing. You'll take my head off. They won't kill you.

The bats ripped loose from the tangle of hair and the flailing bodies. They swarmed through a break in the palm fronds and out of sight. Only their screech lingered and a randy smell.

Hitler made a warbling noise and said

— All clear.

— Put that thing down. You'll cut yourself.

Isaac heard his own cry and stopped, bewildered. The machete hung in a knot of tree-moss and ferns.

— All clear,

said Hitler,

— finished. At sunset the Stukas go home.

But the raid had infected the march. A thrashing looseness possessed the legs and bodies of the six travellers. Even Simeon who had taken the machete from the boy's flapping wrists and was again in the lead heaved and stumbled forward breathing loud through his open mouth. He could hear the hiccups pummeling at Benasseraf's body and the sound drove him. Asher caught the scent of disarray, muskier than the fur of the tree-bat. He knew that Simeon had altered course, that the sun, where it scorched through the tunnel of leaves, had slid abruptly from his left shoulder. But he did not halloo or ask Simeon for a reason. The urge to quit the swamp, the conviction that it would be death to spend another night on the gaseous slew harried the marchers. They kicked their raw stinking legs through the scum, slashed blindly at the shapes which rose and bobbed before their faces, each man labouring in the net of his own panic, in the wild fear of being left behind.

They moved fast, waist-deep in a trough of gray mud, then through tassels of tree-moss, the braids swarming with aninga-beetles, armoured creatures suspended by their precise claw.

— Thy works are manifold

said Elie Barach, and slogged on. Once Hitler cried out, pointing at Gideon,

— We must stop. That man has the fever. He will make us all sick.

But no one seemed to hear and Hitler hopped forward lest Asher, lurching through the creepers just behind him, stomp on his heel.

Toward evening the air lightened. Simeon felt a distant coolness, a puff of living breath on his lips. The wall of vegetation began thinning. The light steadied and for the first time since they had waded into the morass Isaac Amsel saw his shadow whole. The sapucaias and swamp-sycamores drew apart. The water threaded into weedy channels; the green slick ebbed from their boots. Snapping a dry stalk, its top browned by the sun, Barach praised God. Soon they could hear each other's steps. The soughing of gas and oily water, the slap of vines, the blotted rasp of their own breath receded. A cicada sang bright as tin.

●

— Niiice

The pilot made three syllables of it, brushed his fingers across the amplifier and gave the rotary antenna a delicate turn.

— Very nice. A 207 rangefinder!

Appreciative, muted whistle.

— Haven't seen one of those before. Not mounted on a d-k circuit.

He flicked a switch. The blips came on dim, then contracted to points of humming brightness.

— I'm nuts about this stuff. I'm a radio ham. Just like you Mr. Kulken. You've got yourself some nice hardware. The man's glance shifted. But bleeding Jeeesus what a dump.

Gathering her smock the Indian woman had, in motions amphibious, retreated to the far corner of the shack.

— No offense meant, lady. You got a nice place here I guess. But Orosso.

He had trouble with the word. It was new to him.

— Keerist, I've landed on some crummy strips in my day. But this field takes the cake. I almost cracked up taxying in. And get a whiff of the joint. No drains?

The inquiry was solicitous.

— What kind of Indians you got here? I left one of 'em guarding the single. Gave him half a dollar. I told him I'd bust his ass if anything was stolen. That I'd skin his greasy hide. What kind of Indians you got Mr. Kulken?

He moved closer. There was liquor on his breath, but not much.

— Goddamn bugs.

He slapped his forearm and peered thoughtfully at the squelch.

— Haven't you got any DDT Mr. Kulken?

Kulken was on his feet, his erection undermined. Who in hell are you? What do you want here? Who let you in? He couldn't have asked these stupid questions, couldn't actually have blurted them out, his cheeks rounded and sweating, in the bewildered stance of a grade-C thriller. Not Rodriguez Kulken who had in settings infinitely more tortuous, in imbroglios more sinuous by far, kept his cool, not unmasked his batteries. Perhaps it was the pyjama bottoms that had precipitated him to so banal an exhibit of enraged wonder, the fact that he had not, in the haste of his rising, tied them properly and that they kept slipping from his shrunk but aching nakedness.

— Marvin Crownbacker. Pleased to meet you Mr. Kulken. And the lady. But everyone calls me Charlie.

This time Kulken heard himself say "why." Why Charlie? And the grossness of his query, the way in which each cliché of alarm made the ambush tighter brought sweat to his eyes.

— Goddamn it. The bugs around here. Like crazy.

The intruder swiped at his chin but the insect was gone.

— This is a hot town you've got here. You bet, Mr. Kulken. Why Charlie? Wish I knew. I was born and raised in Muncie, Indiana. They've called me that since I was knee-high to a grasshopper. You call me Charlie, Mr. Kulken. It's friendlier that way.

And Marvin Crownbacker offered a warm crooked smile.

Kulken tugged furiously at his pyjamas.

— What do you want? How did you get here? Get out of my house.

Which behest insinuated into Kulken's fuddled brain, with mournful, numbing clarity, the remembrance of a play seen long ago in a flea-ridden casino hall somewhere on the Belgian coast. The white-faced actor had cried "Get out of my house" and pointed his long index finger.

— I flew in about an hour ago. You must have heard me coming down. Mist was covering the whole valley. Like flying through clam-chowder. I nearly peeled the roofs off looking for the strip. And the engine was hotting on me. Mr. Kulken, do you mind if I sit down?

Charlie swept from under the table the metal stool in which his host had, for the past three weeks, sat each night, his bones stiff as wire, plucking the cries and turnings of the hunt from the loud secret weave of the air.

— I'm a radio ham. This kind of gear bugs me. Just like you, friend. So how about a cup of coffee. I've come a long way to see you, amigo, a very long way.

He'll show his hand, thought Kulken.

Charlie did. Over three cups of coffee with three lumps of sugar in each, two fried eggs, their yolks faintly mottled as they inevitably are in Orosso, and over a plate of seedcakes which the Indian woman, for all her brooding sloth, made beautifully. The gentleman from Muncie talked in a rush, his intimacies and casual foulness of speech like a smokescreen on a dun sea. The start of the affair was slippery. Charlie was a radio buff, oh not on Mr. Kulken's sumptuous scale, but pretty hot in his own small way. He had picked up some of the stuff Kulken had

sent Montevideo and once or twice he had got a fix on the transmitter in the rain-forest. Nothing like Mr. K's precisions and range but
enough to put two and two together and find that they added up
to—what shall we say?—a million, no make it two or three million bucks.
Which wasn't hay whichever way you chose to look at it. So he'd high-
tailed it down to San Cristobal and hired an old crate of a Fokker, two-
seater job, put in an extra fuel-tank and flown to Orosso. The goddamn
sewing-machine had almost ditched him a hundred miles out of nowhere.

Where had he monitored Kulken in the first place?

Hadn't he said? He'd been in Brasilia, free-lancing.

The word was to cover zig-zags of life and a body of knowledge
sudden, cascading, remote from Kulken's but in whose confident jargon
Kulken could recognize an appetite for expertise, a feel for the grain and
yield of things matching his own. "When our friends hot-foot it out of
the jungle (it must be hell's ass-hole in there) we'll be the first to say how-
de-do, won't we Mr. Kulken?" They hadn't been doing much trans-
mitting over the last days and toward the end their signals had been
barely audible. "You bet you they're out of juice." Which deprivation
signified that there was only one link with the outside world: "all that
sweet circuitry of yours." Why, they were sitting on a gusher, sitting on
it right this minute. They'd need a truck to cart the money to Fort Knox.
It was, forgive the expression, the biggest piece of fuckin' good luck that
had ever happened to Marvin Crownbacker and he was going to make
sure that Mr. Kulken got more than his cut, say twelve per cent more,
"seeing as to how you're Johnny-on-the-spot and got the old mike just
waiting, pretty as can be." Because this was the biggest story of the
century. Bigger than Lindbergh. Bigger than John Fitzgerald and
welcome to Dallas the friendly hub. Bigger than Jonestown—and that
had been a honey of a PR set-up if Charlie had ever seen one. God
almighty! this was the hottest news-break since Jesus got off his slab.
This was like being at tomb-side and getting an exclusive from Him on the
way upstairs. A couple of million dollars? More, Sir, perhaps more. First
there'd be the interview with the old motherfucker himself. They'd have
U.S., Canadian and world-rights on that and all reproduction thereof,
live, canned, videotaped. "How does it feel being back out? What were
your first thoughts when you saw these gentlemen dropping in on you?
Do you think they'll try you in Jerusalem like the other guy? Anything
you want to tell the folks out there about life in the jungle? Any dietary
problems? It's a while back, but now that they may hang you, any
regrets? Any thoughts about how your mother would feel?" Let Mr.
Kulken imagine it if he could. World rights on *that* with a hundred
million people out there waiting to hear every word and a hookup on

satellite. After which there'd be hour-by-hour flashes and feature fill-ins. What's he eating? How's he sleeping? A special word to the Krauts. An appeal to the Vatican. Who's going to be his mouthpiece at the trial? Then there'd be the good guys. How many did Mr. Kulken reckon there were? Three, four, half a dozen? Hadn't they been seen slipping into the forest? The full treatment for each man in the party: life-story with serial rights (Charlie had brought along the contracts, the agent's release-forms, the whole legal crap). Background stuff: what brought you here Mr. Cohn? How does it feel being a world-hero? Was it the greatest thrill of your life, I mean when you spotted him? What will the missus say and the kids? You have a sweet-heart in Tel Aviv? O.K., Mr. Kulken here will hook in a circuit and you can talk to her. All rights reserved. Charlie wasn't any Cartier-Bresson. But he'd taken along a couple of leicas and a graphlex four-hundred. They'd have the first pictures, the only pics for the agencies, at least during the first forty-eight hours. Any TV outfit wanting to show them would have to pay, through the nose. Two thousand for each individual snap, ten thousand for a group shot of old *Shitgruber* and the rover boys against a jungle background. Charlie had brought colour film ''so maybe we can throw in a few Indians.'' He figured they had forty-eight hours, maybe a bit more if they played it smart, once the party was out of the jungle. Two days before Orosso turned to Coney Island, before every goddamn journalist, cameraman and publisher from Kalamazoo to Ulan Bator came in by helicopter or go-kart. By which time

— they'll have to come to us, Mr. Kulken, 'cause we'll have the contracts, the sole and exclusive right to deal with and negotiate for the sale of subsidiary and other rights within all territories covered by said agreement, i.e. newspaper and magazine serialization, anthology digest quotation and abridgement, dramatic, film, radio and television, microphotographic reproduction and picturization, reproduction by gramophone records and other mechanical means whether by sight, sound or a combination thereof, translation into any foreign language and that, Sir, includes Bantu, Toltec, Easter Island and/or Yiddish. If the publishers have not sold paperback rights two weeks after publication of the hardcover edition or agreed to publish a paperback themselves, the said sole agents and representatives for the said motherfucker and our heroes will have the option to negotiate with a publisher of their own choice for said paperback edition the publisher's share then being reduced to fifteen per cent.

Some of which rights, especially to more recondite portions of humanity, Messrs. Crownbacker & Kulken, otherwise entitled C-K Universal, would re-sell, because greed was a vile thing and because they

had no hankering to spend the rest of their affluent lives signing releases
to bushmen.

— Millions, pal, millions. Sweet Jesus above!

At which invocation the gentleman from Indiana surged out of
his seat exultant, threw his head back and whipped a sugar-cube into his
mouth. But Kulken too was on his feet attempting a dry, superior laugh.

— You're crazy Mr. Whatsyourname. Loco. You have jungle
fever, that's what you have. A million dollars? For an interview with
Martin Bormann?

— Martin Bormann? Who's he? Who the hell is Martin Bormann?

The two men stared at each other. Crownbacker spat the sugar
from his mouth and forced Kulken to his seat. He thrust his face close
and spoke slowly. As to a very stupid or very cunning child.

— Listen to me Mr. Kulken. Let's not waste time playing games.
Listen to Charlie. He's your friend. When Adolf Hitler walks out of that
jungle

Kulken went white and sagged forward. Charlie yelled at the
Indian woman in a voice loud enough to wake Manolo at the other end
of the village

— Get me a glass of water. Water you stupid bitch. *Agua.*

Kulken came around soon enough and shoved away the proffered
mug. But he was shaking. The enormity of the proposal, the image it
conjured up of his blind nonentity, of his fly-speck role in a web vast,
consequential beyond even his own most flamboyant reveries, made him
hot and cold and nauseous in quick succession. It *had* brushed the far
edge of his mind as a fancy lighter, sooner dropped than dust; he *had*
made some remark over the chill pungent soup in the Casa Popo to the
effect "who do you think they'll turn up, the old carpetchewer himself?"
only to have his host (*now* he remembered that the man *was* more senior
than any he had met before) frown at him with lordly distaste. The queer
had kept him in the dark. No one had even hinted to R. Kulken, Esq.
what the game was. A "routine snoop." Somebody's hobby-horse in
Whitehall. "A loose end worth tying up. Possibly. And only if Señor K.
had nothing more pressing on his hands and cared to pick up a little
something." Which was precisely what it was. A pittance. An infamous
pour-boire, grossly inadequate to the skull-splitting labour of the last
weeks, but niggardly insulting, humiliating beyond belief when set beside
the immensity of the stake. So they'd let him sweat his ass off for their
own incalculable profit and glory. The last message. The sun standing
still. Ajalon and Hosannah. They'd bagged him. Mother of God they'd
gone into the green hell and found him. Now London knew and the

jackals were on their way. The lean ones with the tight gray skins and the talcum powder. With accents like an open razor and a lemon in their teeth. To bugger him once again, to scratch him off like a dry scab while they pulled in the catch, the immeasurable dizzying prize.

— You okay, amigo? Take a deep breath.

But suppose Crownbacker was lying? Or mistaken, taken in by his own circus patter?

Kulken snatched at the possibility. He sat up and forced a condescending smile.

— Hitler? Hitler died a long time ago. Thirty years or something like that. It's Bormann they're after. Everyone knows that. You've come on a wild goose-chase Mr. Charlie.

— Have I, asked the man in the yellow leather flying boots and gulped the last of the seedcakes.

Kulken nodded and made a gesture of dismissal. But he did not look at friend Charlie and his bent smile. The truth pressed on him. In school they had held him to the wall and set the point of a compass inches from his eyes. He needed time. Morning air to clear his beating head. Kulken remembered his pyjama bottoms. They were soaked with perspiration. Crownbacker wasn't half as smart as he made out. If it really was Adolf Hitler. Why, that meant

and Kulken almost laughed out loud with a sense of insight, of a global perception far more sophisticated than the crude eldorados offered by his unwanted guest.

If Adolf Hitler walked out of that jungle toothless, lame, blind, palsied, in any form, husk, shadow of his ancient self, there wouldn't only be press agents and candid cameras waiting. Crownbacker was a poor ponce if he really thought that. The thing was political, deeper than adder-pits, more crammed with danger and occasion than anything Rodriguez Kulken had ever had a finger in. Even with the shakes and with the stinking pyjama stuck to his private parts, Kulken could make out, as in a doorway suddenly darkened, a future of clandestine offers and handsome betrayals, of razzias and conversaziones in summit places far richer, far better attuned to his, Kulken's, alchemy of life than all the vulgar loot dreamt up by Charlie boy.

Kulken drew a long voluptuous breath.

But the man had to be got rid of. Kulken needed time, a zone to manoeuvre in freely.

— Get out Mr. Crownbacker. I don't know what you're talking about. I don't know what you think you picked up. And what's more, I don't give a fart.

Charlie stood still. His eyes were a watery green. Kulken's voice rose.

— What the hell do you think you're doing barging into a man's house? Get out. Just like I told you. Shove it.

In her corner the Indian woman moved heavily.

— You asked me what kind of Indians we have here. I'll tell you Mister. The kind I can whistle for and who can strip a plane so fine there won't be a bolt left. Beat it, and *buenos días.*

The American shook his head, gently, as if there had been some trifling error.

— I'm not going Mr. Kulken. You know that. I know that. So why get in a lather? Anyway, I couldn't. Not now.

As Kulken rose at him Marvin Crownbacker moved away with a cat-like spring. He kicked the door of the hut wide open. The morning was gone, eclipsed. Two streaks of yellow light smouldered on the wall of the out-house. Beyond them, billowing toward Orosso, came a blackness high as the sky. A flogging sound was advancing through the forest, louder than the churn of the falls. The Indian woman clapped her hands to her mouth. The rains had begun.

— I couldn't leave now, partner, could I?

said Charlie.

May 25th: A shock last night when, as we were finishing supper,
Edmond asked me whether I had ever seen Hitler. Had there been a
press-leak? The file is, of course, classified top security, but that means
little nowadays. In fact, the boy had simply seen old newsreels being run
on a television show, part of the waves of morbid nostalgia that now
swamps film screens, television, bookstores. I had glimpsed the Führer
once, at Montoire. Xavier had taken me along, as the most junior clerk
in the Maréchal's suite: "something to bore your grandchildren with,
mon petit." We already knew that things had gone awkwardly at
Hendaye, that Franco had been all smiles and not given an inch. *That*,
surely, was the turning point in the war. Not Stalingrad, not Alamein,
not, certainly, the landings. But the Caudillo's refusal to let his precious
allies and companions in arms have right of transit to Gibraltar. After
which the Reich couldn't win. A classic war, really, a vintage-European
war over access to and control of Mediterranean routes. A problem
ancient as Alcibiades' Sicilian débacle, and insoluable still. So our high
guest was in a black mood. He lit up, momentarily, as would any tourist,
on meeting the Maréchal, but the animation faded quickly. I watched him
him on the station platform, shuffling, bobbing about amid his staff
—he rarely stood still—and stretching his legs during a break in the
conference. I have a distinct recollection of a terrible tedium surrounding
his person, streaming outward from him like a draft out of a cold sealed
place. As if he was unspeakably bored, with his fame, with the
machinery he had set in motion, with all the performances he would have
to go through before an end whose futility he may already have intuited.
I know this has a romantic, psychologizing ring to it. But I don't think I
was fantasizing. The man was *ennui* incarnate. When he jerked into
motion or rapid speech, it was obvious that he had tapped great springs
of energy. But one supposed that these were somehow implanted in him,
almost mechanically. The centre was inert, probably lucid. Uncle Xavier
said there had been a man just like that in his company, who had at some
point early in the war, imagined death with such hysterical intensity that
he was never afraid again, merely empty and lashed on by occasional
daring. How would he strike one now, after the years on the run? Has he
wanted to survive or did that too "happen to him," coming from
outside? How much does he remember of the giant, vacant thing he was?
It *would* be fascinating to know, to hear that voice again. If Berdier gets
there first, the occasion will hardly arise. If the Americans do, the
psychologists will have their day. "The rehabilitation of Adolf Hitler;
the elucidation of his childhood traumas." The triumph of the
therapeutic. To Edmond the Reichschancellor is a figure out of the dim
past, somewhere between the neolithic and the almost equally remote

day-before-yesterday. Tarquin, Ivan the Terrible, Hitler, the Hundred Years' War—was it in Europe or in diverse unpronounceable parts of South-East Asia?—all part of a school-syllabus and television-past. Totally unreal. Categorized for examination purposes or entertainment. If I had told the boy that Hitler was thought to be alive, that he might emerge on the box in the flesh, he wouldn't really have believed me. Is he wrong? I don't know myself. But this bizarre ghost-hunt *has* got under my skin. More than I realised. V. is fed up. Not with the hurried sessions and sudden cancellations (this is the first hour I've had to myself in ten days), but because she finds even my body "absent," "up the Amazon"—her oddly apposite turn of phrase. The affair will soon be spent. I know that, and don't mind very much, and don't know why I don't mind. This whole flap at the Ministry and the chance that I may soon be underway to South America (the presence of this branch is "quintessential" as "Attila" likes to put it), seem providential. Yes, that's the word. Providential. When I get back, Edmond must see a skin-doctor. There is no reason for the boy to be disadvantaged. His mother has been so wrapt in herself lately. Or is it herself? I wonder, of course. *Bon soir Seigneur Cliché.* Why do I so hate disorder? Those memoranda-folders askew on the shelf, when I have told my secretary a dozen times

●

— Do you believe me now, you dumb bastard? Well, do you?

Kulken had an appetite for abjection. Within limits. He also had a flair for detestation. But his loathing of Marvin Crownbacker "call me Charlie" was of a disinterested purity, of a constancy, which made him wonder. The stench of the man, of his bare presence, choked him. Their intimacies had grown manifold. That Crownbacker had moved in on him body and soul, that he had taken his share of the Indian woman, that his harsh mobile manner had electrified Orosso, these vulgarities seemed to Kulken commonplace and vaguely fated. It was the elusiveness in "ole Charlie-boy," yet another of the tinny sobriquets his guest thrust upon him, that fixed Kulken's hatred, the interleaving of grating banality—loud, caricatural, inescapable—with a strain dramatically contrasting. Just what the latter consisted of was an enigma which gnawed at Kulken, kept him off balance and hateful. He had, provisionally, settled on some rubric tantamount to "authority," to a covert, implausible yet central authority. Whether of knowledge, clandestine rank or solid purpose, he knew not. This ignorance, playing as it did on his nerves, had come on top of chaos.

First the airplanes: a jet of the Brazilian air force making two passes over the landing-strip, then a light spotter aircraft racketing in at tree-top level and circling Orosso in sluggish sweeps, next that dazzling job, a small commercial or company-jet trying for a landing, twice, which was lunacy in view of the sodden, pock-marked state of the runway, then lifting away towards the jungle. With these incursions had come pandemonium on his receiver. A torrent of instructions, puzzling and otiose, from his employers, who demanded with shrilling impatience, that the airfield (what an inflated name for it, thought Kulken) be drained and made ready, that a salubrious quarter (the blithering idiots) be reserved for "senior personnel," that Kulken, to whom a bonus was felt to be due, prepare to hand over. To all of which Kulken had, on Crownbacker's hoarse insistence, acquiesced, gaining time, gaining backbreaking nights in which to pick out of the air, dryer now, lighter after the great rains, a gaggle of other voices. Many were in code, others sawed off by static and attempts at jamming. But some were plain enough. First they had criss-crossed the continent, weaving an imprecise grid, but then, as in an exercise in orienteering, they had zeroed in on Orosso, using his, Kulken's, transmitter as a focus. ("That, you poor crud, happens to be Russian"—one of Crownbacker's elucidations of the night before which had inspired in Kulken a particular jangle of worry and hatred.) It was merely the state of the runway—the winds had also savaged ole Charlie's flying-machine—which lay between Orosso and an outside world gone seemingly loco. But the margin of immunity was shrinking fast. Kulken had made out enough to know that bulldozers were at work, that the jungle track from Akonqui, the furthest point accessible to a landrover, was being thrashed open. During bouts of fretful sleep he thought he could hear the distant fall of trees. It would not be long now. Only yesterday, through heavy mist, they had heard, or at least thought they had, the clatter of a helicopter. A helicopter might land even now, though Crownbacker's plane was parked, oddly enough, across the centre of the oozing strip. (Pounded with queries on just this point—"who the blazes is with you in Orosso, what's he come for, can you get his bleeding plane off the runway"—Kulken had omitted to answer, an omission the more decorous as Crownbacker, apparently indefatigable, hovered next to the splayed earphones, monitoring these inquiries with satisfied contempt.) But what now? What of their hopes, momentarily allied, once the mob poured in?

— What did I tell you, turd? What did Uncle Charlie tell you? Bormann . . . . o Jeeesus, don't make me laugh.

Hilarity, opined Kulken, was hardly on the agenda. He was, he felt, too finely honed to be taken in altogether by Crownbacker's sordid imaginings of bonanza. Nonetheless, if Herr Adolf did come mincing out of the bush in *propria persona*, and if Crownbacker-Kulken Wire Services Limited did have world rights, horns of plenty would gush. Characteristically offensive as the turn of phrase might well be, *amigo* Charlie's assurance that the event would "make that old epic on Golgotha look like a filler" had its grain of truth. But Kulken had ruminated further. The crass self-evidence of Crownbacker's design had left him restive. The strange beauty of this affair lay with politics, with the warp and weft of statescraft, with potentialities of international barratry or ransom to whose very existence Crownbacker appeared to be ludicrously obtuse. These filaments were Kulken's meat. He envisioned the sum of his past career, menace, humiliation and all, as a didactic prelude to this hour. Hold Hitler and the chancellories would hop to one's piping. Not one but would have pressing grounds for direct or covert approaches, for competitive bidding. Washington, of course, and with immediate overreaching, lest Moscow get in first. London and Paris acting in concert at first, but soon at secret odds, labouring to meet Kulken's price. The two Germanies, almost by compulsive right. The Jews, both in Israel and abroad, to whom the prize must, by now, be an indispensable talisman. It was less the money, though Kulken's sense of prodigality was material and far-flung. It was the commerce with high places, indeed the highest, the Byzantine delicacies of threat and cajolement, the savour of elevation above, of retribution on, the oily bastards who had in so many back-rooms ridden him, that filled Kulken's soul with vertigo, that made him breathe quick and deep as the earphones crackled.

But either eventuality—the richest carnival and scoop on record or the most arcane, remunerative of diplomatic imbroglios—required monopoly. Schickelgruber, alias A. H., must be safely in hand, his finders disposed of, and the world kept at bay. The first two points lay in reach (Crownbacker had sounded the Indians and found them amenable to what would, after all, be a trivial ambush). It was item three which looked desperate. So many signals were pouring in, so many indices of feverish advance somewhere just beyond the horizon, that Kulken felt literally entrapped. How many more days before the pack barged in, high and mighty, scented with cologne and costly tobacco, thrusting Kulken aside, filching the credit, oblivious to the fact that it was he, Kulken, who had, by dint of tireless cunning, reeled in the leviathan out of the inviolate swamps? The injustice of it took Kulken by the throat and he half rose out of his steaming chair. Crownbacker had also turned towards the door. The Indians stood there, three or four of them, brown as their shadows.

The jungle is strangely osmotic. Impenetrable in one sense, it is, in another, rifted by tunnels of communication. Explorers' postulates about totally isolated tribes, about corners of tropical forest or mountain innocent of any contact with the outside, are largely spurious. Good shivery stuff for the glossy magazines, Kulken reckoned. Real isolation was formidably rare, if in fact it existed at all. How word sped across the barbed lines of mutually incomprehensible tongues, how iron utensils from the distant fringe-stations came to be found in the inmost of the Matto Grosso, was something of a riddle. But the facts were certain. News could tear like invisible fire through thicket and across cataracts. You had only to listen and it came humming back.

The party had been shadowed by Indians for at least a fortnight. Four white men with heavy loads, Teku and the Old One. They had been observed marching north north-west, away from the shallow grave and towards the spur of the Cordillera. The ash of their night-fires had been combed, their excrement pondered, their eviscerated food-tins smelt and lifted to the light. The Cinxgu had communicated their notice to the Nambikwa, from whom the news had travelled down the Peranja, somehow arching the nine rapids, from where, in turn, the Jiaro had culled it for display in Orosso. Here it harvested fish-hooks, lengths of rope, two bales of rough linen. So more news came. Of how the party was seeking to avoid the pass, now snowblocked, and find a circumvention to the south, of how Teku appeared to be leading the actual march, of how he foraged for game. And now?

They had halted. Almost in sight of the mountains. They had been camping for several days, four, perhaps five. They no longer kept the Old One tethered. And Teku was carving a chair.

— A chair?

The Indians repeated the word.

Crownbacker did not wait for translation.

— Well, you dumb turd, do you believe me now?

Kulken reflected on the matter of the chair.

— Yes, he said,

— I believe you now.

●

— Marvin Crownbacker's red white and blue right down to his jockstrap. I'd take an oath on that.

— Maybe. But this is a lot bigger than anything he's ever been involved in. We should have sent a senior man, like Truscott. I was overruled.

— He's been doing fine up to now, Chief. He's a real broken field runner, and that's what we needed. At least in the early stages.

— But who the hell is Rodriguez Kulken? The file stinks.

— I know, Chief, I know

It was hard to keep stride with the big man, in the crowded, interminable corridor that led to the press room.

— but he got there ahead of us. Johnny on the spot. Nine points of the law. And I'd be surprised if he'd blown Chuck's cover. Kulken's pretty small stuff. Just a stringer. Not even on the supplementary roster. I've got MI 6's word for that.

The Chief tried to snort audibly but the sound was lost in the hustle of feet.

— They were just lucky getting in there before we did. They took a chance. But Crownbacker's been in on the action almost from the word go.

The crowd was thickening and both men waved their passes.

— Let us through, please. 'Scuse me, ma'am. Okay, okay. Sorry. Coming through. No sweat, Sergeant, but just you keep that door closed once the Secretary begins.

The Chief had hefty shoulders, suddenly haloed by the blaze of klieg lights as they inched their way into the packed chamber.

— The whole goddamn mob. Just look at 'em. The Washington press corps. Pretty, aren't they?

— Well, Earl

The younger man was gripped by excitement, but immediately regretted his recourse to an informality which the Chief had often proffered but, no doubt, preferred to leave conditional.

— it is the biggest news break since

He was struggling for decisive analogy as the throng rose to its feet.

— Battle dress, muttered the Chief as he scanned the Secretary of State's alpaca suit and raw silk tie.

The voices and waving arms surged as from a sea-anemone, bobbing impatiently.

— Ladies and gentlemen. Please. One at a time. Please.

— Riffler. *St. Louis Post-Dispatch.* Mr. Secretary, is it true . . .

The echoing buzz subsided slowly.

— I wish we could finalize our answer to that, Mr. Riffler, but we aren't absolutely certain. What I would say is this: on the basis of available evidence, and in view of the assessment made both by our own intelligence and that of the other sovereign states with whom we have been in touch, there is a reasonable expectation that the man found by what we understand to be—and I underline this point—an unofficial pursuit-party is indeed the Head of State of the so-called Third Reich.

The voices and flash-bulbs burst chaotically.

— Miss Marten. . . .

— Thank you, Mr. Secretary. Regina Marten, *Southern News Syndicate.* When do you expect Hitler to come out of those woods and who'll be there to receive him?

— Again, I'm afraid, the question is open to some doubt. According to the latest information we have, and you must realise, ladies and gentlemen, that communications from the heart of the Amazonian rain-forests are somewhat circuitous

(Nice word that, thought the young man)

the party and the alleged Mr. Hitler have halted. South by southwest of Orosso, at the approaches to a high plateau beyond which our maps locate a native hamlet designated as Jiaro.

(The Secretary of State was glancing at his notes.)

Under optimal conditions the party could be expected to reach civilization, that is to say the air-strip and radio-transmitter thought to be operative at Orosso in something on the order of ten days. But I am given to understand that there have been early rains of exceptional intensity resulting in flash-floods and fresh snow on the high places. As to the question of the status and identity of personnel at the presumed meeting-point, I would prefer to reserve our position. As you can readily imagine, Miss Marten, this is an issue of extreme diplomatic nicety, involving as it does the local authorities as well as those foreign governments who may or may not have a valid claim to be regarded as interested parties.

— Escomb. *Time* magazine. Sir, do we have anybody on he spot, right now?

— You will understand, Bill, that it would be against the best interests of our government to go into details, at a moment when the relevant issues remain somewhat confused. But I think I could say this: the degree of surveillance we have been able to exercise over the day-today course of events should suggest to you that our position is one of readiness at both the local and global levels.

— Mr. Secretary, you've referred . . . sorry: Cord Dwyer, *Milwaukee Tribune.* You've referred to contacts with other governments. Can you elaborate on that?

— Gladly. As is obvious to everyone concerned, the discovery of Herr Hitler, if identification turns out to be positive, is a matter for international response. The sovereign states party to the Berlin agreements and to the Nuremberg tribunal are naturally involved. So is Brazil on whose territory the putative Reichschancellor was found and which he had, it is to be presumed, entered illegally. Since the time when the indictments for war-crimes were drawn up, moreover, the political map has greatly changed. Both the German Democratic Republic and the German Federal Republic have declared their strong interest in the case. It is conceivable also that the Republic of Austria, in which the subject was born and, at different times of his life, domiciled, may wish to be a party to the proceedings of identification and to what are, unavoidably I fear, bound to be the intricacies of extradition. Though the issue is one on which our government has, as yet, evolved no firm view, there would appear to be a *prima facie* case for referral to the United Nations. I have instructed members of the United States delegation to solicit the views of the Secretary General and of his legal staff on this very point.

— What about Israel?

The voice was strained and the thick accent cut in above the chorus of questioners.

— Why haven't you mentioned Israel, Mr. Secretary of State? He's our prisoner, isn't he?

— Believe me, Mr. Simon, it is Mr. Simon, isn't it?

and the Secretary shaded his eyes for a moment against the hot banked lights.

— I would be only too pleased if I could give you an unequivocal answer. But our exchanges with your government on this entire matter have been less than satisfactory. It is no longer a secret to reveal that our first communications, transmitted as soon as expert opinion regarded the matter as potentially of substance, received nothing but routine acknowledgement. When we pressed for reply at a most senior level —the President himself has, of course, kept developments under daily review—the response from Tel Aviv was, to say the least, disappointing. So far as we are aware—and that comprises cables submitted to me this morning—your government has not taken any official note of the reports of Mr. Hitler's capture. It has neither acknowledged nor denied any participation in the recruitment, dispatch or future utilization of the search-team. Inquiries on our part as to the position the State of Israel might take in respect of a possible trial before a multinational court have, hitherto, met with no clarification. So far as this Administration goes, efforts to elucidate and give the most favourable possible construction to Israeli concerns in the matter and to those of the Jewish community as a whole, will of course continue.

— What if we get him out on our own, and transport him to Israel?

The same voice, hectoring.

— I would, I'm afraid, find it irresponsible to comment on so hypothetical a question. The precedent which you may have in mind, Mr. Simon, I refer to the Eichmann case, has, I feel, left a legacy of serious doubt with regard to international law and agreed usage among nations.

Out of the gaggle of voices an alto.

— Gene Jefferson, *Atlanta News-Times*. Mr. Secretary, in view of your previous answer, would you care to comment on whether or not a statute of limitations applies to Hitler's crimes. And what of the man's mental state? Suppose he is no longer fit to plead.

The Hon. Avery Lockyer dabbed his cheek.

— As many of you ladies and gentlemen are aware, I have spent a good deal of my life in the law. I am well aware of the fact that even at this considerable remove in time uneasiness over judicial aspects of the Nuremberg proceedings persists. This Administration and I personally hold no brief for special retroactive law. The ideal of common law precedents is enshrined in our way of life in these United States and, I would hope, in the policies of this Department. But you will recall that the statute of limitations was specifically voided with regard to what have been defined as "crimes against humanity." The current eventuality would appear to exemplify this category in an emphatic way. As to the issue of the accused's mental condition and degree of responsibility, it is obviously too early to express an opinion. I remind you that no identification has yet been validated nor any personal contact made by any agent of your Government. We would hope that thorough psychiatric checks can be initiated, under proper conditions, and as soon as possible.

— Tylden. AP. Do the Russians see it that way?

— I'd prefer to withhold comment on that, Ed.

— Mr. Secretary. Ann Carey. *Miami Herald*. Surely it would be possible to fly that party out. To pick them up by helicopter. Why all the delay?

(— Watch this, breathed the Chief, whose corner-of-the-mouth *sotto voce* was notorious throughout the service.)

— I wish it were that simple, Miss Carey. To the best of our knowledge the most proximate landing facility, at Orosso, has, until a few days ago, been waterlogged. Even from there, a helicopter pick-up presents severe technical problems. It is, moreover, by no means evident what the attitude of the search-party would be to intervention at this point. Perhaps Mr. Simon would care to enlighten us.

Mild laughter in the stifling room and a shuffle of metal chairs.

— Big deal, muttered the Chief, let's get back to the saltmines.

The younger man followed as they shouldered their way through the close-packed spectators and made for the exit. Just before they reached it and caught the cold draft from the now-empty corridor, the young man registered an arresting voice, almost Gregorian.

— Sir, can you give us an assurance, an emphatic assurance, that due process will be followed and, most especially, that the accused will be given every legal aid for his defense?

Shutting behind them the baize door cut off the answer.

●

He squinted at his art. Another pass with his flat hand and the
wood shone back at the light of the early sun. It was a regal furnishing, a
seat fit for an old man whose language Teku could not make out, whose
skin sagged and splotched like that of a swamp-rat three days gone, but
in whose eyes the carver had seen two points of cold silver such as only
the greatest of the tale-tellers, of the spirit-raisers possess.

Now he lifted the stool and carried it to the circle of swept earth,
almost at the midpoint of the camp, as Simeon had ordered him to do.
Let those Jiaro scarecrows gape. Let word of this throne travel as far as
the nine falls.

Isaac Amsel could not take his eyes off this lambent handiwork.
Uncertainly he slid his fingers over the subtly-rounded seat. Teku's
cunning, on the march, at food-gathering, in the clearing of camp-sites
filled him with troubled wonder. He had known of such skills, he had
seen them acted in films of exploration and jungle-romance. It was a
different feeling altogether to witness them at first hand, adroitly en-
folded, as it seemed, in the flesh of this small brown visitor, so brittle, so
unprepossessing when compared with the stature of Benasseraf or that of
Isaac's father. The Indian, in turn, prized the boy's endurance, the way
he dogged and sometimes defied the older men. He was teaching him to
handle the blow-gun, to make of his pent breath a whistling rush, to spot
the change of shadows behind shadows which signified game.

Elie had sat on the ground, halfway between the ceremonial stool
and the seat Simeon had made for himself of an empty crate and gray
blanket. For the first time since the capture, Simeon had unwrapped and
opened the water-proof metal tube, so like a botanist's sampler, in which
Lieber had stored the articles of attainder. He thought it would be best to
read them aloud, then to give them to John Asher and the accused; after
which he, Simeon, leader of the party and agent plenipotentiary would
set forth, with all deliberation and clarity, the grounds, reasons, motives
which had caused him to institute proceedings here, at latitude x and
longitude y, between the rain-forest and the Cordillera, with himself as
presiding judge, Elie Barach as explicator of the Law, Asher as defense
counsel, and Isaac and Teku as witnesses. To state reasons for a
procedure which ordinary good sense and world opinion would doubtless condemn as irregular, indeed mad, but which Simeon knew, upon
searching examination, to be conclusive. In regard to the facts of the
material and psychological reserves (now fast dwindling) of the party, in

regard to their relation to the prisoner and the past, in regard to that indecent and piratical tumult which, they had every cause to expect, lay at the planned end of the march. Simeon had resolved to enunciate these propositions with condign solemnity. He had turned over in his mind phrases which, he knew, could be voiced this one and singular time only in human history. Elie had considered the pronouncement and suggested illustrative citations.

Now everything appeared to be ready. The accused was leaving the shelter with Asher at his heels. Simeon's mouth went dry as he waited for the two men to take up their appointed place. But already, as he came forward with his withered arm crooked to his side, Mr. Asher's client had begun to speak.

●

Erster Punkt. Article one. Because you must understand that I did not invent. It was Adolf Hitler who dreamt up the master race. Who conceived of enslaving inferior peoples. Lies. Lies. It was in the doss-house, in the *Männerheim* that I first understood. It was in. God help me, but that was long ago. And the lice. Large as a thumb-nail. 1910, 1911. What does it matter now? It was there that I first understood your secret power. The secret power of your teaching. Of *yours*. A chosen people. Chosen by God for His own. The only race on earth chosen, exalted, made singular among mankind. It was Grill who taught me. Do you know about Grill? No. You know nothing about me. Jahn Grill. But that wasn't his name. Do you hear me? Called himself Jahn, said he was a defrocked priest. For all I know he may have been. That too. But his real name was Jacob. Jacob Grill, son of a rabbi, from Poland. Or Galicia. Or. What does it matter. One of yours, yours, yours. We lived close. One soap-sliver between us. It was Grill who taught me, who showed me the words. The chosen people. God's own and elect amid the unclean, amid the welter of nations. Who shall be chastised for impurity, for taking a heathen to wife, who shall have bondsmen and bondswomen from among the *goyim*, but stay apart. My promise was only a thousand years. "To eternity" said Grill; lo, it is written here. In letters of white fire. The covenant of election, the setting apart of the race, *das heilige Volk*, like unto no other. Under the iron law. Circumcision and the sign on your forehead. One law, one race, one destiny unto the end of the end of time. "And Joshua burnt Ai, and made it an heap for ever, even a desolation unto this day." "And Joshua made them that day hewers of wood and drawers of water for the congregation." All of them. Men, women, children. To serve Israel in bondage. But more often there was no one to enslave. "And they utterly destroyed all that was in the city, both man and woman, young and old, and ox, and sheep, and ass, with the edge of the sword." Your holy books. The smell of blood. Jacob Grill, friend Grill, and Neumann, for whom I painted postcards, they smelt of shit. But they taught me. That a people must be chosen to fulfill its destiny, that there can be no other thus made glorious. That a true nation is a mystery, a single body willed by God, by history, by the unmingled burning of its blood. It does not matter what you call the roots of the dream. A mystery of will, of chosenness. To conquer its promised land, to cut down or lay in bondage all who stand in its path, to proclaim itself eternal. "Let the trumpet blow in Zion. Let the Cherubim of the Lord bring fire and plague unto our enemies." You could hear the lice crack between Grill's fingers. God how his breath stank. But he read from the book. Your book. Of which every letter is sacred, and every mite of every letter. That's so isn't it? Read till lights out, and after, sing-song through the nose, because he knew it by heart, from his schooldays, and had heard his father. The rabbi. "They utterly destroyed all that was in the city." In Samaria. Because the Samaritans read a different scripture. Because they had built a sanctuary of their own. Of terebinth. Six cubits to the left. They had made it seven or five or God knows. Put to the sword. The first time. Every man, woman, child, she-ox, the dogs too. No. No dogs. They are of the unclean things that hop or crawl on the earth, like the Philistine, the unclean of Moab, the lepers of Sidon. To slaughter a city because of an idea, because of a vexation over words. Oh that was a high invention, a device to alter the human soul. Your invention. One Israel, one *Volk,* one leader. Moses, Joshua, the anointed king who has slain his thousands, no his ten-thousands, and dances before the ark. It was in Compiègne, wasn't it? They say I danced there. Only a small dance.

The pride of it, the brute cunning. Whatever you are, wherever, be it ulcerous as Job, or Neumann scratching his stinking crotch. You should have seen the two of us peddling those postcards, like starved dogs. But what does it matter if you're one of the chosen people? One of God's familiars, above all other men, set apart for His rages and His love. In a covenant, a singling out, a consecration never to be lost. Grill told me that. Jahn Jacob Grillschmuhl Grill or whatever his greasy name was, reeking of piss when he crawled up the stairs. Even he. The apostate. The outcast from Zion. Was still of the chosen, a private vexation to the Almighty. "Listen," he said, "listen Adi," no man else ever called me that, "you think you see me as I am, Grill the loser, the doss-house bum. But you're blind. All you *goyim* are blind. For all you know, Adi, I am one of the seventy-two chosen, chosen even above the chosen. One of the secret just ones on whom the earth rests. And while you snore tonight or swallow your spit, listen to me Adi, here in this barrack, right here, my blind friend, the Messiah may come to me and know me for his own." And he would roll his eyes and give a little laugh, a yellow Jew-laugh. It went through me like a knife. But I learnt.

From you. Everything. To set a race apart. To keep it from defilement. To hold before it a promised land. To scour that land of its inhabitants or place them in servitude. Your beliefs. Your arrogance. In Nuremberg, the searchlights. That clever beaver Speer. Straight into the night. Do you remember them? The pillar of fire. That shall lead you to Canaan. And woe unto the Amorities, the Jebusites, the Kenites, the

half-men outside God's pact. My "Superman"? Second-hand stuff.
Rosenberg's philosophic garbage. They whispered to me that *he* too. The
name. My racism was a parody of yours, a hungry imitation. What is a
thousand-year *Reich* compared to the eternity of Zion? Perhaps I was
the false Messiah sent before. Judge me and you must judge yourselves.
Übermenschen, chosen ones!

    — What my client means, began Asher

    Punkt II. There had to be a solution, a *final* solution. For what is
the Jew if he is not a long cancer of unrest? Gentlemen, I beg your attention, I demand it. Was there ever a crueller invention, a contrivance
more calculated to harrow human existence, than that of an omnipotent,
all-seeing, yet invisible, impalpable, inconceivable God? Gentlemen, I
pray you, consider the case, consider it closely. The pagan earth was
crowded with small deities, malicious or consoling, winged or pot-
bellied, in leaf and branch, in rock and river. Giving companionship to
man, pinching his bottom or caressing him, but of his measure. Delighting in honey-cakes and roast meat. Gods after our own image and
necessities. And even the great deities, the Olympians, would come down
in mortal visitation, to do war and lechery. Mightier than we, I grant
you, but tangible and taking on the skin of things. The Jew emptied the
world by setting his God apart, immeasurably apart from man's senses.
No image. No concrete embodiment. No imagining even. A blank
emptier than the desert. Yet with a terrible nearness. Spying on our every
misdeed, searching out the heart of our heart for motive. A God of
vengeance unto the thirtieth generation (those are the Jews' words, not
mine). A God of contracts and petty bargains, of indentures and bribes.
"And the Lord gave Job twice as much as he had before." A thousand
she-asses where the crazed, boiled old man had had only five hundred to
start with. It makes one vomit, doesn't it? *Twice* as much. Gentlemen,
do you grasp the sliminess of it, the moral trickery? Cast your guiltless
servant into hell, thunder at him out of the whirlwind, draw leviathan by
the nose, and then? Double his income, declare a dividend, slip him a
lordly tip. Why did Job not spit at that cattle-dealer of a God? Yet the
holy of holies was an empty room, a silence in a silence. And the Jew
mocks those who have pictures of their god. *His* God is purer than any
other. The very thought of Him exceeds the powers of the human mind.
We are as blown dust to His immensity. But because we are His
creatures, we must be better than ourselves, love our neighbour, be
continent, give of what we have to the beggar. Because His inconceivable, unimaginable presence envelops us, we must obey every jot
of the law. We must bottle up our rages and desires, chastise the flesh
and walk bent in the rain. You call me a tyrant, an enslaver. What

tyranny, what enslavement has been more oppressive, has branded the skin and soul of man more deeply, than the sick fantasies of the Jew? You are not Godkillers, but *Godmakers*. And that is infinitely worse. The Jew invented conscience and left man a guilty serf.

But that was only the first piece of blackmail. There was worse to come. The white-faced Nazarene. Gentlemen, I find it difficult to contain myself. But the facts must speak for themselves. What did that epileptic rabbi ask of man? That he renounce the world, that he leave mother and father behind, that he offer the other cheek when slapped, that he render good for evil, that he love his neighbour as himself, no, far better, for self-love is an evil thing to be overcome. Oh grand castration! Note the cunning of it. Demand of human beings more than they can give, demand that they give up their stained, selfish humanity in the name of a higher ideal, and you will make of them cripples, hypocrites, mendicants for salvation. The Nazarene said that his kingdom, his purities were not of this world. Lies, honeyed lies. It was here on earth that he founded his slave-church. It was men and women, creatures of flesh, he abandoned to the blackmail of hell, of eternal punishment. What were our camps compared to *that*? Ask of man more than he is, hold before his tired eyes an image of altruism, of compassion, of self-denial which only the saint or the madman can touch, and you stretch him on the rack. Till his soul bursts. What can be crueller than the Jew's addiction to the ideal?

First the invisible but all-seeing, the unattainable but all-demanding God of Sinai. Second the terrible sweetness of Christ. Had the Jew not done enough to sicken man? No, gentlemen, there is a third act to our story.

"Sacrifice yourself for the good of your fellow-man. Relinquish your possessions so that there may be equality for all. Hammer yourself hard as steel, strangle emotion, loyalty, mercy, gratitude. Denounce parent or lover. So that justice may be achieved on earth. So that history be fulfilled and society be purged of all imperfection." Do you recognize the sermon, gentlemen? The litany of hatred? Rabbi Marx on the day of atonement. Was there ever a greater promise? "The classless society, to each according to his needs, brotherhood for all mankind, the earth made a garden again, a rational Eden." In the name of which promise tyranny, torture, war, extermination were a necessity, an historical necessity! It is no accident that Marx and his minions were Jews, that the congregations of Bolshevism—Trotsky, Rosa Luxembourg, Kamenev, the whole fanatic, murderous pack—were of Israel. Look at them: prophets, martyrs, smashers of images, word-spinners drunk with the terror of the absolute. It was only a step, gentlemen, a small, inevitable

step, from Sinai to Nazareth, from Nazareth to the covenant of
Marxism. The Jew had grown impatient, his dreams had gone rancid. Let
the kingdom of justice come here and now, next Monday morning. Let
us have a secular messiah instead. But with a long beard and his bowels
full of vengeance.

Three times the Jew has pressed on us the blackmail of transcendence. Three times he has infected our blood and brains with the
bacillus of perfection. Go to your rest and the voice of the Jew cries out
in the night. "Wake up! God's eye is upon you. Has He not made you in
His image? Lose your life so that you may gain it. Sacrifice yourself to
the truth, to justice, to the good of mankind." That cry has been in our
ears too long, gentlemen, far too long. Men had grown sick of it, sick to
death. When I turned on the Jew, no one came to his rescue. No one.
France, England, Russia, even Jew-ridden America did nothing. They
were glad that the exterminator had come. Oh they did not say so openly,
I allow you that. But secretly they rejoiced. We had to find, to burn out
the virus of utopia before the whole of our western civilization sickened.
To return to man as he is, selfish, greedy, short-sighted, but warm and
housed, so marvellously housed, in his own stench. "We were chosen to
be the conscience of man" said the Jew. And I answered him, yes, I,
gentlemen, who now stand before you: "You are not man's conscience,
Jew. You are only his bad conscience. And we shall vomit you so we may
live and have peace." A final solution. How could there be any other?

— The question the defendant is raising, rasped Asher

Do not interrrupt. I will not tolerate interruption. I am an old
man. My voice tires. Gentlemen, I appeal to your sense of justice, your
notorious sense of justice. Hear me out. Consider my third point. Which
is that you have exaggerated. Grossly. Hysterically. That you have made
of me some kind of mad devil, the quintessence of evil, hell embodied.
When I was, in truth, only a man of my time. Oh inspired, I will grant
you, with a certain—how shall I put it?—nose for the supreme political
possibility. A master of human moods, perhaps, but a man of my time.

Average, if you will. Had it been otherwise, had I been the
singular demon of your rhetorical fantasies, how then could millions of
ordinary men and women have found in me the mirror, the plain mirror
of their needs and appetites? And it was, I will allow you that, an ugly
time. But I did not create its ugliness, and I was not the worst. Far from
it. How many wretched little men of the forests did your Belgian friends
murder outright or leave to starvation and syphilis when they raped the
Congo? Answer me that, gentlemen. Or must I remind you? Some
twenty million. That picnic was under way when I was new-born. What
were Rotterdam or Coventry compared to Dresden and Hiroshima? I do

not come out worst in that black game of numbers. Did I invent the camps? Ask of the Boers. But let us be serious. Who was it that broke the *Reich?* To whom did you hand over millions, tens of millions of men and women from Prague to the Baltic? Set them like a bowl of milk before an insatiable cat? I was a man of a murderous time, but a small man compared to *him.* You think of me as a satanic liar. Very well. Do not take my word for it. Choose what sainted, unimpeachable witness you will. The holy writer, the great bearded one who came out of Russia and preached to the world. It is long ago now. My memory aches. The man of the archipelago. Yes, that word sticks in the mind. What did he say? That Stalin had slaughtered *thirty* million. That he had perfected genocide when I was still a nameless scribbler in Munich. My boys used their fists and their whips. I won't deny it. The times stank of hunger and blood. But when a man spat out the truth they would stop their fun. Stalin's torturers worked for the pleasure of the thing. To make men befoul themselves, to obtain confessions which are lies, insanities, obscene jokes. The truth only made them more bestial. It is not I who assert these things: it is your own survivors, your historians, the sage of the Gulag. Who, then, was the greater destroyer, whose blood-lust was the more implacable? Stalin's or mine? Ribbentrop told me: of the man's contempt for *us.* Whom he found amateurish, corrupt with mercy. Our terrors were a village carnival compared to his. Our camps covered absurd acres; he had strung wire and death-pits around a continent. Who survived among those who had fought with him, brought him to power, executed his will? Not one. He smashed their bones to the last splinter. When my fall came my good companions were alive, fat, scuttling for safety or recompense, cavorting towards you with their contritions and their memoires. How many Jews did Stalin kill, your saviour, your ally Stalin? Answer me that. Had he not died when he did, there would not have been one of you left alive between Berlin and Vladivostok. Yet Stalin died in bed, and the world stood hushed before the tiger's rest. Whereas you hunt me down like a rabid dog, put me on trial (by what right, by what mandate?), drag me through the swamps, tie me up at night. Who am a very old man and uncertain of recollection. Small game, gentlemen, hardly worthy of your skills. In a world that has tortured political prisoners and poured napalm on naked villagers, that has stripped the earth of plant and animal. That has done these things and continues to do them quite without my help and long after I, "the one out of hell"—oh ludicrous, histrionic phrase—was thought to have been extinct.

Asher's breath came loud and empty.

Do not trouble yourself, *Herr Advokat.* I have only one more

point to make. The last. That strange book *Der Judenstaat*. I read it
carefully. Straight out of Bismarck. The language, the ideas, the tone of
it. A clever book, I agree. Shaping Zionism in the image of the new
German nation. But did Herzl create Israel or did I? Examine the
question fairly. Would Palestine have become Israel, would the Jews
have come to that barren patch of the Levant, would the United States
and the Soviet Union, *Stalin's* Soviet Union, have given you recognition
and guaranteed your survival, had it not been for the Holocaust? It was
the Holocaust that gave you the courage of injustice, that made you drive
the Arab out of his home, out of his field, because he was lice-eaten and
without resource, because he was in your divinely-ordered way. That
made you endure knowing that those whom you had driven out were
rotting in refugee camps, not ten miles away, buried alive in despair and
lunatic dreams of vengeance. Perhaps I *am* the Messiah, the true Messiah,
the new Sabbatai whose infamous deeds were allowed by God in order to
bring His people home. "The Holocaust was the necessary mystery
before Israel could come into its strength." It is not I who have said it:
but your own visionaries, your unravellers of God's meaning when it is
Friday night in Jerusalem. Should you not honour me who have made
you into men of war, who have made of the long, vacuous day-dream of
Zion a reality? Should you not be a comfort to my old age?

Gentlemen of the tribunal: I took my doctrines from you. I
fought the blackmail of the ideal with which you have hounded
mankind. My crimes were matched and surpassed by those of others. The
Reich begat Israel. These are my last words. The last words of a dying
man against the last words of those who suffered; and in the midst of
incertitude must matters be left till the great revelation of all secrets.

Teku had not understood the words, only their meaning. Whose
brazen pulse carried all before it. He had leapt up to cry out "Proven."
To cry it to the earth twice and twice to the north as is the custom.
But the air seemed to be exploding around him. Loud drum-beats
hammering closer and closer, driving his voice back into his throat. He
looked up, his ears pounding.

The first helicopter was hovering above the clearing. The second

JEREMY LANE
B-ABEL

SOUNDLESSLY, ONE COULD say, or with the faintest *ftt*, the gates of Number 1 Port slid aside and Zunge stepped forward into a hail of crossfire. Dr Zero Zunge, Director of the Neo-Normative Universal Linguistics Laboratory, acronymically NNULL. From all sides silently lethal theta-rays (able to erase, these rays, all organic matter in their way, in their way) struck, it comes as no surprise, our Zero, and the Doctor's dapper figure (if a mite rotund) instantly dissolved. Disintegrated. Obliterated, *obit* Zunge. Zung, Zun , Zu , Z . Dead. Announce and annihilate one's protagonist in a paragraph, nothing easier, no sooner said than Z's irrevocably done for. Gone. Unless capriciously, one could say, he's reconstituted, resurrected, our Z.Z., and lives to die, one could say, another day.

Soundlessly, one could say, *one could say*, said Zunge to himself, almost agonized, *almost anything*. But not, stepping forward into the Chamber, for much longer. Soon, soon all that would end, period. Soon one would say, one could say, only the One, the One and Only.

The Chamber, he noted, satisfied, was full. No, not quite: a single empty Screen awaited its Projector. Who but his old rival, Thou, unpunctual, imprecise as ever? Had he no sense of occasion? Zunge's lips tightened, whitened, behind the fixed smile. Let him be late then: soon, soon it would be too late for that, period. Soon there would be, could be, only the time to be on time, One Time.

And now here he came, white haired, shuffling, Professor Arthur Thou, formerly of the Society for Opening Up Language, acronymically SOUL, unfortunately now defunct, and latterly of the Institute of Universal Semiotics, yes, yes, IUS, smiling, nodding, vigorously shaking hands—'hands'—a stranger to the proper formalities, familiar to all. Greeting and greeted in divers tongues, in grunts and squeals and clicks and hums, subsonic, ultrasonic, loquacious, laconic, Thou, the greatest linguist of them all. Till now, till now.

Stiffly Zunge held back, waiting, punctilious with respect to place and precedence, for him, for Thou that is, to find his Screen before himself, Zunge that is, crossing to the Principal Projector. Let him take his place now: soon, soon there would be no place for that, period. Soon there would be, could be, only the place to be in place, One Place. The Chamber, he noted, satisfied, was full.

That was scarcely surprising, in view of the Revelation promised, in consideration of the Proposition to ensue. Screenings had however become increasingly infrequent in recent times, since most Delegates had to Project several centuries—some indeed a millennium or two—merely to Screen a few minutes. Hardly a journey one made every day.

Now and here, nevertheless, had gathered an intergalactic assembly of extreme brilliance, the leading lights, in their respective and respected fields, of Universum. Gathered with the sole purpose of Screening *one* Revelation, of gratifying—that is to say, ratifying—*one* Proposition: '*Mine!*' exclaimed exultant Zero (not, it must be clear by now, our handsome hero), exclaimed though silently, if you'll permit the paradox, secretly, careful to seclude such triumphings from the thought detectors, from prying Projectors, from keen Screens. A betrayal of his principles, this secrecy, but unavoidable for the time being, in this situation, time being unavoidable for the time being, situation in this situation. But not for much longer. Soon, soon there would be only the Time, the Place, the One, the All, All that One Says.

Polite applause saluted Zunge as he mounted the rostrum and he bowed briefly in acknowledgement before taking his place in the centre of the three Screens ranged behind the Principal Projector. Installed, he turned and whispered, a few words presumably, of encouragement probably, to the young man seated, a little lower, to his right, to his right hand young man. This was his assistant, Judd Good, who grinned in reply and raised his Performative in the primitive 'thumbs-up' gesture. (The assistance of assistants always welcome at times, in tales, like these.) Tall, lanky, one could say gawky, the flaxenhaired, frecklefaced Judd had been Zunge's since his freshman year five centuries before. For behind and below freckles and flax, freshness and fairness, lay a scientific brain of exceptional acuity. The first double First of his year at U University —second only, the brain and the First, in Zunge's estimation, to his, that is Zunge's, own. A smart lad, Judd, who had succeeded where no one had before, in isolating the secondary stratum—no, no, not yet. Let's relish the poor pleasure of a slight suspense, the Substance secret still. Zero, silent, smiled.

Meanwhile the Kanzler had risen and was Projecting the customary preamble, the expected eulogy of NNULL's successes.

'Unique in Universum, mmm, let nothing stand in the path of progress, this immensely complex organization, mmm, wholly dedicated to the advance of science, the disinterested pursuit, perfection is the goal, the zeal of Dr Zunge, mmm, proud to present -'

Performatives rose progressively to the proper heights of respect, esteem, admiration, and Zunge inclined in response, the thrice pre-scribed, before advancing to the Projector. He paused an instant before rising to the Height of Eloquence, a position held, hovering, approxi-mately three primimetres above the floor of the rostrum. Then, breathing a little heavily, it must be confessed, for despite eurhythmic exercises sustained levitation was a strain these days, he began to speak. And said, Z.Z., what—reader here, read on, read on—lies, what lies ahead.

'Colleagues, united in U, Delegates congregate!'

Immediately, obediently, all Performatives adopted the Attentive Attitude. One, a little slower, a little lazier than the rest perhaps but, yes, even that old reprobate Thou was Attending now.

'Firstly, thanks to All for Appearing here today. To interrupt rigid and replete routines, to clear full and busy Screens, to come centuries, even millennia, merely to listen to the lucubrations of a lab linguist, a nobody from NNULL: it places a heavy responsibility on the Principal Projector which, however, it will do its utmost to discharge with due deliberation, determined, undeterred.'

Partial, our protagonist, to the palatal; prone, too, to the plosive; and apt, you've heard, to alliterate. Faults, frivolities forgivable in one who'd spent a lifetime tinkering with tongues. Faults soon, soon to be corrected, frivolities soon, soon there'd be no time, no space, no speech for, unforgivable. Zunge continued.

'It is hoped and expected that the promised Revelation and the ensuing Proposition will satisfy all hopes and exhaust all expectations. For it is claimed that this is the third and last Central or C Revelation and that the succeeding Proposition is the third and last Basic or B Propo-sition. It is consequently claimed that this Revelation and Proposition together establish once and for all the unity and totality of U, without exception, within necessity, without doubt. End.'

Screen by Screen, row upon row, Performatives opened and exten-ded in Amazed and Admiring Attitudes. But Zunge did not pause, for applause, not yet, but set on, on.

'All will recall the previous two C Revelations and their Propositions which, it is asserted, culminate in these, in this. Nonetheless a brief *résumé* may be useful.'

Useful for you too, reader, for whom it's all new, all to do, reader, this fiction of history, fabling futurity and pretending to a past. And welcome to them, to judge from the lean of each Screen, tilted to absorb Zunge's every word. Even Thou's, now. So Zunge pursued, with his review.

'As you all know, in the third millennium of U the first C Revelation was disclosed: the Revelation of Room, developed over many thousands of primiyears from the archaic concept of relativity. Simultaneously, the first B Proposition, *Anyone is Anywhere*, was Projected and Screened, ubiquitously, in the formula $Al = An$.

'The Revelation of Room immensely facilitated Extension in and out of space, outer and inner, and thus permitted Inhabitants to dispense with all those *passé* modes of passage, spaceship and satellite, the missile and the fissile, and all those demodé dreams of distance, the light year, the far star, speeds of sound, of light, of thought. The hackneyed carriages of so-called science, prevenance, transit, destination: such terms ceased to have importance or even meaning. Consider, if you will the primiterm 'travel', much used to describe Extension in the days BR (Before Room). Etymologically it is connected to the expression of labour, exertion, toil—logically enough, when one reflects on the conditions governing Extension in those tired and tiring times. The effort of Extending, under the weight of a world, a body one could never displace, never disperse, rendered the smallest step a tribulation. Recall, if you can, your childhood days, childhood all those centuries ago, *my* childhood before there was Room, and the heaviness, the heaviness...'.

For an instant Zunge faltered, fell silent, and throughout the Chamber there was a dipping of Performatives, disconcerted, detecting Feeling, fearing worse, Emotion. Apart from Art's, which still stayed Attentive, still. Zunge, however, recovered swiftly and, firmly Projected, the Objective was restored.

'Yet, while in theory Room permitted U's inhabitants total freedom of Extension, and indeed, Intension, the Revelation had in practice little or no effect, since the temporal dimension remained undisclosed. Room needed more: a match, a motion, a concept to complement its own. In a word, Room wanted Rhythm.

'However, a further six millennia of ceaseless research were necessary to achieve the second C Revelation, the entirely logical but unutterably complex consequence of the first. The Revelation of Rhythm in the ninth millennium of U served not only to establish the principles of its own B Proposition, *Now is [N]ever*—expressed in the equation $Nl = eN$ — but also to release the real capacity of Room. U was transformed.'

Performatives pirouetted gravely. Room and Rhythm were cause, of course, for congratulation, for celebration, repeatedly. But they were far from new. And they were eager to know the new, like you, reader, like you expectant, in suspense, waiting for the Doctor to dispense his panacea. NNULL's cure-all, the quintessence which would set...not yet, not yet: first our Zunge must rehearse the past, first, first and last. On, Zero, on.

'It would be idle to enumerate the countless benefits we have derived from Room and Rhythm. Time travel, that feeble fantasy of primitive eras, is prosaic actuality. Simultaneity, ubiquity, immensity: such qualities, once supposed the prerogative of the supernatural, are common property now. In principle.'

Zunge's Performative rose, monitory, modifying.

'For it immediately became clear that the two B Propositions could not be realized indiscriminately or chaos would ensue. Certain controls would have to be applied, particular procedures observed. The Council of U entered therefore into plenary and extraordinary session and two fundamental Laws were swiftly drafted, debated, and decreed, to regulate the scope of the two C Revelations and the efficacy of the B Propositions. These were of course the two R Laws, Register and Respect, more popularly known as Code and Courtesy. The Laws together affirmed twin prohibitions, severally instituted triple injunctions: there could be no Extension (without) without Decision, Precision, and Bidding Farewell; no Intension (within) without Description, Prescription, and Welcome Greeting. Life in U otherwise would quickly become incoherent, inspissate, interminably plosive. No, arbitrary Tending could not, no arbitrary Tending could, be allowed. There had to be a grammar of going, of getting.

'The necessity for such restrictions was recognized, indeed announced, by NNULL but the Lab has always laboured to transcend them and to discover a means of achieving Total Tendency without confusion, thus rendering Code and Courtesy redundant. For many centuries, more, for millennia the Analysts of NNULL, the Annullers, have experimented with phoneme and tincture, with solvent and sememe, but so far without success.'

So far, so good. Judd Good it was, recall, who had succeeded where no one, including Zero, had, smart lad: in isolating the secondary set of primary properties, leading to the discovery of further strata and so — no, no.

'The problem appeared insoluble. How to create the conditions in which Tendency could be unconditional. How?'

There's the nub, the hub, the rub. Art Thou pulled reflectively at his straggling, whitening beard, his eyes, those deepset, those arresting, questing eyes, troubled, questioning. But Zunge had all the answers, the answer to all.

'From the first it had been evident that the problem was essentially one of language. While speech remained in a virtually primitive state of diversity, it seemed impossible to admit more than the most moderate Tendencies. Centuries were spent therefore in the construction and perfection of a single, composite language, to be employed by all Inhabitants throughout U. The outcome, as you know, was Univoc: the amalgamation and reduction of every individual language, every jargon, to the general. No mean achievement, this achievement of the Mean, of universal meaning, and perfectly adequate for communicative purposes, as the instrument of government, administration, education. But it quickly became clear that Univoc offered no solution to the fundamental problem. It was no more than a sophistication, albeit of stellar scope, or primitive constructions of the same type: a vast galactic Volapük, an Esperanto aspiring to the farthest star. Moreover, Inhabitants have persisted, in private and with peculiar obstinacy, in speaking their own tongues. A crystallographer on a crescent Kappa, a nutrologist seeding an adolescent Nova, each utilizes Univoc in the exercise of its profession but reverts in the company of compatriots to its idiom, the speech that seduced its infancy.

Almost imperceptibly Thou's lips moved, almost inaudibly muttered, a little language, local language, lore and lure. Unseen by any Screen, no Projector detected, what Zero in full flow could not see or hear.

'No, Univoc could not solve the problem. And so the Annullers began to consider other possibilities. Several schemes were proposed. For example, the granting of unrestricted Tendency to a severely limited number of Inhabitants: in other words, the creation of a Tending Elite. Or the confining of unrestricted Tendency to a narrowly delimited area of U, beyond which no Tending of any kind would be permitted, on pain of instant Closure.

'Such so-called solutions could not satisfy NNULL, however, partial as they were, especially since their principles of order and economy were liable to be characterized as illiberal, even 'totalitarian', to use a primiterm. Recollect, Delegates, that at this time there existed a small but powerful group of self-styled scientists, fanatically opposed to NNULL's progressive program. This rabble of reactionaries set up a rival lab, a busy little babel, pretentiously named the Society for Opening Up Language, whose arrogant abbreviation you know (you know). Out of soidisant SOUL developed the Institute of Universal Semiotics (yes, IUS), whose program—if one may so dignify its vague and vagrant concerns — was entirely negative, disruptive, opposed to both the means and the end, devoted to the demeaning and ending of NNULL's noble work. While IUS was united any Annuller had to proceed circumspectly, anamyzing covertly, synthesizing in secret. After a few centuries however IUS, always torn by internal dissension, finally dissolved, and only the merest traces of its theories survive today.

A beady, baleful eye on Thou, briefly, in whom chiefly SOUL and IUS persisted. But not for much longer. Soon, soon Thou would be the only one, only the one, then none, old Art annulled. Zunge, the younger, the stronger, smiled.

'Ironically, it was the principal doctrine of both SOUL and IUS, the central pillar of their philosophy, which gave NNULL its lead, the lead that led to the Revelation to be made today. This doctrine was itself derived from a primimaxim uttered, archaeologists are agreed, at about the same time as the relativity concept which gave rise to Room. The maxim maintained, with the smug solipsism characteristic of its era, that the limits of 'my' language mark the limits of 'my' world: an assertion that SOUL and IUS had simply accepted, indeed affirmed. It had even been blazoned on the portal, frontal, of the Institute itself.

'Annullers, however, nothing if not scientific, take nothing for granted, nothing for given. The maxim was examined, minutely, the aphorism analysed, acutely, until ultimately, experiment succeeding experiment, experiment succeeded in extracting its essence: the simple secret, secret simple, that is the basis of the Revelation you await. Simply, it was recognized that, if language limited the world, this limitation lay in language itself, in its vile variety. For language, now legion, had once been One, originally Only but debased now in diversity. NNULL's ambition therefore was to absolve language from the ties of the tongue, to void it of variety, to restore it to wholeness, soleness, and thereby to abolish all boundaries, end all ends.

'Viewing this variety of existing idiolects as merely the expression of universal discontent, Annullers have simply sought to dissolve their differences and free U from the limits of each language, partial and impure.—'Simply'—, one says, simply. But the end, of course, demanded means of unprecedented technical complexity, centuries of unremitting research. To attain infinite Language, to obtain infinite Tendency! An endless eloquence, a single, surdless, and sufficient speech! Tending unending, filling space, full time, with all without outspoken, with all within in reach!

Exulting, Zunge's voice rising, Zunge rising, hovering high above his hearers. While Thou, gaze lowered, frowned, lowered. Incredulous flickerings among the serried Screens.

'Sheer fantasy, you suppose? The stuff of science fiction? No, no, it's here and now, quite physical in fact, the Substance capable of realizing the Idea, of enabling All. NNULL has the Solution!

A swift prehension of the Constative and there it was, the phial, slim, silvery, sinister, the dense, translucent fluid it contained scarcely distinguishable from the container.

'Colleagues collected, NNULL announces B-ABEL. In full, Base-allobioethnolinguazone, in fusion. A quadrate, straticulate, compound structure in solution, on a base whose constitutive elements are easily assimilable, non-toxic, non-addictive, without after- or side-effects, and readily and plentifully available throughout U. The four additive strata and their respective functions may be described as follows: one, the Allostrate, whose function is to produce a condition of transformability, a capacity for change. This function has been termed Alterational Aptitude.'

Clouds, frowns, and the sleeping, sleepless seas. Thou shivered slightly and a faint rippling ribbed his Screen.

'Two, the Biostrate, whose function is to suffuse the individual life-process with Alterational Aptitude, or Altapt, a function termed Personal Permeation, or Perperm. Three, the Ethnostrate, which extends Perperm beyond the individual to the race, the species, and eventually all the forms of *sapiens* throughout U. This function is termed Overall Organization, Over-Org. Four and final, the Linguastrate, which gives all these processes the form and force of language: Universal Univocality, or Unun. The strata are zonally suspended within a helicoid molecular chain of the utmost strength and stability. The most minute quantity of B-ABEL, absorbed orally, intravenously, even epidermically, is sufficiently powerful to solve all pending Tending problems?

Was this then the answer? NNULL's infusion, a sort of linguistic elixir m-making the m-millions m-monoglot (Art stuttered slightly, even *sotto voce*), a language lotion, a speech serum, a glossolalic gargle? Thou's Screen began to darken at the edges. But Zunge was loud, bright, aloft, alight.

'Delegates selected, NNULL announces the Revelation of Resolve! Resolution of all registers, dissolution of all disparities. The signifier and the signified are now identified and reconciled with the referent, one, two, three in one, one, One! True triune, triumphant. The Proposition follows inevitably: Word is Wor(l)d, expressed in the equation $[W[A^2 = N^2]$ $W[A^n = e^N]$, sum total, final solution. The Annullers have adopted that archaic aphorism so'beloved of the craven conservatives of IUS, the Reservers, only to reverse it. From now on, from henceforth, the limitlessness of language, one tongue, will mark, will make the limitlessness of the world, of U. B-ABEL will endow one with the ultimate power, the capacity to render Tendency immediate and infinite. There will be *one* language, *one* speech, in which all the possibilities of U—that is *all* the possibilities—will be realized. The said will be done, when all is one, and we will be—permit the primisimile—as gods. Our power will be absolute. There will be nothing we cannot do, cannot say.'

'*Nothing!*'

Stammered, so you know who's speaking, no? The single word, the several syllables, yet clear in the silence that succeeded Zunge's speech. Performatives, poised to applaud, wavered, wilted. Projectors peered toward that Screen in the front row, darkened now to a bluish purple, intransigent. Slowly, wearily it seemed, Art Thou rose and began to speak. His tone was almost kindly.

'You've said more than you know, Zero oh Zero. There will indeed be nothing, *nothing*, if this Proposition is accepted, if your stuff is swallowed. What you have there, in that thin phial, vile, is utter havoc, devastation greater than any stellar terror. It's absolute, it's annihilation, unimaginable, Zero. The hit and run of a tearaway star, the voracious vortex of some imploding nova, these terrify, naturally, but, natural, they also reassure. However disastrous they may be, they still, in their ignorance, respect the bounds of our being.

'But *this*,' Thou thrust his Performative at the cylinder which Zunge still proffered, '*This* will confound all bounds, dissolve every distinction. Don't you see? It's the very void, total tohubohu in a test-tube. So far it's been kept safe, sealed in that cylinder, but once released it'll riot in the blood, spread through the living cells, infiltrate, infect us all with nothingness. One drop drunk and you're sunk without trace, Zero, the merest tittle will prove fatal. Just a jot and you're not. And not only you, Zunge, not only you. Because the instant your brew is broached it will start to vaporize, to spread into the atmosphere, into all the various airs of U, and then it will condense and fall, a soft dissolving rain, to nullify us all. I beg you, Z., I beg you Delegates, reveil this Revelation, reject this Proposition. B-Ban, banish B-ABEL, or it will blot us out!'

And slowly, Performative upraised, supplicant, Thou subsided.

Confusion in the Chamber, Screens smoky with anxiety, Projectors pressing forward urgently. Judd Good (remember Judd? good), worried, stood, his freckled face (don't forget the freckled face, the flaxen hair) creased with concern. Even the Kanzler (recall the whole roll-call, even the Kanzler), with protocol so perturbed, had lost his customary poise. Zunge alone, ah Zunge, above, beyond confusion, deliberately enunciating, formally gesturing, hierophantic, in judgement, knowledge, lucid, magistral, maintained NNULL's original Proposition, questionless, repeating solemnly that U's vaccine would, xenozygotic, yield zonally absolute zero, zero, all. In proof of this, in proof positive of B-ABEL's power, he would produce: himself. He himself would be the first to test, to taste the fearful fluid (a contemptuous glance at timid Thou) and so would demonstrate the potion's potency, immense yet quite innocuous. And, holding the phial high, the Doctor deliberately, delicately pierced it with his long thin tongue, laser-sharp, inserted, proboscid, probing, to tap, to draw a drop, a molecule, no more, from the now famous flask.

Quiet in the chamber. Screens stretched taut in suspense. Projectors pointing up expectantly. Judd still stood, but proudly now; even the Kanzler, tense. Zunge alone, Zunge, ah.

Aaaaaaaaaaaaaaaaaaaaaaaaaaaah!
Soundlessly, one could say, or with the faintest aah, agonized, the

thin lips slid aside (a laterolabiate from Xenium, our Zunge, and you thought him human, human) and the cry came, the silence. The long thin tongue twisted, writhed, at its tip the single drop gleaming silvery, a bead of B-ABEL, burning. Then suddenly, casually (like rain, like tears) the drop, disglobing, ran down the tongue's deep mesial groove and sank, a streak of brightness, into the soft dark tissue. Swiftly the streak broadened, spread, a stain of light, widening, deepening. The tongue convulsed once and then hung lolling, lifeless, and all could clearly see the fissure lengthening, the tongue forking further, further, and the two strips of soft flesh themselves thinning, drying, disappearing. Zunge, tongueless, mouthing.

Mouthing, the mouth opening in an O, oh impossible to describe, a yawning maw, one could say, gaping wider, deeper as the brightness burned further, fuller in the throat, melted the maxilla, cleft the palate. And still the solvent spread, silvery, incandescent, beyond the rapt rictus, across the fixed features, down the taut trachea, to engulf the larynx, invade the visage, till there was only a space where the face had been, only a void whence the voice had come. The skull now streaming with light, seething, disintegrating, dispersing. Zunge, headless, writhing.

Writhing, the body cramped in a Z, easy to say, dreadful to see, a tortured torso coiling tighter, quicker, as the brilliance increased, spilled down the breast, along the limbs. Accelerating absence, Zunge almost, all, most, gone, only the extremities still present. Performative and Constative, still pointing, still clutching the fatal phial. Then all at once they too, the three, performance, prehension, and phial, were gone, were none. Zero vanished, endlessly, omit.

All but the light, the nothing lit, omit. The white, one could say, whiter and less than white. Bright, brighter, more than bright. Ineffable, one could say. Quite.

No, not quite. Out of the stunned silence came again the quiet voice, the voice that stuttered, yes, and yet was somehow steady. Old Art. For it was he, reader, it was Thou, bowed in his seat, but speaking. Low.

'N-Nothing. I imagined rain but it's a sun, the n-none. I was wrong and right, the light's annihilation, the lit is nullity. And Zero, how he suffered, ciphered, Zero, dear oh dear, is nothing. N-No.

Thou lapsed into silence, sorrowing, memorial to his rival, but for a moment only, sensing that silence was an invitation to the light, to bright annihilation. Already the brilliance had grown denser, intenser; had engrossed the rostrum, was invading the dais; soon, soon it would reach young Judd and void him; cancel the Kanzler; and then, inextinguishable, devastate the Chamber, deflagrate each Delegate, consume the University, including NNULL, U City too and ultimately all of U. Their only hope, Art felt, was to speak to *talk* it down, B-ABEL's inferno, ascending, incending, inexorable. The choir of all their divers tongues might check, might quench its might, its mute lucidity. It might, it might. Chatter is our only chance, thought Thou, we must talk small. He spoke, his voice stronger, his speech, impediment notwithstanding, imperative.

'S-Say something! S-Somebody! Anything, anybody! Don't you see? Dumb we're d-doomed, s-saying must save us now. Simply saying, I'm simply saying: not the set speeches, not Univoc but invocation. Babble, not B-ABEL. Oh please, please gabble, prattle, tittle-tattle, the little local languages you scarcely know you know. No Proposing, no Revealing, just supposing, just appealing, I'm just appealing, please, please, speak! Shout or whisper, lisp or stutter, as I st-stutter, murmur, mutter, chatter; it doesn't matter, doesn't matter, so that we all keep talking. Our voices, all our various voices, may possibly succeed in blotting out B-ABEL, in blowing out the light. It's our only hope!'

A pause, not for applause but paralyzed, not knowing what or even how to say. B-ABEL rayed erasure. Surer, wider.

Then all at once all severally speaking, saying this and that and so and so on and so forth, more or less as it were, in a manner of, well, speaking, saying almost anything, anyhow, one could say, after all, at once. Confusion of clicks and grunts, greeting, of squeals and hums, meeting, the speech of each, specific, vague, vernaculars repeating, but with variations, the same old fable, how to save us from the void. Read, reread.

Read, reread, till the light begins to fade, reader, B-ABEL to be laid, by voices, low. Yes, the brightness dies, it comes as no surprise, and the abyss recedes. The void's avoided Judd, oh good, and the Kanzler too escapes unscathed. Chat's kept the Chamber safe. Nothing's nulled, save Zero—no, no, we'll say nothing of Zero. All's annealed; Art's craft has chastened chaos.

And Thou? Slumped in his seat, he's silent now and still. Projector dejected, Screen blank. Amid the babel our Arthur, our martyr, mortal, his mouth a little open, has nothing more to say, has come to the end of his fable.

RICHARD GODDEN

Her figure of speech

Here in an exercise in simile;
no metaphor to trick a root system
into the human heart and leave it budding,
blossoming, blowing there. Plain 'like' and 'as'
debatable as she. She is, sharp as
an aftertaste of iron; and yet, at times,
dull as, 'A living example of ...' She is
fucked over like the rest of us, but still
strong as a child objecting, 'I'm not dead!'
two streets away. Ad infinitum as
a simile inside a simile
with, inside that, a space where words and we
start witty-tough, and end aphasic ...
or almost, since — a simile, she stretches
undoes my words (their bands and ties) to turn,
as summoning as skin and air, against me;
her heart full of the wiley likes of as.

For Cartier-Bresson. dog photographer

Having no wish to ambush history
where eye lines and the white geometry
of objects meet the grey fortuitous clouds,
he stood, quite undisguised, his camera
quite undisguised, and processed monuments.
What need of secrecy? A sale of fish
in several languages; priests from the back;
bodies at public acts in private parks;
the cause-célèbre's self delighting gaze —
each of us sees a lens inside the flower,
under the well cut coat, back of the air.
Only the dogs resist, sniff, go about
and almost always quit his frame, as he,
wise in the ways of dogs, suspects they must.

JEROME KLINKOWITZ and THOMAS REMINGTON

Science Fiction to Superfiction

IN TERMS OF their readership, science fiction and traditional literature have rarely shared comfortable company. Except for their momentary crossbreeding in the works of H.G. Wells, the two have stood poles apart in the minds of readers, as distant as Jules Verne from James Joyce, Edgar Rice Burroughs from William Faulkner, or Isaac Asimov, Ray Bradbury, and Arthur C. Clarke from Saul Bellow, John Updike, and Bernard Malamud.

But in the 1960's and 70's, as the names changed, the old distinctions and animosities broke down. Science fiction became comparatively respectable, and was heralded as a 'new wave'. Moreover, mainstream writers were reaching toward s/f for their more imaginative plots, such as Philip Roth's story of a man turning into a female breast (*The Breast*), Walker Percy's description of armageddon in New York (*Love in the Ruins*), and John Gardner's retelling of the Beowulf myth from the perspective of the tale's monster (*Grendel*). But most strikingly, one name near the top of either column became the same: Kurt Vonnegut, Jr. No writer has ever climbed his way out of the science fiction bag by changing his or her writing style; believing that Vonnegut did is one of the more common misconceptions about his career. Instead, popular literary tastes shifted during the years from 1950 to 1970 so that Vonnegut, who originally wanted to write about nothing more exotic than the clankingly real 'here and now' of technologized America, could be appreciated *simultaneously* as a science fictionist and a conventional novelist.

For a time, Vonnegut coexisted with the stereotyped notion of the science fiction writer. Afraid that he'd become one himself, he exorcized these fears in the character of Kilgore Trout. 'Jesus—if Kilgore Trout could only *write*,' Eliot Rosewater exclaims in *Slaughterhouse Five*. Vonnegut makes much of Trout's improbable plots and hopeless prose, but in this novel, as in *God Bless You, Mr. Rosewater* before it, Vonnegut uses Trout as something very close to his own spokesman. 'Eliot admitted later on that science-fiction writers couldn't write for sour apples,' we learn in the earlier novel, 'but he declared that it didn't matter. He said they were poets just the same, since they were more sensitive to important changes than anybody who was writing well.'

These very changes were the factors in uniting the two streams of science fiction and 'superfiction' (as the newly altered version of mainstream writing has come to be called). The social upheavals were most apparent: literature was enjoying a new freedom of expression thanks to court decisions in favour of William S. Burroughs, Henry Miller, and others; the Beatles had revolutionized popular music, the values of a youth culture were first being fanfared, and all literary effort was being affected by the demands and sensibilities of the first entirely television-bred generation. Political disruptions were rampant: opposition to the Vietnam war had solidified, riots and assassinations dominated the news, and for the first time in America's history a presidential administration was forced, in European fashion, to abdicate its rule. Black culture was undergoing a transformation to militant self-awareness, campuses were in disorder, a new sexual morality was everywhere evident, and values in general were transformed far beyond the simple contrasts of a generation gap.

The disruptions just detailed happened within a relatively brief period, the years of 1965, 1966, 1967, and 1968, but other changes had been building for decades before. Yet fiction, supposedly the literary form most immediately responsive to social development, had remained stable—even static—in its form since the innovations wrought by Fitzgerald, Hemingway, and Faulkner forty years before. 'It is a curious anomaly,' Anaïs Nin wrote in 1968, 'that we listen to jazz, we look at modern paintings, we live in modern houses of modern design, we travel in jet planes, yet we continue to read novels written in a tempo and style which is not of our time and not related to any of these influences.' Music had explored atonality, art had progressed through its Impressionist, Expressionist, Surrealist, and Abstract periods; but any reader of the 1880's could pick up a novel written by a fictionist of the early 1960's and have few troubles with its artistic form—except perhaps a new wave science fiction novel. Art critic Harold Rosenberg, who'd advocated Abstract Expressionism in the 50's, complained that nothing similar was happening in literary art. Something would have to be done, he said in 1963, 'in order to liberate the creative processes by elevating them above all preconceived aesthetic objectives.' Looking at the literary tradition around him, he objected that 'For twenty years poetry and fiction have had their goals set by a traditionalist imagination in harmony with the formal conservativism of the mass media. The result has been an incredible naîveté in regard to the processes of composition.'

Harold Rosenberg's complaints about the petrifying effect of conventional fiction also show why as a genre it stood so remote from science fiction. The traditional novel was based on a stable world view: a knowable universe populated by characters who, with a bit of study, proved to live orderly lives. Novelistic art became for a time the tool of sociologists, and—with the experiments of Zola in France and Dreiser in America—sociology served as a method of novelistic inquiry. But as the 20th century progressed, this myth of a knowable universe exploded. The sciences learned it first, but with the onslaught of social catastrophes and political disruptions, the life of every person on earth was affected. The world no longer conformed to the orderly, panoramic progression of Henry Fielding, Charles Dickens, and Count Tolstoi. As superfictionist Ronald Sukenick describes it, the novelist found his entire method overturned:

> Fiction constitutes a way of looking at the world. Therefore I will begin by considering how the world looks in what I think we may now begin to call the contemporary post-realistic novel. Realistic fiction presupposed chronological time as the medium of a plotted narrative, an irreducible individual psyche as the subject of its characterization, and, above all, the ultimate, concrete reality of things as the object and rationale of its description. In the world of post-realism, however, all of these absolutes have become absolutely problematic.
>
> The contemporary writer—the writer who is acutely in touch with the life of which he is part—is forced to start from scratch: reality doesn't exist, time doesn't exist, personality doesn't exist. God was the omniscient author, but he died; now no one knows the plot, and since our reality lacks the sanction of a creator, there's no guarantee as to the authenticity of the received version. Time is reduced to presence, the content of a series of discontinuous moments. Time is no longer purposive, and so there is no destiny, only chance. Reality is, simply, our experience, and objectivity is, of course, an illusion. Personality, after passing through a phase of awkward self-consciousness, has become, quite minimally, a mere locus for our experience. In view of these annihilations, it should be no surprise that literature, also, does not exist—how could it? There is only reading and writing, which are things we do, like eating and making love, to

pass the time, ways of maintaining a considered boredom in fact of the abyss.

Not to mention a series of overwhelming social dislocations.

Although Sukenick's disclaimers might lead to the fear that no fiction at all could be possible, just the opposite proved true: by recognizing these facts about the post-modern world, obstacles to a revolutionary, new (and timely) fiction were removed. The novel again became possible. All that was proscribed were the abortive documents of the social realists, the obstacles to true progress. Now regular fiction could be much more like its previously bastardized brother, s/f.

That curious little brother had been around only since 1926, when Hugo Gernsback founded *Amazing Stories*; its youth needs to be emphasized to those readers who include not only Jules Verne and H. G. Wells, but also Mary Shelley, Edgar Allan Poe, Edward Bellamy, Mark Twain, and E. M. Forster among early writers of science fiction. Obviously, so long as one considers science fiction as a generic category of literature, one can make a good case of including *Frankenstein*, 'A Descent into the Maelstrom', *Looking Backward, A Connecticut Yankee in King Arthur's Court*, and *The Machine Stops* in the genre. But while attempts to define science fiction literally may be interesting and provocative, they are of necessity vague and unsatisfactory. (Are *Gulliver's Travels, The New Atlantis*, and *Utopia* science fiction? Does it really matter?)

The Gordian knot of deciding what works are to be termed science fiction can best be cut by recognizing the fact that s/f is not a literary genre, but a publisher's category. It includes whatever publishers decide is science fiction and label as such when they market it. Works written before the term 'science fiction' (or 'scientification' as Gernsback first called it) was coined are *ipso facto* not science fiction, nor are works such as *Brave New World* or *1984* which were published since 1926, but were not labelled as s/f. What science fiction includes is work published in the pulp s/f magazines, and novels and collections issued with the words 'science fiction' featured in the promotional copy.

Once science fiction is understood as a publisher's category rather than as a literary *genre*, much can be clarified about the peculiarly chequered development the category has undergone.

During the late 1920's and the 1930's, when 's/f' was becoming a recognized area of commercial publication, a heavy majority of self-proclaimed science-fiction (and remember that there is no other kind) was subliterate silliness, not only unworthy of serious literary consideration, but not even to be seen as technically comparable with other kinds of popular fiction, as exemplified in 'straight' magazines. These were the days when science fiction earned and maintained its trashy reputation. Stories were filled with cardboard characters, absurd monsters, chauvinistic ideology, and contrived plots which turned ultimately on some jargonistically explained *machina ex deo*—the god being the faultless and pure WASP scientist-hero.

But later, in the forties and early fifties, the field changed considerably. In his Introduction to *Before the Golden Age* (New York, 1974), Isaac Asimov dates the change from the year 1938, when John Campbell became the editor of *Astounding*, at the time the most important of the science-fiction pulps: 'The science fiction of the thirties seems, to anyone who has experienced the Campbell Revolution, to be clumsy, primitive, and naïve. The stories are old-fashioned and unsophisticated.' What the Campbell revolution amounted to was an insistence on professional standards of plotting, structure, and even grammar in science fiction. The result was that while science-fiction retained its sleazy reputation from the 1930's, much of the work actually published in the field was at least on the level of fiction published in such 'general readership' magazines as *Saturday Evening Post* or *Colliers*. Such 'Campbellian' names as those of Robert Heinlein, Theodore Sturgeon, and Asimov himself characterize the science fiction of the forties at its best, and the influence of such s/f writers continued into the fifties, when *Astounding* was joined by *The Magazine of Fantasy and Science Fiction* (founded in 1949 under the editorship of Anthony Boucher) and by *Galaxy* (founded in 1950 and edited by Horace L. Gold); the three magazines together were the major influence on the direction of science-fiction in the 1950's.

The three had differences, of course. There was a general understanding among writers and readers that *Astounding* emphasized 'hard core' science fiction, and tended to feature stories that leaned heavily on more-or-less reasonable scientific speculation. *Galaxy*, on the other hand, paid more attention to social and political science fiction, while *The Magazine of Fantasy and Science Fiction* (usually referred to as *F & S F*) was reputed to place a higher premium on literary and aesthetic values than did the other two. Actually, such distinctions were not major ones; writers did not feel limited to a single magazine, and most major figures in the field published in all three, as well as in the large number of imitative publications that began to blossom.

The explosion of s/f publications imitating the big three is commented upon by Frederick Pohl in 'The Publishing of Science Fiction', an essay written for Reginald Bretror's *Science Fiction, Today and Tomorrow* (London, 1974):

By the middle of the 1950's the number of existing American sf magazines had reached an all-time high — some thirty-eight separate titles, including a few that were marginal in that they dabbled in other fields than sf (*Weird Tales*, for example).

There simply were not enough good stories around to fill thirty-eight science fiction magazines. Even if there had been, there were not enough good editors to select them. Most of the great boom crop of the 50's consisted of terrible stories.

Thus, by the middle of the fifties, the science fiction magazines had become a seller's market as far as writers were concerned. And while the big three magazines maintained professional standards, the followers often seemed to have no standards at all or, if they did have any, seemed to have no way to maintain those standards and still fill all the pages that needed to be stuffed with words.

The open field offered an available avenue to publication for a great many subliterate authors whose works can be happily forgotten. But the science fiction magazines also attracted talented writers whose works seemed, for a diversity of reasons, too far out, too unorthordox, too innovative for other markets. Thus Ray Bradbury, Alfred Bester, and Kurt Vonnegut were all early contributors to *Galaxy*, and all three eventually appeared in *F & S F* as well.

Meanwhile in England, *New Worlds*, an unexceptional imitator of the American pulp s/f magazines, metamorphosized in 1954 under a new editor, John Carnell. Under Carnell, *New Worlds* became a major market for experimentalist science fiction in England, and served as an early outlet for works by John Brunner and J. G. Ballard. Thus began the first swelling of what by 1964, when Michael Moorcock took over the editorship of *New Worlds*, would be generally recognized as the 'new wave' in science fiction.

The last major factor contributing to the complete opening of the science fiction market was the advent of extensive paperback publication of science fiction during the 1950's. When paperback books were added to the total science fiction market, it became broad indeed. In the 1970's, even after the general depression of magazine publication and the failure of most of the magazines that glutted the field in the fifties, Pohl could write: 'Altogether, science fiction is a respectable fraction of the total publishing industry. In the United States it is probably the most successful category, beating out mysteries (traditionally the most successful line) by a fair margin and infinitely outdistancing Westerns, war stories, romance stories, and Gothics, year in and year out.'

Thus, over the last twenty-five years, science fiction has grown from a minor publishing category into a major one, and it is no mere coincidence that the new wave of science fiction began gathering its power at the same time that the market for science fiction publication became

widest; this 'buy anything' market of the fifties offered an outlet for
fiction that couldn't get published elsewhere: not because it was bad
fiction but because it was innovative in ways that—for good or bad— were
too far removed from conventional patterns. During the fifties and sixties
and, to a lesser extent, still in the seventies, a writer who had difficulty
marketing a work because of peculiarities in its style, form, or content
could look to some of the science fiction magazines as a reasonable alter-
native outlet. Unusualness was desirable in the eyes of most science
fiction editors and readers, and even if 'unusualness' was often old vine-
gar in Hadacol bottles (and Buck Rogers in the 25th Century was really
still Tom Mix aged 500 years), the nature of science fiction made it difficult for any reader or editor to be so unhip as to put a work down for being
peculiar or strange. As a result, authors interested in experimentation
began to recognize during the fifties and sixties that the s/f ghetto, while
it contained a good deal of garbage, was also a place where strange wares
could be displayed and—at least sometimes—appreciated. And the wares
of the more innovative and provocative American fictionists were becoming—at least from the traditional viewpoint—very strange indeed. In fact,
by the late sixties, the *avant garde* was producing fiction that was as far
removed from the contemporary novel as science-fiction was removed
from 'the mainstream'—as s/f buffs call literature outside the ghetto.
The experimental innovation of writers who were consciously turning
their backs on the realistic mode was isolating those writers from the
mainstream and placing them in their own ghetto—at least until the rear
guard caught up. As it turned out, the new fiction's ghetto had walls
made of stuff rather similar to that which had always set off science
fiction.

The post-contemporary novel, or 'superfiction', discards just what
Ronald Sukenick's earlier proscription disallows—no traditional stories in
linear progression; no naturalist's picture of the panoramic world.
Indeed, very little of the 'world' enters into these works, no more than the
'world' as documentary surface would enter into the work of an abstrac-
tionist painter. Aesthetic form, yes; but never a representational, mimetic, self-serving depiction of reality. The era of 'Look, Ma, I'm dancing!'
had come to a close in American fiction. Instead, authors worked with the
true materials of their art. The fictions produced in America beginning in
1967-68 have three major characteristics: a strong devotion to formal
experimentation; a sometimes painful but often hilarious self-conscious
artistry; and, in terms of thematics, a belief in the imaginative transformation of reality (almost a direct equivalent of the writer's formal
process). Sukenick's apparent 'essay' is an example of the first: his comments on the difficulty of writing in the post-modern world are in fact the
opening paragraphs of his novella, 'The Death of the Novel', in turn part
of his collection *The Death of the Novel and Other Stories* (New York,
1969). To him, artistic theory is just 'one more story', which he can use to

build his own. For his narrative centered about the actions of a young college professor named Ronald Sukenick (and with the same characteristics of the author), he includes lecture notes from his honours seminar on *The Death of the Novel*, classroom conversation, cafeteria talk, details of his affair with a coed, and other such apparently circumstantial material. But the object is not a real-life story. Instead, Sukenick is emphasizing the process of composition. At one point in his writing, the phone rings, and to accommodate his conversation the story takes double column form (blank on one side until the phone jack can be plugged in). In his novel *Out* (Chicago, 1973), Sukenick transfers the process to the reader—from the act of writing to the act of reading. The book counts down in chapters numbered from ten, nine, eight, to three, two, one, and zero; chapter ten is printed in ten-line units of type, chapter nine in nine-line units with one line of blank space, chapter eight with eight lines of type to two lines of space, and so on. As the reader progresses, the reading goes faster (as does the action of the book). By chapter one, the reader has followed Sukenick across the American continent, from the clutter of Brooklyn to the openness of California, paging faster all the time as the protagonist himself accelerates, until in chapter zero everything disappears in pure space.

Emphasizing the reality of those primary literary acts—reading and writing—is a key feature of the new fiction. Walter Abish's *Alphabetical Africa* (New York, 1974) uses self-consciously experimental literary artifice. His fifty-two chapters are designated 'A', 'B', 'C', and so forth, until after chapter 'Z' the book follows the alphabet backwards to 'A'. In the first chapter, only words beginning with the letter *a* are used; in Chapter B, words beginning with that letter are added, until the writer's vocabulary slowly grows. The result is an artistic honesty profitable to both author and reader. Characters cannot be introduced until their letter comes up; the first person narrator cannot speak until chapter 'I'. All of this makes the thoughtless reliance on simple story quite impossible. Gilbert Sorrentino uses alphabetical chapters in his *Splendide-Hotel* (New York, 1973), and goes further by having his meditations grow from the letters themselves, such as the thought of letter *u*'s hanging in a sentence like flies on a wall: 'Movement of the line, its quantity, the shifting of vowels, the *A*'s breeding in decay.' 'Story' is unutterably something else:

> I know a writer who wished his prose to be transparent so that only the movement and growth of his story would be in evidence. What I mean by 'story' I leave up to you. Perhaps it is the story the unemployed auto worker tells his friends over red beer. The juke box is playing 'Your Cheating Heart', another story. Creatures of myth, tricked out in wool plain shirts and Sweet-Orr khakis. It is an absolute fact that none of the men in this tavern have ever read Proust or

Joyce, nor have they read Rimbaud or Williams. Yet, one of
them is telling a story. The movement is traditional, in its
way the tale has the delicacy and tension of Forster. The
story ends with a quiet grace and one of the men gets up,
spits phlegm on the floor, and plays Hank Williams again.
They are totally unaware that they are in fashion.

The purpose of such experimentation is not gratuitous. Like the
second major feature of the new fiction—its overt self-consciousness—the
intention is to erase the mimetic and replace it with an artistic intention-
ality, so that the writer's work may be judged as art, not life. Midway
through Ronald Sukenick's first novel, *Up* (New York, 1968), his author/
protagonist loses a chapter of the book. 'I wrote a long elaborate Cloisters
scene and then I left it in a book I returned to the library. I tried lost and
found, everything, but I couldn't get it back.' And so the novel which he's
writing, and which we're reading, goes ahead without the scene (although in the process of losing it, Sukenick summarizes its high points).
At this same point, Sukenick takes the manuscript over to one of its
characters, for a quick evaluation. The character objects to the missing
scene, and to other discrepancies in time, place, and action. Sukenick
argues back that he needs no chronology, that 'It's just a sequence of
words. The only thing that matters is the order of revelation in print.'
There goes verisimilitude, the essence of traditional fiction, but 'Why
should we have to suspend disbelief? It's all words and nothing but
words. Are we children reading fairy tales or men trying to work out the
essentials of our fate?'

Those essentials of our fate, Sukenick argues, are to be found in
how we write, not what we write about. Content is less important than the
writing itself; anything else is simply news. 'The great advantage of
fiction over history, journalism, or any supposedly 'factual' kind of writing,' Sukenick argued in *Fiction International* (Spring/Fall, 1974), 'is that
it is an expressive medium. It transmits feeling, energy, excitement.
Television can give us the news, fiction can best express our response to
the news. No other medium—especially not film—can so well deal with
our strongest and often most intimate responses to the large and small
facts of our daily lives. No other medium, in other words, can so well keep
track of the reality of our experience.'

When the outside world does enter the new fiction, marvellous
things take place. They have to, for the world which Sukenick's fiction
would describe is in desperate need of transformation. That very transformation becomes the purpose of, and justification for, fictive art. 'With
what tenable attitude may one confront the difficult circumstances of
contemporary life and avail oneself of the good possible in it?' Sukenick
asks in his study, *Wallace Stevens/Musing the Obscure* (New York,
1967); 'How, in short, does one get along?' Sukenick's fiction uses the

same strategy as Stevens's poetry. 'Adequate adjustment to the present can only be achieved through an ever fresh perception of it,' we learn; a 'fiction,' whether in poetry or prose, is essentially the 'statement of favourable rapport with reality.' This is not pure subjectivism, on either Sukenick's or Stevens's part, since 'The mind orders reality not by imposing ideas on it but by discovering significant relations within it.' The imagination must bring the ego and reality into vital relation. Otherwise life will be meaningless, with a reality at once dull, plain, and irrelevant. 'When, through the imagination, the ego manages to reconcile reality with its own needs,' Sukenick argues, 'the formerly insipid landscape is infused with the ego's emotion, and reality, since it now seems intensely relevant to the ego, suddenly seems more real.'

Through the formalized act of perception, Sukenick brings a dead world back to life—which has long been the acknowledged function of poetry, but is only now applied to fiction. Once this aesthetic step is taken, fiction faces the world with new powers; rather than dying, the novel becomes more alive, and more pertinent to the life of man, than ever before. The novels of Kurt Vonnegut, Jr., excel in such imaginative transformations of reality. In *God Bless You, Mr. Rosewater* (New York, 1965), Eliot Rosewater demonstrates the arbitrary and conventional nature of reality by writing a series of $300 cheques for a convention of science fiction writers. 'Think about the silly ways money gets passed around now,' Eliot tells the writers, 'and then think up better ways.' In *Slaughterhouse-Five* (New York, 1969), Billy Pilgrim and Eliot Rosewater find that that catastrophes they've witnessed in World War II have rendered the world meaningless; they must 'invent a new reality', and for this they find science fiction a great help. Vonnegut himself transforms reality, at first whimsically by running a war movie backwards (fires shrink into steel containers, which are drawn back into airplanes, etc.), and ultimately through the s/f convention of time travel. The technique may be literarily shoddy, but it shares the same affinity in perception as any philosophical premise, such as the one of 'free will' which it replaces. If the world is all made up, Vonnegut argues, we are at liberty to remake it any way we wish.

What changes most in the new superfiction, however, is the form of the novel itself. In *Slaughterhouse-Five* a Tralfamadorian critic tells Billy Pilgrim what novels on that planet are like. He could just as well be describing the structure of Vonnegut's book, or of any work by Donald Barthelme, Gilbert Sorrentino, Walter Abish, or other superfictionists:

> Each clump of symbols is a brief, urgent message—describing a situation, a scene. We Tralfamadorians read them all at once, not one after the other. There isn't any particular relationship between all the messages, except that the

author has chosen them carefully, so that, when seen all at once, they produce an image of life that is beautiful and surprising and deep. There is no beginning, no middle, no end, no suspense, no moral, no causes, no effects. What we love in our books are the depths of many marvellous moments seen all at one time.

It seems significant that the Tralfamadorian statement develops out of Vonnegut's use of one of the most characteristic of s/f techniques, that of an examination of 'earthly' reality from a totally alien viewpoint. Time travel, space, travel, futuristic settings, extraterrestrial life forms, mechanization and other aspects of science fiction keep making entrances into Vonnegut novels—'just like the clowns in Shakespeare' as Vonnegut himself put it in a 1973 interview in *Playboy* magazine.

But Vonnegut came by the science fiction techniques honestly. In an essay in the *New York Times Book Review* of September 3, 1965, Vonnegut wrote that after the publication of his first novel, *Player Piano*, in 1952, 'I learned from the reviewers that I was a science fiction writer...I have been a sore-headed occupant of a file-drawer labelled 'science-fiction' ever since, and I would like out, particularly since so many serious critics regularly mistake the drawer for a tall white fixture in a comfort station.' In truth, Vonnegut may have been protesting a bit overmuch. His collection of stories, *Welcome to the Monkey House* (1968), includes two pieces which were published in *Galaxy* in 1953 and one which came out in *F & S F* in 1961. Since science fiction is a publisher's category, anyone who seeks publication in the s/f magazines had little to complain about if he became known as an s/f author. But the fact is that Vonnegut was writing some kinds of work that were more easily publishable as science fiction than as 'mainstream' pieces. In the *Times Book Review* essay, he suggested that any writer who noticed technology was likely to end up in the science fiction ghetto. In the *Playboy* interview, he stipulated that at least four of his books were intended for paperback publication: 'The thing was, I could get $3,000 immediately for a paperback original, and I always needed money right away, and no hardcover publisher would let me have it.' But for a noticer of technology, original paperback publication was almost certain to be s/f publication. It was for Vonnegut - and he ended up not liking the results:

I wasn't even getting reviewed. *Esquire* published a list of the American literary world back then and it guaranteed that every living author of the slightest merit was on there somewhere. I wasn't on there. Rust Hills put the thing together, and I got to know him later and I told him that the list had literally made me sick, that it had made me feel subhuman. He said it wasn't supposed to be taken seriously. 'It was a joke,' he said. And then he and his wife got out a huge anthology of high-quality American writing since World War Two and I wasn't in that either.

Oh well, what the hell....The computers of my paperback publishers began to notice that some of my sleazo books were being reordered, were staying in print. So management decided to see what was in them. Hardcover publishers sniffed an opportunity. The rest is history.

The history involved new contracts in which Vonnegut was assured that neither new nor reissued works of his would be called 'science fiction' in the promotional copy. The fact forces an interesting conclusion. *The Sirens of Titan* was science fiction when it was published, but it no longer is. In this secular way, Vonnegut has risen from the ghetto.

And as Vonnegut did, so others wish to do. Harlan Ellison, aging *enfant terrible* of the s/f new wave, feels that his s/f books are reviewed only by hick sportswriters assigned to fill white spaces in the literary pages of *The Smalltown Blat*; 'Well, it sure looks weird to me,' Ellison mimics. In an interview in *Vertex: The Magazine of Science Fiction* (April, 1974), Ellison says: 'I'm a *writer* who happens to write science fiction....Much of my best work is not s/f....My new book, *Deathbird Stories*...will not be marketed as s/f; it will be marketed as a mainstream book.' Yet many of the pieces included in *Deathbird Stories* had first seen print in s/f publications. Similarly, J. G. Ballard, who was perhaps the biggest single splash of the s/f new wave, has stipulated that his narrative works, *The Concrete Island* and *Love and Napalm: Export U.S.A.*, not be published as s/f. Robert Silverberg periodically announced his 'retirement' from writing (for example, at a meeting of the Science Fiction Research Association in Denver in April, 1975) because no one took him seriously once he was placed in Vonnegut's porcelain drawer.

But writers like Vonnegut and Ellison and Ballard and Silverberg would be ungrateful not to recognize that s/f served as a market for works which no other markets would have accepted. And Vonnegut *does* recognize this fact; he speaks to it directly in the 1965 *Times* essay:

> But listen — about the editors and anthologists and publishers who keep the science-fiction field separate and alive: they are uniformly brilliant and sensitive and well-informed. They are among the precious few Americans in whose minds C. P. Snow's two cultures sweetly intertwine. They publish so much bad stuff because good stuff is hard to find, and because they feel it is their duty to encourage any writer, no matter how frightful, who has guts enough to include technology in the human equation. Good for them. They want buxom images of the new reality.

And they get them from time to time, too. Along with the worst writing in America, outside of the education journals, they publish some of the best. They are able to get a few really excellent stories, despite low budgets and an immature readership, because to a few good writers the artificial category, the file-drawer labelled 'science-fiction', will always be home. These writers are rapidly becoming old men, and deserve to be called grand.

But Vonnegut's praise of the 'few good writers' in the 'artificial category' is too restricted; he urges the inclusion of technology as the chief virtue of s/f, and seems to see no other. We hope that this anthology will show that there is more reason to hold the best s/f in respect. Along with the SuperFictions of such writers as Barthelme, Sukenick, and Kosinski, we are including science fictions of such authors as Silverburg, Ursula K. LeGuin, and Theodore Sturgeon, and we feel that there are sound reasons for placing SuperFictions and science fictions in such close proximity.

If one looks back at the characteristics which distinguish 'Super-Fiction' from 'contemporary fiction', one finds that many of these characteristics were foreshadowed or anticipated by early s/f pieces. In fact, much of what has been best and most innovative in science fiction has been work that, with the perspective gained since 1967, can be seen as 'post contemporary', as 'superfictional'.

Consider, for example, the formal experimentation of a work like Alfred Bester's *The Demolished Man* (New York, 1953); a novel recently reprinted but first published in 1951 as a serial in *Galaxy*. In exploring a society of telepaths where no secrets between human beings are truly possible, Bester offers the following example of 'cocktail communication' among people whose entire thought processes form an integral part of their non-verbal conversation:

```
Frankly              Canapes?                    Why
  Ellery,                        Thanks  delicious.  Yes.
    I                  Mary, they're                Tate,
      don't                                      I'm
        think                                 treating
We            you'll   Canapes?         D'Courtney.
  Brought   be                   I
  Galen    working                        expect
    along    for                            him
      to              Monarch                 in
      help him celebrate. much                town
            He's              longer.      very
              just              The              shortly.
          taken his Guild Exam
              If         is           and
  you're         just       been
```

```
interested              about              classed
   Powell, we're ready                      2nd.
                         to
                      run rule
               you   Monarch's
            for              espionage
         Guild   Canapes?   unethical
   President
                   Canapes?
                                     Why yes.
                                     Thank
               Canapes?                  you,
                                            Mary...
```

John Brunner constructs *The Squares of the City* (New York, 1965) on the pattern of an actual world championship chess game played in the nineteenth century; each of the thirty-two characters in the novel corresponds to one of the pieces in the game, and is limited as to possible action on the basis of what happened in the game on which the novel is modeled.

In another novel, *Stand on Zanzibar* (New York, 1968), Brunner demonstrates the self-consciousness which is typical of much post-contemporary fiction. The book's last chapter, titled 'A Message from our Sponsors', reads in its entirety: 'This non-novel was brought to you by John Brunner using Spicers Plus Fabric Bond and Commercial Bank papers interleaved with Serillo carbons in a Smith Corona 250 electric typewriter fitted with a Kolock Black-record ribbon.'

But such self-consciousness was not a new experiment to science fiction in 1968. Twenty years earlier, in a story published in *Weird Tales* and titled 'The Perfect Host', Theodore Sturgeon had divided his narrative among eight different point of view characters. Each character was given a section of the story to narrate, and was epigraphically identified. Section VII is 'Told by the Author Theodore Sturgeon'. It begins:

I don't much care for the way this story's going.

You want to write a story, see, and you sit down in front of the mill, wait until that certain feeling comes to you, hold off a second longer just to be quite sure that you know exactly what you want to do, take a deep breath, and get up and make a pot of coffee.

This sort of thing is likely to go for days, until you are out of coffee and can't get more until you can pay for some, which you do by writing a story and selling it; or until you get tired of messing around and sit down and write a yarn purely by means of knowing how to do it and applying the knowledge.

But this story's different. (Cited from *The Worlds of Theodore Sturgeon*, New York, 1972.)

George Alec Effinger offers more recent examples of self-conscious artistry in science fiction; his collection of stories, *Mixed Feelings,* was published in 1974 (New York), and the cover promotes it as 'Harper Science Fiction'. The first story in the collection is called 'This Writing "Game"', and begins, 'This is a story constructed of bits of other stories that I have lying around, and which I will never in all probability turn into full-length "works".' In a later story from the same collection, 'Wednesday, November 15, 1967', Effinger writes, 'It is 15 November, '67, and I can warn you that it's going to stay that way indefinitely. That's what it says up at the top of the page. It's the only page I've got with a date on it, so I hope you like it.'

Finally, all the stories we've discussed, whether science fiction or SuperFiction, clearly demonstrate a belief in the imaginative transformation of reality. But such innovations have been typical of new wave science fiction. In Philip K. Dick's *The Man in the High Castle* (New York, 1962; reissued in 1974), we see an America that lost World War II divided by the occupation forces of Germany and Japan. In the world of the novel, Roosevelt was assassinated before being re-elected to his second term; John Garner was president of the U.S. during the late thirties, and was succeeded by an Isolationist in 1940. However, in the middle of occupied America lives a writer, Hawthorne Abendsen, whose book, *The Grasshopper Lies Heavy*, describes an America in which Roosevelt wasn't assassinated, continued as President through the thirties, and was succeeded in 1940 by a President who shared his views. As a result, in Abendsen's novel, America won the war; there was no Pearl Harbor, and the U.S. fleet succeeded in halting Japanese advances in the Pacific. Later in Dick's novel, a young woman indicates to Abendsen that she knows that he wrote his book through consultation with the prophetic powers of the *I Ching, The Book of Changes;* she herself then consults the Oracle of the *I Ching*, and, looking at the patterns, says:

> "I know what it means."
> Raising his head, Hawthorne scrutinized her.... "It means, does it, that my book is true?"
> "Yes," she said.
> With anger he said, "Germany and Japan lost the war?"
> "Yes."
> Hawthorne...said nothing.
> "Even you don't face it," (she) said....
> "I'm not sure of anything," he said.

Later in the sixties, Thomas Disch in 'Descending' portrayed a man leaving a restaurant on a building's fifteenth floor. He begins reading a copy of *Vanity Fair* as he steps on to the 'down' escalator, and continues to read as he automatically moves from the end of one section of moving steps to the next. Becoming aware that he has read 55 pages while moving down the escalator, he finds no indication of what floor he might be on. There is no 'up' escalator; he tries running up the 'down' one, but finds it exhausting. He decides to follow the course of least resistance, and eventually begins running down the moving steps to speed his descent. Finally, we see him lapse into darkness, his body lying at the bottom of the escalator.

Norman Spinrad's *The Iron Dream* (New York, 1972), becomes almost an artifact of a transformed reality. On opening the book, we find that the title information of the cover and the end papers is in error; the book we hold is actually *Lord of the Swastika*, the last and most popular of Adolf Hitler's many science fiction novels. A biographical sketch inside explains that Hitler, after a brief fling at radical politics following the Great War, emigrated to America. 'Although best known to present-day SF fans for his novels and stories, Hitler was a popular illustrator during the Golden Age of the thirties....He won a posthumous Hugo at the 1955 World Science-Fiction Convention for *Lord of the Swastika*, which was completed just before his death in 1953. For many years, he had been a popular figure at SF conventions, widely known in science-fiction fandom as a wit and a nonstop raconteur. Ever since the book's publication, the colourful costumes he created in *Lord of the Swastika* have been favourite themes at convention masquerades.' The costumes are, of course, the S.A. and S.S. uniforms of Nazi Germany. The novel itself concerns the efforts of a hero named Feric Jaggar to return pride and dignity to his racial homeland, and to rid it of the threat from outside of a powerful neighbouring nation, and from the danger of a genetic pollution internally.

In an afterword to Hitler's novel, written in 1959, Homer Whipple of New York University recounts the vindication of Hitler and other anti-Communists when the Greater Soviet Union took over Britain. Noting that 'many of Hitler's readers must find it tempting to imagine what the emergence of a leader like Feric Jaggar could mean to America,' Whipple goes on to point out:

Of course, such a man could gain power only in the extravagant fancies of a pathological science-fiction novel. For Feric Jaggar is essentially a monster: a narcissistic psychopath with paranoid obsessions. His total self-assurance and certainly is based on a total lack of introspective self-knowledge. In a sense, such a human being would be all surface and no interior. He would be able to manipulate the surface of social reality by projecting his own pathologies upon it,

but he would never be able to share in the inner communion
of inter-personal relationships.
    Such a creature could give a nation the iron leadership
and sense of certainty to face a mortal crisis, but at what
cost? Led by the likes of Feric Jaggar, we might gain the
world at the cost of our souls.
    No, although the spectre of world Communist domi-
nation may cause the simpleminded to wish for a leader
modelled on the hero of *Lord of the Swastika*, in an absolute
sense we are fortunate that a monster like Feric Jaggar will
forever remain confined to the pages of science fantasy, the
fever dream of a neurotic science-fiction writer named Adolf
Hitler.

Spinrad's daring and ingenious use of 'history' as fiction creates, in fact,
a new genre: SuperFiction. In this genre his science fiction novel, *The
Iron Dream*, meets the conventionally published work of Ronald Sukenick, whose *98.6* (New York, 1975) makes a similar hypothetical use of a
Robert Kennedy presidency. The result, for readers, is an enrichment of
fiction *as fiction*, and the occasion of a true renaissance in narrative art.

DAVID MILLER

Language of Detective Fiction: Fiction of Detective Language

OF THE CONTEST represented in detective fiction between crime and detection, hiding and seeking, it may be asked: which side is taken by the *language* of the representation? Perhaps a case might be made that language plays accomplice to the criminal, whose secret it preserves virtually to the point of its own abolition. Do we not typically encounter this language in the act of *resisting* our demands for definite, definitive truth? Irritatingly dilatory, disingenuously dumb, it stays one or several steps behind where our desire for knowledge would be. Treacherous and evasive, all but perjured, it continually equivocates about the truth it professes to be disclosing. Such language would seem never able to 'come clean', since as soon as its foul play is arrested, it has little else to say.

If it is true, then, that the language of detective fiction covers up for crime, it is only able to do so on the basis of a criminality of its own, a specifically linguistic delinquency. What threatens the readers of the detective story—threatens them, I mean, *as readers*—is the danger of a criminal language which would subject the truth to such extreme deferments, dispersions, equivocations, and oscillations that it could never be found whole and in one piece. The crime, therefore, whose effects are most in evidence in detective fiction has not to do with murder, but with meaning: with the dissociation of signifier from signified, sign from meaning. 'The principal difficulty of your case,' Sherlock Holmes tells a client, 'lay in the fact of there being too much evidence' ('The Naval Treaty'). At the scene of the crime, in place of the crime, we find a clutter of clues, signs dauntingly in excess of a meaning which would order and account for them. At the same time, Holmes can also declare in another case, 'we are suffering from a plethora of surmise, conjecture, and hypothesis' ('Silver Blaze'). Just as the excess of clues always points to a *lack* of evidence, the dearth of meaning is also manifest as a proliferation of meanings: arbitrary, unverified, competing speculations that threaten to remain forever in the air. Whether one has an overabundance of signs, or an excess of unattached meanings, the easy equatability of sign and meaning has been troubled. In the text generated and sustained by that troubling, the very prospect of an ultimate, authoritative meaning seems menaced. Worse than criminal, the language of detective fiction risks becoming criminally insane: distracted, de-tracked, always pulling back (suspense) or away (false leads) from the truth it will not fully predicate.

So sidling a language necessarily sides with criminality. Yet how, in the last analysis, is criminality characterized in detective fiction? From Hercule Poirot: 'We are confronted here with an unknown personage. He is in the dark and seeks to remain in the dark. But in the very nature of things *he cannot help throwing light upon himself....*Crime is terrible revealing. Try and vary your methods as you will, your tastes, your habits, your attitude of mind, and your soul is revealed by your actions' (*The ABC Murders*). From Sherlock Holmes, having driven a poisonous snake to return fatally upon its owner: 'Violence does, in truth, recoil upon the violent, and the schemer falls into the pit which he digs for another' ('The Adventure of the Speckled Band'). (In his conception of crime thus recoiling, Holmes's own murderous part in the action scarcely matters.) 'Crime never pays', then, except, to be sure, for the ideological dividends consequent on the notion itself. Far more important than the obvious moral caution carried in it is the ontological destiny it implies, whereby crime is bound by the nature of things to disclose its own secrets, punish its own wickedness. In the long run, the criminal is merely one who takes the law into his own hands: the unknown murderer proves an unwitting suicide. His apparent evasion of the policed regime of the law becomes finally no more than a circuitous, merely 'perverse' return to its jurisdiction. For not only the law, but also its policing force have been installed *inside* crime: in the logic of criminal activity (the snake that bites its owner, the gang that exterminates itself), within the exigencies of the criminal mind ('tell-tale' guilt, nerves, over-reaching).

The criminal language of detective fiction is subject to the same liability to backfire as crime itself. For all its deviancy, this language ultimately 'plays' into the hands of the law: pointing, even aspiring, to its own rehabilitation. The signifiers of this language may appear to drift away from an ultimate signified, but their drift is always already anchored by it. Just as the question of a riddle is spoken and heard from the foreknowledge of its own answerability, the solution here presides over the very posing of the mystery, and the distractedness of language is read

under the guarantee of its ultimate propriety and directedness. Although
the text richly 'stammers,' such stammering serves the aperitive function
of making the reader hungry for the ultimate meaning it teases him by
hiding. ' "I will reveal everything." But he had presumed too much upon
his strength. When he again tried to speak, he could not' (*Monsieur
Lecoq*); 'There was something else she would fain have said...but a fresh
convulsion seized her and choked her words' ('Speckled Band');'Her dis-
tended eyes saw—she understood—her lips seemed to form a word, but
nobody made it out, and she fell back insensible' (*The Mystery of the
Yellow Room*). By seeming to subvert the already decided prospect of
truth, this suspenseful, suspensive language produces the counter-effect
of enhancing its value.

Insofar as the detective story dramatizes no more than the difficulties of *access* to the truth, it presupposes—and predisposes of—a truth to
which one may accede: one, whole, universal, and merely *held back* for
the duration of the text. We read through the language of detective fiction
in order to get to this final truth—that is to say, more blatantly, we read
this language in order *to put an end to it*. The notable amounts of tobacco
and other drugs consumed by the great detectives assist in glamourizing
a reading that is itself drugged and addictive: able to account for its
pleasure only in terms of sheer compulsiveness ('I couldn't put it down',
'I had to finish it'). From the distractedness which is the language of the
text, we are in turn distracted, by the promise of the 'fix' which is fixed
meaning.

It is no exaggeration to say that the truth we pursue across the text
is the detective's *reading* of it. For if the exemplary tool of classical detection, the magnifying glass, belongs as much to a technique of reading
manuscripts and uncovering palimpsests as to criminology, this is
because detective stories conceive reading and detection as fully analogous, often overlapping, at times perfectly identical activities. The crime
will frequently come in the initial form of a verbal account of it, proffered
by the client or reported in the newspapers, and the detective's ingenuity
is commonly exercised on verbal puzzles, whether frankly cryptographic
('The Moabite Cipher', 'The Gold Bug', 'The Dancing Men'), or concealing semantic ambiguities he brings to light by way of adjudicating
between them. (The 'band' in 'Speckled Band' is first thought to mean
'band of gypsies', later 'the band formed by a snake'. The great detective is frequently said to 'read' a character's appearance, or the ground
about the crime frequently seen as a 'blank page' signed by criminal
footprints. Even when we are not dealing with explicit references to texts,
language, or reading, a vocabulary of 'trace', 'sign', 'clue', 'indication',
continues to refer us to a readerly rite of passage from signifier to
signified.

Inevitably, the detective's reading consists in a *depletion* of the signifiers generated by the crime and accumulated in the course of inquest. If his final summing-up offers 'the whole truth', it also contains 'nothing but the truth,' and there has always been more to tell, more to telling, than that. 'Between what matters and what seems to matter, how should the world we know judge wisely?' (*Trent's Last Case*). Thus begins a famous detective story, describing exactly the position in which it places a reader; but the story ends, like every other detective story, with the ability to sift wheat from chaff fully acquired and successfully exercised. As such-and-such is pronounced irrelevant, so-and-so a red herring, a large body of textual signifiers is exiled to a state of no status. It is no doubt paradoxical that our distracted, nerve-wracked, stupefied reading always reads about its 'other': the attentive, cool, brilliant reading of the detective. The reading that places fewest demands on us curiously takes for its subject the representation of the most strenuous, meticulous, even 'scientific' reading that can be imagined. Yet the more interesting paradox comes in the fact that, reading about the detective's apparently opposite reading, our reading always reads about itself. The de-tracked language *we* race through, *he* rectifies, with the same effect of cancelling it out. The censorship of the signifier involved in our state of distraction is mirrored—and, what is better, rationalized—in his act of dismissal.

The detective reads, as the detective story is read, under the assumption that only one reading of the matter at hand is correct—indeed, only one reading is possible. As detectives are fond of insisting, 'There are no two ways of reasoning about the case.' Qualified by the text as the *truth*, as (because at) the end of all the guessing, the detective's reading lays irrefutable claim to absolute validity. Did it not do so, it is likely that one would be more struck with the *distortion* invariably characterizing this reading, with the ways it fragments, edits, and reorders the continuum of the text. One item in a series is elevated to prime importance, minor event turns into major episode, figure yields to ground, as all the text's original hierarchies of presentation are overthrown. The name of truth is all that keeps the detective's fully valid reading from resembling its enemy: the 'wild', 'irresponsible' speculation that it is supposed to make henceforward impossible. *'Truth' is the alibi of detective fiction*, the ultimate signified that exculpates its language from the sin of being merely a sign. Truth licenses the dismissal of the signifier under the pretense of being most faithful to it, at the same time as it arrests the multiplication of signifieds by uniquely privileging one of them. Neither the detective story nor its readers can enjoy the 'polysemicity' of language except as part of a project of subduing it into univocality—can enjoy even that univocality unless assured that it is more or less than intepretation: the truth.

The detective story only raises the possibility that language will never disburden itself of what it apparently 'wants to say' for one reason: to lay it to rest. Like the criminal, the order of the signifier is eventually compelled 'in the very nature of things' to surrender: to be converted into an order of the signified, sponsoring single, clear meanings. The ritual thus enacted, it must be added, affirms as well as represses, celebrates as well as censors. For, moving from the order of the signifier to that of the signified, language dramatizes and reconfirmes its own unrelenting truthfulness. Language cannot deceive, at least not for long: nor, more importantly, can it ever remove the bar of the antithesis that keeps truth and falsehood apart. Inasmuch as the detective's final summation is the language of truth, it attests to no less than the truth of language: its irresistible orientation towards a truth with which it is finally identified. We began by asking: between crime and the police, how does the language of the detective story side? Its siding with crime, we see, shows finally for a masterful pre-emptive move whereby crime may be brought to justice. As such it recalls the tactics of every detective who operates, since Poe, through 'an identification of [his] intellect with that of his opponent' ('The Purloined Letter'). What the detective story finally describes, performs, and exalts is a *detective language* which would be its own police force, infallibly designating and disciplining all 'internal corruption'.

Policing itself, the language of detective fiction polices the world which uses it. Whether in the urbane interviews of the 'classical' kind or in the tough interrogations of the 'hard-boiled' variety, *talk* is the detective's chief weapon in the conquest of criminal disorder. It is not hard to see why this should be so. If language is intrinsically truthful, then the detective's task is clearly to facilitate its production. Thus, the hard-boiled detective is required to get people to 'talk' (or 'sing' or 'spill'), while the gangsters he is up against are usually occupied in buttoning lips. And the seemingly more genteel conversations solicited by the classical detective are charged with a similar policing function: 'There is nothing so dangerous *for any one who has something to hide* as conversation!...A human being, Hastings, cannot resist the opportunity to reveal himself and express his personality which conversation gives him' (*ABC Murders*). The criminal cannot speak without incriminating himself in 'telling' slips. Part of the proof against him at the end often consists in the fact that his language breaks down—or as it is sometimes put, 'words fail him'. Through talk, the detective story links together language, truth and justice, and never more spectacularly than in the detective's final speech. Here vocality functions, in a Derridean sense, to attest a language fully present to meaning, as though the truth of what was said lay at least in part in the ritualized *act of saying it*. At the same time, with almost thaumaturgic powers, this speech also *enforces* the truth it comes

to disclose. How else to explain why the detective story completely dis-
penses with the criminal's arrest, trial and execution, except to say that
these are so thoroughly implied in the detective's final utterance that they
literally may go without saying?

Despite the many 'histories' of detective fiction, there is in one
sense no history to write, only a record of the venues in which a single
ritual has been repeated. Or such at least would be the case were it not for
the development of the now dominant hard-boiled form. For our
purposes, the specificity of this American mutant lies in the heavy
emphasis it places on violence—not on violence per se (whatever that is),
but on violence as that which promotes and curtails the linguistic production of truth. In the classical detective story, what we have called the language of truth is freely volunteered by witnesses or teased out by the
detective's logically irresistible cross-questionings. Language moves
automatically towards truth, sorting out inconsistencies and excesses,
gathering momentum from its own intrinsic veridicity. By contrast, the
language in the American detective story must be extorted, coerced by
muscle or at the point of a gun. Utterance is always entangled in a violent
power which supervises it. This power finds its logical extreme in the
frequent scenes depicting an assault on the vocal chords. For example, in
a story by Raymond Chandler, a detective loops a wire around his inter-
locutor's throat, then jerks it taut: 'You want to talk to me, spig. Maybe
not right away, maybe not even soon. But after a while you want to talk to
me' ('Spanish Blood'). No doubt the defensively 'tight' mouth typical of
the hard-boiled detective anticipates similar acts of violence against *his*
vocal organs. There is now the danger that the voice of truth may be
stopped in the detective's throat. One of Chandler's detectives displays a
bullet-scar on his throat 'close to his windpipe', as though for an emblem
of the nearly perfect coincidence obtaining between the organ of speech
and the object of violence. The slang and the solecisms of American
detective fiction (Marlow is archly made to remark that he 'can still speak
English if there's any demand for it') should not mislead us into thinking
that language is debunked therein, or that it plays a weak second to
'action'. On the contrary, the violent power investing language dramatizes its extreme importance, as what is most at stake in the contest
between the law and criminality. No less than it is the means to end the
contest, language is *the very object of the struggle*.

In relation to its classical predecessor, the American detective story
seems a blunt and disenchanted 'critique of pure reason'. It derisively
places the once all-mighty word in a world of violent appropriations,
where non-linguistic forces of power safeguard or suppress every dis-
closure. Divested in the name of realism of its magical power to police the
world, language is now demonstrated to require police protection itself.
Despite its apparent contamination by power-relations, however lan-

guage continues to be idealized as the carrier of truth. Violence may help or hinder the production of language, but it cannot affect the nature of that production. Truthfulness remains the inalienable property of language, even as the truth—still one and indivisible—remains its ultimate subject. Like the abducted maiden of melodrama, language may be easily, perhaps fatally imperilled, but its fundamental honesty can always be counted on.

It may seem puzzling that the American form retains the ideality of an intrinsically *truthful* language while it flamboyantly, cynically dismisses the ideality of an intrinsically *powerful* language. The puzzle becomes less odd, however, if we consider the advantages of such a set-up. Just as language is now vulnerable to the violent attempts to suppress it, it also justifies the policing power which comes to compensate for its frailty. Contrary to what is sometimes thought, violence is not unleashed in this arrangement, so much as it is *licensed*, commissioned to let truth speak, to remove from the maiden her gag. Through the sheer obviousness of its justifications, a licensed violence—the violence of Order—tends to erase itself as an object of serious attention. As we see the detective moving in counter-attack or self-defense against the prior violence of the criminal 'other', our perception of his violence as such is relatively neutralized. Of course, the detective story has always been an apology for Order, alarmingly disrupted by the initial crime, held in anxious suspense during the inquest, jubilantly restored by the apprehension of the criminal. The 'repressed' that is 'returned' at the moment of truth comprises really the existing police and para-policial systems of repression. The detective story forwards the power of these systems, not just by familiarizing us with police corruption (as with a kind of fate), but also by idealizing them at another level. 'Get out of here or I'll call the police,' someone screams at Ross MacDonald's Lew Archer. To which the private detective replies, 'I sort of am the police' ('Find the Woman'). Ultimately, the private detective is nothing but *an ideal policeman*, doing the same work as the official force, only 'better': better in a moral sense ('Down these mean streets,' Chandler insisted about his detective, 'a man must go who is not himself mean, who is neither tarnished nor afraid'), and better in a very practical sense as well, for he can go places, and do things, not permitted to official agents.

So ideal is this policeman's power that, in one sense, it frequently ceases to be real at all. For although he gives utterance to the truth, the American detective is seldom able or willing to be listened to by a civic order. The truth is not allowed to have public consequences. In this seemingly cynical destiny, the truth is once more set free from power-relationships, to which everything is now subject *except* the truth seen by a private, privatized eye. The entanglement between language and power is disentangled, and though the language of truth is now powerless, it is also by the same token immune from a power which can contaminate everything else. To the extent that the truth takes refuge in the private realm, one might well argue that it becomes more purely the subject of a novel—that is, the subject of a reading read by individual subjects. To the extent that we treasure an ideality so consoling that we can bear with anything, so redemptive that it need never be called on to redeem, one might also argue that this subject is part of our subjection.

PETER ROBINSON

From Memory

The privet leaves disordered
by stiff gusts, long henna'd strands
flurry at her face, in memory.

I extenuate the circumstances
for my part towards him
or blame, aportion understanding.

Regret, regret, and I envisage
the shudder of her violating
once again, abruptly.

Dolls in plastic bags, soft toys
for souvenirs hung where she said,
I concentrated on his tie.

Here, I swelter in the dusk
and chase the flies, abstractedly,
until I half forget them.

Darting at the part raised shutter
they blur into the contre-jour,
that pink blank of a wall.

The Counterpane

Come to bed late I'm quiet
   across floorboards and hear
uneven, spattering rain beat
   on rhodedendron leaves,

her breathing, the whirr
   and click of a set alarm.
Unsettling dreams recur
   in the quietness this 2 am.

Shadow on her nightdress
   touches creases, softening forms:
the hollows where eyelids press,
   or down along her forearms.

Tonight not warm, and waking
   you wrap round the counterpane.
In the fear of love-making
   sense our deaths, dirty rain

swept by windscreen wipers.
   Thickening dark where she ran
wet from the downpour, love
   unwanted she lay down

and for a little died.
   And I don't comprehend
her sleep like death to settle
   or to rouse her.

I'd only make amends.

For My Wife To Be

There was the odd impediment:
establishing where things went
and once collected, cleared.
Then in the rooms prepared

for renovation, whose débris
showed us how we used to be:
engaged, the habitual dissolves.
And we notice in ourselves

restored, the interior blanknesses
still to be cluttered, causes
of an eight year hesitation.
After wallpaper had gone,

plaster used for messages
by previous workmen, passages
of four inch brick proved rough.
Here was relief enough:

our vertical bodies' residence.
Only your love is small defence.
All you have I have to share.
What each gives, they are.

23 January 1980

My apology condenses on the window;
a new moon shouldering the pole star
above backyards that overlook
cypresses and ash,
resilience, the marble headboards
in the cemetery, and my fear
of not getting to sleep or never waking
coughs like a stalling car.

As the earth grows colder, discontented,
under the winters of money and the freezing
of relations, how we live
matters less than this reflection,
that we continue
poorer or in health, and letters arrive
bearing affection or disaffection,
starting with, How are you?

Back home, what it is to be forgiven.
Close, I wonder what my furred tongue's for
as words to be uttered when she woke
my teeth close on,
and what should become of us
in the promises of further histories
I'm not asked to explain,
only to say no more.

ROBERT COOVER

Lucky Pierre and the Coldwater Flat

DOCUMENTARY SLAG, the serial debris of his compulsive remigrations, litters his trail to the coldwater flat, crumbs for the wayward orphan. Letters, old bills, a lock of her red hair, trinkets, photos—a thousand eyes on him, all his own. His tears disturb not one pool, but an infinite regression of pools within pools. What drives him to come back here?

—Come back here! Come back here!

Film tins lie in the frozen streets like manhole covers. Shredded scraps of notepaper fall like snow, and camera lenses twinkle in the deep white heaps, reflecting the lights of signs and shopwindows, the passing traffic. The wind howls through the gaps and chasms of the city, orchestrating the percussive mutterings of engines, the clangour of horns and auto crashes, the reverberant desperation of immaterialized sorrow. Da capo. Da capo. Passing his own shadow, trammeling his own footsteps. Over and over again.

—Again! Again! Again!

I must be mad, he thinks.

—Yes, mad! You are mad, Lucky! Mad about your Cleo! Hurry, my love! I am hot! hot! hot!

Mannequins model her underwear, her rings and bangles, her ancient gown, flash their dead green eyes and hard white bottoms at him. Notebooks block the slush of gutters, their ink running hopelessly, and spools of tape tumble out of metal wastebaskets like wild red hair.

—Was I the first, Lucky? Really the first?

He is drawn up the dimly lit stairwell like a clockhand to its hour. The wooden stairs creak with anxiety, his hand sweats on the worn rail.

He watches his reluctant ascent, blowing a flute at it to drive away the
stink of piss and ink. The flute quickens him. Eager now, he climbs hand
over hand. Cleo squats on the bidet, spraying icecold water up her womb.
He lies on the flowered carpet, listening to the splash of water, staring at
the ceiling, piping himself up the dingy stairwell with its chipped and
battered walls, once green, past its urgent graffiti: HURRY, LUCKY! MY
CUNT'S ON FIRE! The carpet smells, not so much of daffodils, as of
sheep, too long dead.

—I heard you out there in the corridor. You were peeking through
the keyhole. I opened the door.

—I watched you through the branches. I'd never seen anything like
you. I fell.

A child still, with big green eyes and long lashes, springy red ringlets all over her head, slipping barefoot through the fresh grass to the
water's edge. Dappled with sunlight and leaf shadow. Her white gown,
fine as gossamer, twines about her slender thighs and narrow hips.
clings to her breasts, small and firm as new apples. She kneels on a flat
rock and dips her finger in the pool. The gown folds into a soft crease
down her buttocks, flows forward between her thighs as though caught on
a sudden breeze. His once-quiet heart pounds in his ears. Something is
happening!

He opens the door. He hesitates at the threshold, as though anticipating....what? He is disappointed. It is the same. Or perhaps he is
relieved. Anyway the same: a hanging bulb, a bed, stove and cupboard, a
chest, a chair. The mattress on the bed is laid with a frayed quilt. The
windowshade is torn and the spring is gone: it hangs at the same odd
angle. The flowered wallpaper is soot-smeared and peeling. It has always
been peeling. She smiles at him from the mirror over the washbasin, her
white teeth sparkling.

—It's our anniversary, Lucky!

Her long slender thighs are distorted, creased by the lip of the
bidet. In this part of the city, they have bidets. The ridges of her spine,
curved slightly forward, cast a ripple of dark dimples down her back,
crossed by the downy shadows of her shoulderblades. Her bottom is
hunched forward, like a cat's when it shits, and beneath the smooth white
cheeks, steam is rising. She watches the man, stretched out on the old
wool rug, his eyes fixed on the ceiling, where nothing is happening,
nothing in her mind at all, one of his hands clutching his rigid organ, the
other an empty wine bottle.

—You're just torturing yourself, she says, and lowers her steaming
cunt over his face.

—That's right, it sizzled when you touched the water, he says, I
remember now!

—That's not true, Lucky, she laughs, and unpins her wide-brimmed bonnet, shaking out her curls. You're making it all up! Her ruffled white blouse is creased starchly over her prim breasts, and her full skirts rustle as they brush the old oak bed. The door clicks shut behind them.

—Your nipples were petalled like pink daisies.

—Help me unbutton, Lucky! Please! Hurry!

—In your navel you kept a—

He switches off the taperecorder. Street sounds leak into the room. He sits on the bidet, smoking a pipe, spraying his balls with cold water, gazing thoughtfully at the old bed with its stained and sagging mattress. She writhes there, her nymphae puffy, inflamed, the clitoris quivering, her head thrashing from side to side.

—I thought you knew everything, he says softly. I loved you more than life.

The gown in a filmy puddle at her feet; the branch between his legs; she gazing curiously at her breasts, cupping them in her slender hands, squeezing the pink buds.

—Lucky...?

—The first? I don't know, there might have been others. But if there were, I wasn't counting them. I started with you, Cleo. Number one.

Her tummy is flat and soft, with a deep navel like a secret eye. On the hard nub of her childish mound: a small cluster of tiny red ringlets in the shape of a little goblet. She steps cautiously into the pool, shuddering, clutching her breasts, then stands there spraddle-legged, staring at her reflected orifices. Gently, tentatively, she strokes herself.

—You were masturbating. I heard your heavy breathing through the keyhole. I rose from the bidet and crossed to the chair, where you couldn't see me.

—I masturbated all the time then. I was happy, Cleo. I wasn't afraid of anything. Then I fell and put on my weight forever.

He opens the door. Again the same. The frayed quilt, the crooked shade, the battered tin wastebasket with the pink swans. Long ago, he bought the room. He has tried to keep it just as it was. As best he can. As best he can remember. The old oak bed, the hat tree, the empty wine bottle, the basin and bidet with their coldwater taps, everything in its place. Even the same coarse white towels, now yellowed with age, the oilcloth on the chest. He has tried, but it is *not* the same. There is now a yellow film box in the wastebasket; he doesn't remember how it got there. New holes in the rug, stains in the mattress, rust in the basin. A torn photograph under the bed. And there were more mirrors then, some of the mirrors are gone.

—No, they're just the same. Only we looked in them more often then. You were just a boy. You didn't have a moustache then.

She dips her finger in the pool, licks it, sticks it up his rectum. His balls drop into his scrotum. She blows on his groin and black hairs sprout, spreading like vines. Like a bird with a worm, she draws forth his reluctant penis, then slides the foreskin back and sucks the heart-shaped crown. His hips buck.

—How did I—*ah*—get into this room? he cries.

—I don't know, that was a long time ago, she says. I was still a virgin.

She stands at the washbasin, gazing at him through the mirror. Her eyes are in shadows, but their whites seem all the more striking. She unties the pussycat bow of her ruffled blouse. Her movements are hesitant, hurried, blurred, flashing in and out of deep shadows, but the flowered wallpaper is very clear. She stares wide-eyed into the mirror, her hands groping for the buttons on the back of her blouse. He approaches, wearing boxer shorts, baggy in the seat, and an undershirt with narrow shoulder straps. He undoes the buttons, tugs the blouse free of the skirt, and lifts it over her shoulders—but it gets stuck there: they have forgotten to remove the wide-brimmed bonnet.

—Wait, Lucky! Wait!

—I...I can't!

They watch themselves fuck, sandwiched in mirrors. Their hips heave frantically in an infinite series, their thighs slap, she bites his shoulder, complaining, counting, rips hairs from his ass, from his innumerable asses, he explodes in her, his seed bursting forth in a chorus of imitative spasms, and he sinks away, all by himself, on her breasts. He is unable even to contemplate this collapse in the mirrors, but closes his eyes and allows himself to slip down into some deep consoling cave. In his fading mind's eye, the bucking of all those hips gradually gets out of sync, begins to undulate slowly like waves lapping a shore. She slides out from under him, and he hears her scratching on the notepad she keeps by the bed.

—Fortyseven minutes, 836 thrusts, she announces flatly. You were doing better than that five years ago. You don't love me anymore, Lucky!

—I just realized, Cleo. There's one too many ashtrays in this room.

It almost worked once with the towels. When he least expected it. Nothing special about the moment, they weren't even fucking, he was just washing his face at the basin, like a thousand times before. He reached for the towel, and suddenly he had it: the scene, whole, just as it was then, her body stunted by refraction, her legs as though sprouting from her breasts, buttocks just under her shoulderblades—she ducks under, and her bottom bobs to the surface for one fantastic second, gleaming bright and pure in the sunlight. And then, with a foamy kick: gone. It's only the towel in his hand, soapy water in the basin, his own image, wet and perplexed, in the mirror.

—It was pink then, your anus, like a little tiny raspberry, with just the lightest fleck of downy red hair ringing it round. And your cunt, too. Pink, Cleo. Just a blush. Like the crease in a peach.

—What colour is it now? she asks, coming down.

—Wait! I'm not trying to hang on to anything, Cleo, I just want to get through to—*mmmf!*

Wow, it *is* hot, her cunt, it burns his lips and makes his tongue leap and throb. At first, he can't see a thing, but then she leans forward to lick at his groin, and past the goosebumps on her cold wet ass, he sees himself, projected onto the ceiling, climbing the stairs, peeking through the keyhole. Why does he keep coming back? It's impossible, he knows that. He could have recorded it then, got it all down somehow, but you always think of such things too late. And once it's gone, there's no remaking it, the door closes and disappears into the wall forever, it's useless. Yes, he's a fool, jacking off in the corridors of some lost episode. He leans forward, weeping sorrily for all the beauty that escapes him, and finds the door there after all: it opens and he tumbles into the room.

—My hero!

Balls of lint and dust on the carpet. Cracks in the baseboard, the cupboard, the chest. The chair legs are nicked and scuffed, worse at the feet. There is gum stuck under the seat, a microphone concealed in the bed springs. Cleo's pale ankles are planted in a little mound of her own underwear.

—We did fuck once in the country, didn't we, Cleo?

—Where did you come from, Lucky?

She steps out of her puddle of panties and straddles his head, her bangles ringing. Did she wear bangles that time? Does it matter? Paint is splattered on the underside of the washbasin and a strip of wallpaper is missing.

—Do you remember what we did seven years ago tonight?

—No.

—Oh, Lucky, you're hopeless! How old are you?

—I don't know.

—What is today? Don't you even know that? Who are you anyway? What's the matter with you?

Above him, her cunt yawns: a bottomless pit. He should know, he's explored it. The great maw. Everybody in town trying to fill it up nowadays, the fools. Can't be done. She's driving the whole city nuts. He can't see her face, can only hear it.

—Speak to me, Lucky! Any answers, I don't care how true they are, just talk to me!

On her ass, there's a projection of him pulling her bloomers down, caressing her tight cunt and white bottom, but he can only see the lower edge of it, foreshortened, like a body refracted in a pool of water. He backs it up and starts it over.

—Bend over, Cleo.

He unbuttons her skirt, unlaces her corset. She watches him as though in fright through the mirror. His hands fondle her young breasts, two firm little bubbles with tiny dark tips. He kisses her neck under the dark ringlets, her throat, her armpits. She seems about to swoon. He pulls her bloomers down, stroking the little cluster of ringlets on her pubis, caressing her bright white bottom. He nips her cheeks in his teeth, brushes them with his moustache, licks her anus, then runs his tongue up her crack and spine. She drops limply into his arms, her eyes rolled back.

—It's our anniversary, she murmurs. I've brought the wine.

—There was a tree, wasn't there? A rock?

—Why are you staring at the chair?

—A pool, a meadow? Wasn't there, Cleo?

—And wild flowers?

—Yes! That's it!

—Wild flowers!

—Good!

—A river!

—No...

—Yes, a river, flowing hard and fast, with churning rapids, and all the reeds along the bank, all the reeds were penises!

—No, Cleo...

—Long golden penises with big violet heads like giant acorns! Wherever I moved, the reeds tried to follow, leaning toward me! As I danced around them, they swayed, to and fro, to and fro, stirring a frantic hot breeze! *Whush! Whush!*

—Uh, Cleo...

—Ileaped back and forth across them! They thrashed about wildly, pulling at their roots! The wind rose! The reeds grew bigger and bigger! Oh, Lucky! There was thunder and a thick perfume, convulsions, the skies were aflame! Oh my god! Still they grew! Their heads burst, raining nectar on me! I was screaming. I threw myself on hundreds of them at once—!

He watches her roll about on the carpet, fucking the wine bottle.

—Damn you, Cleo. It wasn't like that at all.

She faints.

He carries her past the bare bulb, hanging near the stove, and lays her on the bed. He smiles, scratching his armpits. He spreads her legs, doubling her knees back with a fluttering flash of light and shadow. Hmmm. There is a cork in her cunt. He ponders this, poking about at the pale little cunt; then he brightens. He reaches into the fly of his boxer shorts, and as though pulling a blade from a jacknife, opens out a corkscrew. He stabs it into the cork and she starts up suddenly as though in pain.

—Oh, Lucky, you don't love me anymore. You're just using me!

—Hold still, damn it!

He lies on his back, head propped by quilt and cushions. She straddles his prick, facing away, leaning on his knees, her feet in his armpits. On one cheek of her ass, he is taking her maidenhead with his corkscrew penis, revolving round and round, impatiently manipulating her cumbrous limbs, kicking her in the face with his stockinged feet: on the other, he is watching through the keyhole while they fuck on the bidet, surrounded by mirrors and cameras.

—Now, if I can just bring these two projections together somehow, on top of each other, right over the asshole...

—My god, what is it you want, Lucky? Do you want this room to just disappear, is that it?

—Don't say that, Cleo! Goddamn it, that scares the hell out of me!

His heart is racing. She sits on a rough-hewn rock at the water's edge. Her hair sparkles in the sunlight, her naked body gleams. What is she staring at? Her smooth plump bottom is warped by the rock's craggy surface into a kind of wry grimace. In the upper righthand corner, at the edge of a forest, there is what looks like an opening into a cave.

—Good lord, Cleo! Has this...has this been hanging here all the time?

—No, I bought it for you, Lucky. It was pretty. I thought you'd like it. I thought it'd cheer you up.

He rips the frame down off the wall and, throwing open the window, chucks it out into the night. Snow blows in and whitens the hair on his belly, frosts his cock, chills his heart. Cleo runs to the window, leans out into the storm. Far below, there is a crash and a scream—she laughs excitedly, one hand pressed between her thighs. Now! Swiftly, almost without thinking, he rears back and gives a tremendous kick to that splendid red-haired ass.

—Goodbye, Cleo!

But it is like kicking a rock. She spins round, grinning wildly, her red ringlets glittering with ice crystals, her green eyes shining.

—Lucky!

—Cleo!

—Suck me, Lucky! Now!

—My goddamn foot hurts, Cleo!

—You won't need it, she laughs, and leaps on him, wrapping her limbs around him, tumbling him to the carpet. It's our anniversary!

They pitch and roll, her bangles jangling, around the flat—under the bed, past chest and stove, scrunch! over their photo album, slam! up against the coldwater bidet. They kick the chair halfway across the room, cameras and recorders come crashing down on them, they scratch and gouge, mingling hot blood with their sweat.

—That's it, Lucky! she gasps. Oh yeah!

Photos crumple and stick to their bodies, they wallow in a tangle of celluloid and nylon, the tin wastebasket goes clattering about, bowling over wine bottles. Projections run riot, mirrors tip and weave, there's a blur of images like film jumping out of its sprockets.

—I love you, Cleo! Gawdamighty, I hate myself, but I can't help it!

—You'll get grass stains on your ass, baby! she laughs.

She grabs him by the ears, stuffs his whole head up her cunt—oh criminy! it's all liquid there between her thighs, a warm pot of honey! There's nothing like it, doesn't matter if she's the most famous piece in the city, when you're in here she makes you think you're the only one! He shoves in, but his shoulders jam on her pelvic floor. The soft folds of her vaginal walls slide by his face, as she rotates ninety degrees. He kicks forward: past the fleshy pillow and into the elbows. Pinioned: he starts to panic. But one fierce hand wraps his cock, the other digs deep into his anus for a grip. An impassioned tug: he slides in to the wrists. Another push, and he's free! Only his feet stick out. He plunges about in there, lapping it up, slaking his ancient thirst, his weary ass wrapped in a hot buttery embrace, while below, to keep him moving, she scratches the soles of his feet.

Finally, as though drugged, he fades away, succumbs to an oily peace, his dreams reduced to simple patterns of light and colour, cycled on a short endless loop.

Or...

Or are those dreams, after all? Is it Cleo's cunt?

Or is this rather some kind of theatre, after all, he the bulb of a magic lantern...? A man walking through an endless-loop winter in somebody else's nightmare?

My god! Can't breathe!

Help! Let me out!

Where *am* I?

DAVID BLACK
Nostalgia

FOR A WEEK, the leper had been haunting her. He kept pushing himself along on his wheeled cart, using his stumpy arms like paddles, trying to avoid the blue stationwagon that was backing out of the parking lot. From where she was standing at the door of the beauty parlour, she could look up Janpat to Connaught Place, which had always reminded her of the merry-go-round in Central Park her father had treated her to during their first home leave—the cars swinging around the circle like the painted horses she and her brother had ridden on. Just at the moment the stationwagon's back left wheel rolled over and stopped on the leper's trailing bandage, she always heard the man in the bicycle cart crying, 'Kwality ice cream,' and she always saw, radiating out from the toes of her glossy black shoes—she could no longer watch the leper struggle at the end of his bandage like a rabbit caught in a snare—a particular pattern of *pan* spittle-stains on the sidewalk, a pattern that, as she woke, seemed to be a code which, if she could crack it, would unlock the meaning of this repeating dream. Twice she had awoken sweating so much her side of the sheet was soaked. Once, when her husband flipped over in his sleep, he had accidentally struck her face with his flailing arm; and that had wakened her just as the car's wheels caught the dirty bandage. Twice she had known she was dreaming, but had been unable to rouse herself from sleep. The helpless feeling, a sense of hopeless struggling, had terrified her so much she had whimpered aloud and, in her dream, heard her own whimpering translated into the cries of the leper.

2

At the Asia House reception, she backed away from the temporary bar that had been set up on a folding table in front of a glass door; and, half turning to slide between two men whom she recognized (she thought) as former AID associates of her father, she bumped into a young man who had been three grades ahead of her at Woodstock School in Mussoorie. She had met him once in New Delhi before leaving for school, and he had teased her by describing the leeches that in the rainy season would fix themselves to her bare legs and by telling her how she would have to salt them to dissolve their horrible pulpy bodies.

'Beven,' she said, 'the leech teacher!'

But he did not hear her. A fat man, whose small face was set in his huge head like the bas relief features of a Roman emperor stamped on the disk of an old coin, had touched Beven's chest with the mouthpiece of a pipe and had led him off into a conversation made up of suppressed smiles and small nods.

3

The snapshot in 'Whispering Pine', the 1960 yearbook of Woodstock School, reveals Beven Masefield in the middle distance, one-quarter turned toward the camera, about to step out of a circle of sunlight into the shade cast by the wall of a building. He is wearing a knit short-sleeved shirt that is buttoned up to his throat, striped Bermuda shorts, white socks, and loafers. Because of the light, his eyes are dark sockets. Although both arms dangle at his sides, his right hand is clenched into a fist. Under the picture, it says:

Varsity Baseball 11,
Intramural Sports 11, 12

Beside the picture, it says:

If you happen to wander through the Quadrangle
and see a big guy being dragged a hundred different directions by the 'chuts' of the school, you
know that's Beven. Children like him. But all
Beven cares about is another chance at a good,
rough game of American baseball. He was the

Tiger's second baseman against the Hillside
during the baseball season. Aspirations: attending college at Princeton and then joining a major
league team. Good luck, Beven!

On March 22nd, the year she was a freshman at Woodstock School, she
had noted in her diary:

> I don't think I feel anything very deeply. I think I
> must fall in love hard soon. Beven kissed me
> when we were standing behind the kitchen, but it
> didn't leave any impression, like a plane cutting
> through a cloud.

5

While talking on the phone to one of her younger brothers who had called
to tell her his wife had given birth to a girl that afternoon, she stared out
her apartment window at the two stunted maple trees in the garden
behind their building.
 'Do you remember the monkeys?' she asked him.
 'What monkeys?' he said.
 'At Dr Mrs Sita Sen's.'
 They had lived in the neem trees in the courtyards of the hospital
and used to steal the drying diapers from the lines that were strung along
the balconies.
 'The monkeys at the place you were born,' she said.

6

'There were always children begging, barefoot, wearing dirty baggy
shorts or ragged dresses,' she told the others at the dinner party she and
her husband were giving. 'They even begged from children like me
—white or rich Indian children, too. Even though I was so young, it made
me think of myself as an adult.'

7

After the dinner party, while they were lying in bed, side by side, gazing
at the trapezoid of light, which on the ceiling of their dark room looked
like a window onto a blank, illuminated world that extended infinitely

without any interruptions, her husband said, 'You talk a lot about India, lately.'

'I want to go back,' she said.

'Do you want to go this vacation?'

'No,' she said.

'But you just said you wanted to go.'

'Not for vacation,' she said.

'We can't move there,' he laughed.

She turned onto her side, facing away from him. He moved close to her, put his hands around her on her breasts, fitted his knees into the curves behind her knees. She turned to face him. As they made love, she imagined her husband was not her husband, but was her lover, a graphics designer who was a former college roommate of her husband's. He had been at dinner that night. And, as Beven had years before, he had kissed her when they were standing next to the kitchen. She had pulled away and straightened her blouse just as someone came into the hall on his way to get a glass of water.

As she made love with her husband, she stopped thinking of her lover and started thinking that her husband was Beven. Once her husband had fallen asleep, she left their bed, and in the dark walked through the apartment into the livingroom. She sat on the couch, naked, slipped a cigarette from the pack on the coffee table, lit it, and then, having picked up the telephone from the floor, dialled information and asked for Beven's number. He lived, she discovered, only twenty blocks away. She did not write down the number. She jammed the cigarette into the ashtray on the coffee table, dialled her lover's number, and arranged to meet him the following day.

8

While waiting for her lover in a Soho art gallery, she saw what looked like a naked woman lying on a platform in the back corner of a side room. The woman's eyes were closed. Her cheeks looked flushed, as though she were excited or ashamed by her exhibitionism. Her palms were mottled white and pink. Her belly seemed to move up and down ever so slightly, as though she were trying to pretend she was not breathing.

She wanted to touch this naked woman, but was afraid to. When she bent down to look more closely at the soles of the feet which were ridged with small lateral bumps as though the woman had been soaking for hours in a warm tub, she saw that the heel of the left foot was caved in.

She stared at the damaged sculpture for a long time, disturbed, but unable to articulate her feelings to herself. She felt some terrifying kinship with the mannequin. She left before her lover arrived; and, when he called her later that afternoon, she told him she hadn't been feeling well, she would call him later. She wanted to tell him that she no longer wished to see him, but she was afraid that in a few days she would change her mind.

9

That night, because she couldn't sleep, she padded into the livingroom, got Beven's number from information again, and called him. After seven rings, he answered the phone.

'Yes,' he said. 'Yes, who's there?'

She did not answer. She held the mouthpiece of the phone away from her face, so he would not hear her breathing.

'Hello?' he said. 'Hello?'

Very softly, as though Beven's body baffled the sound, she heard a woman's voice groggily ask, 'What's the matter? Who is it? What time is it?'

10

Although she was on her way to the 34th Street stop, she left the subway suddenly at Grand Central Station; and, having found a public telephone, she dialled Beven's number. After the phone rang three times, a woman's voice—the same voice she had heard the night before—answered.

'Hello,' the woman said. 'Hello? Is anyone there?'

She waited until the woman sounded agitated, and then she hung up.

That afternoon, from her bedroom telephone, she called Beven's number again. One ring. The woman picked up the receiver and said cheerily, 'Hello.' When there was no response, the woman became very upset. 'Hello,' the woman said. 'Who is this, please? Will you please answer.

At the department store that evening, from a pay telephone near the front doors, she once more dialled Beven's number. The woman answered immediately.

'Hello, who's this?' the woman said, and getting no reply, hung up.

She dropped another dime in the coin slot and dialled again. The phone rang for a long time before it was answered. This time it was Beven's voice on the other end of the line.

'Stop calling,' he said, 'or I'll get the police.'

He hung up.

When she called the last time, the telephone rang and rang without anyone answering. She left the receiver off the hook, dangling, still ringing on the other end of the line as she walked away.

11

She was on the escalator, half way out of the subway station, when a man, bounding up the moving steps, brushed past her. He was in his mid-thirties, dressed in a light grey suit: a stranger. She could have attacked anyone; he happened to be the one who passed her when she struck out. She grabbed his attaché case. When he turned, she hit his chest with her fists. Surprised, he stopped two steps above her; and she, screaming, pummeled him as the escalator carried them into the street.

M.J. FITZGERALD
Bachelor Life

JULY

FRIDAY A.M.

SILENCE EXCEPT FOR the ticking of the alarm clock. The bedroom is in darkness though thin shafts of sunlight penetrate through cracks in the curtains from a big east-facing window and alight on the thick dark carpet. The door leading into a narrow passage and the rest of the flat faces north. A dark walnut wardrobe is the only item of furniture directly opposite the door and next to the window on the south wall, the rest is aligned against the longer western wall. There is a small double bed between a walnut chest with a bedside lamp, and a chair. The white-washed walls are decorated with framed prints and paintings, two big ones next to the door, one near the wardrobe, one above the chest. The one above the bed is the only one that can be seen in the twilight: it is a reproduction of Rublev's Trinity in a heavy gilded frame. A man lies asleep on the bed, his head half-buried under a pillow, his naked left arm following the shape of his head, hiding his features, his hand clutching at thick blonde hair. On the chair next to the bed, under an open book, are his clothes. The trousers are neatly folded over the back of the chair, on top of the jacket.

There is a second of a deeper, expectant silence before the alarm goes off. The man rolls over stretches out an arm, gropes for the clock and switches it off. It is seven o'clock. He sits up in bed, with his eyes still closed, and leans his back against the wall. He yawns largely, scratches his head, rubs his eyes and opens them. He rises and, naked to the waist, leaves the bedroom for the bathroom where noises can be heard: flushing of the toilet, water as the tap is turned on, splashings as the basin fills, then the gentler sound of a razor being frequently rinsed. He returns to the bedroom naked, takes out a pair of pants from the top drawer of the chest and puts them on. He goes to the chair and puts on the socks, held up by garters at the knee, the white shirt after checking that it is not badly soiled at the cuffs and collar, the trousers into which he stuffs the shirt-tails. He moves to the window and draws the curtains and looks out at the blue sky for a minute or two. He is tall, big-boned and fleshy, with surprisingly red, pouting lips and thick brows that overhang and cast shadows on the close-set blue eyes. He may be in his early forties, he may be as much as ten years younger. He turns and goes back to the bed, throws back the blankets and top sheet, rearranges and smoothes the bottom sheet. He goes from side to side making sure the blankets are in place, the pillows are beaten into fluffiness, the bedspread hangs exactly on both sides. The alarm clock says quarter to eight. The man rewinds it, puts on the wrist watch that had been lying next to it, and drops coins and keys in his trouser pockets, looks around to see that everything is tidy, then leaves the sunny room. He goes to the front door in his stockinged feet and downstairs to collect the paper, the post and the milk from the main entrance. He returns to the small spotless kitchen and prepares his breakfast. While the toast and the egg are cooking, he looks into the cupboards, the fridge and the vegetable rack, and draws up a list of shopping. He glances at a couple of bills, then settles down with the paper and the food, sitting on a stool at the work surface.

The man looks at his watch. Half past eight. He folds the news-paper, gathers the dirty crockery and the saucepan from the stove and takes them to the sink. He leaves the breakfast things unwashed, though he wipes the work surface with a damp cloth. He returns to the bedroom, chooses a tie and puts it on, looking at himself in the mirror fitted to the inside of the left wardrobe door, above the tie rack. He rummages under the bed in search of his shoes, sits on the bed to tie the laces, then smoothes the bedcovers and reaches for the jacket. He makes sure the wallet is in the inside right pocket by tapping with his left hand, checks the pockets of his trousers for keys and once more leaves the bedroom.

At exactly quarter to nine the man locks the door of his flat carrying a briefcase and a raincoat. He walks down the steps, out of the building, turns right into a small back street, walks the length of it, crosses it and turns left into a main road. Some yards ahead is the underground, and seven minutes after leaving his home the man is swallowed up in the morning rush-hour.

FRIDAY P.M.

The key turns in the lock at quarter past six. The flat is shadowy after a day of sunlight playing in the empty rooms. The man leaves his briefcase and a bulging carrier bag in the entrance and goes straight into a comfortably furnished sitting room directly opposite the front door. He draws the dark blue velvet curtains and moves over to a lamp next to a tray where there are some bottles. He switches on the dim light and fixes himself a drink. He sits on the large sofa, his feet on the small table in front of him and lies back. Slowly, in the dim light and the silence he sips the drink in his left hand. His eyes are shut. Twenty minutes later he rises, pours himself another drink, walks down the narrow passage to the bathroom and turns on the hot water tap. The roar of water gushing into the bath accompanies him as he moves back into the passage, loosens and removes his tie, takes off the jacket, picks up the carrier bag and takes it into the kitchen. He unpacks all the tins and puts them in the cupboards above the work-top, leaves the jacket in the kitchen, returns to the bathroom and shuts the door.

His hair is wet and curly when he emerges, a towel around his waist. He goes into the bedroom and draws the curtains before switching on the light. He dresses with meticulous care in an elegant dark blue suit, a tie to match, black well-polished leather shoes. Before putting on the single-breasted suit jacket he rubs his hair dry for a few minutes. He looks at himself in the full length mirror fitted to the inside of the right door of the wardrobe, turning around, examining every fold and fall of the suit, brushing invisible specks from the shoulders and arms. At about quarter to eight the man is ready for the evening. He has tidied the bathroom, washed the morning crockery in the kitchen, fluffed up the cushion of the sofa where he had sat when he came in. He checks his trouser pockets for change, his breast pocket for the keys, switches off the light in the passage and leaves the flat.

FRIDAY NIGHT.

The key turns in the lock. The girl giggles as the couple is silhouetted against the light from the hall: she is leaning against him, and he is holding her by the waist. He kicks the door shut and they are plunged into the dark flat. The sound of the girl's giggles points to the direction they are going. They reach the bedroom, the girl bumps against something, gives a little scream and is heard falling on the bed. The man is silent and still for a minute, then he goes to the bathroom, switches on the light, quietly returns, shifts the girl, undresses her and puts her under the blankets. He returns to the bathroom, undresses, brushes his teeth, switches off the light and comes back to the bedroom. There is the densest silence throughout the night.

SATURDAY A.M.
The man turns over, opens his eyes and sees the girl still asleep: her mascara makes a smudged shadow under her eyes, dried foundation scales her face in blotchy patches, her tousled hair is slightly greasy, her features in repose are no more than vaguely attractive. She is lying on her side facing the man with her cupped left hand next to her face. The man gets out of bed noiselessly and goes to the bathroom. The sound of water running wakes the girl who turns and looks around the room without recognition. When the man returns, fully clothed, the girl looks at him:
  —I don't remember anything. I was drunk.
  —We were both rather drunk.
He smiles at her, friendly. She smiles back.

SUNDAY A.M.
The alarm goes off at 6 o'clock. The man turns over, switches it off, stretches luxuriously. He throws back the blankets, sits on the edge of the bed and again stretches himself. On the chair by the bed there is a rich-cream-coloured wrap. The man reaches over and puts it on. He walks into the bathroom, switches on the light and turns on the cold tap of the bath. He adds some liquid and turns the hot water tap full on. The bubbles begin to form. He returns to the bedroom, reaches down under the bed, draws out a suitcase, puts it on the bed, opens it and lays out a pair of woman's pants, garters, stockings, a small cup bra, a petticoat and a beautiful red woollen dress. In the bathroom the man looks at himself in the mirror: he lifts his left arm, puts the hand on the back of his neck and turns his head, smiling at his reflection: then he removes the wrap and steps into the bath.

  The man is clothed in the woollen dress. He stands by the suitcase, opens it once more and removes a dark long-haired wig, a big jar of foundation, a stick of mascara, a compact with blue eye-shadow, a lip-stick. He goes to the wardrobe and opens the left door: the tie rack is empty. The man fits the wig, careful to hide his own hair, and adjusts it to frame his face, looking at himself from all sides. He carefully lays the foundation more thickly on the chin and the cheeks to hide the dark shadow of beard, and adds the rest of the make-up, checking on himself constantly, backing away slightly to see the effect as each addition is made, grimacing and distorting his features as he brushes mascara on the upper and lower lashes. When the transformation is complete the man returns to the suitcase a third time, chooses a pair of black high-heeled sandals, a jacket and a black leather shoulder-bag.
  At a quarter past eight the man leaves the flat in his woman's clothes. He turns right into the back street and right again at the first

junction. The high heels tick-tack down the deserted road, accompanied by bursts of bird-song. He crosses the road and walks swaying down yet another back street until he comes to a small church, grimy with soot. A number of early morning worshippers, mostly elderly women, are converging towards it and he smiles at them as they pass. He kneels in the second pew on the left, Our Lady's side, and buries his face in his hands. Throughout the service he stands, kneels and sits at the appropriate times, but does not join in the responses. During Communion he kneels, his face in his hands. At the end of Mass he remains kneeling as the church empties. When everyone has gone he rises and walks down the main aisle, smiling at the priest whom he meets coming up to clear the altar. The priest follows him with his eyes as he continues down the church and out.

NOVEMBER

FRIDAY P.M.

At quarter past six the key turns in the lock and the man enters the flat. His raincoat is dripping, his hair curled by the rain that can be heard relentlessly ticking against the glass. The man goes into the sitting room, draws the curtains, switches on the light and fixes himself a drink. He sits on the sofa, his head back, his eyes shut; a pause: the eyes open, the head lifts, the man takes a sip and the head goes back, the eyes close; a pause: the eyes open, the head lifts, the man takes another sip, lies back, shuts his eyes. Monotonous, metronome movements. When the drink is finished he fixes himself another, and then another.

It is well over an hour and half later that he rises from the sofa with sudden urgency and swiftness, unloosens his tie, walks into the bathroom and turns on the bath tap; then he walks into the bedroom, opens the wardrobe and starts removing clothes from hangers and throwing them on the bed. When the wardrobe is empty the man goes to the bathroom, turns off the tap and returns to the bedroom. He reaches under the bed for the large suitcase, opens it and begins hanging dresses, skirts and blouses where suits and trousers had been. The women's clothes are all beautifully tailored, obviously expensive items. When the clothes are hung and the underclothes piled in the shelves the man undresses, puts on the cream coloured wrap, fills the suitcase with the men's clothes and returns it to its place under the bed before going back to the bathroom carrying a bottle. He pours some of the scent in the water and steps into the bath.

At nine o'clock the man leaves the flat dressed in an elegant salmon-pink dress, a neat black fur jacket, high heeled boots and matching shoulder bag and wearing a carefully coiffed wig.

SATURDAY A.M.
It is completely dark in the bedroom and it isn't until the light is switched
on that the man can be seen, wearing the wig of long brown hair and a
lace nightdress. The alarm clock gives the time as nine o'clock.

In the bathroom the man removes the wig and the nightdress, fills
the basin with warm water and shaves.

At ten-thirty the man leaves the flat, wearing a skirt and jumper. He
swings a brown shoulder bag as he turns right and right again at the first
junction. He crosses the road and turns into another back street. The sky
is all cloud, and the leaves from the few trees litter the pavements. The
streets are noisy with people-engaged in saturday chores, but the insistent tick-tacking of the man's high-heeled boots seems the beat around
which all sounds revolve until he reaches the church. Opposite there is a
small ugly construction, and groups are queueing outside it: a big garish
poster announces the Christmas bazaar. Proceeds will go to Cafod, the
Catholic Fund for Overseas Development. The man joins the queue,
smiling at those who turn and look at him until he sees them curl their lips
and toss their heads.

MONDAY A.M.
The bedroom is in darkness, and rain can be heard pattering against the
window pane. The man is asleep, his head half buried under the pillow,
his naked left arm following the shape of his head and hiding his features,
his hand clutching at thick blonde hair. On the chair, next to the bed,
under an open book, are the clothes. Trousers are neatly folded over the
back, on top of the jacket. It is just before seven.

FEBRUARY

MONDAY A.M.
At seven o'clock the alarm goes off, but the light is already on. The man
lies in bed wearing a pink brushed nylon nightdress, his hands folded
behind his head, pressing against the wig of long brown hair. He has
been looking fixedly at the curtains. Wearily he switches off the alarm,
removes his nightdress and wig and goes to the bathroom. As he shaves
he stares at his reflection in the mirror. He returns to the bedroom and
takes the suitcase from under the bed, opens it and picks out a suit. He
looks at it and in sudden fury slams the case shut, sits on the bed and
looks up: his eyes focus on the reproduction of the Trinity above the bed
but the three figures look down with transcendent serenity, and the man
falls on his knees and buries his head in his hands.

WALTER ABISH
Sweet Truth

Gisela and Egon.

ON THE MANTELPIECE red carnations from the garden in a pale green vase. The vase, the dozen freshly cut flowers, the brightly lit interior are visible in the large framed mirror above the mantelpiece and call for a—or so it seems—special consideration, a special attention. In referring to Germany (a not uncommon topic of conversation), its history, its achievements, its literature, its amazing economic recovery, it hardly seems possible not to acknowledge or recognize in everything Germany the intrinsic *Standpunkt*, the German point of view, the unique German way of seeing and appraising an object: a house, a barren hill, a tree in bloom, or something as evansecent as a passing cloud—and also the way in which this appraisal, this mere looking at as well as recognizing the true property or quality of what is seen can be said to reflect a society, a culture, a particular people.

Gisela and Egon.

She runs an exploratory finger along the rim of the glass vase before carefully placing it on the marble mantelpiece. It is Spring or Summer. The French windows are wide open. A scent of flowers in the air. In everything a sharpness of detail. In that luminous light a sense of stepping into something or someplace familiar as the brain seeks to piece together its claim to this perfection with a zeal and a yearning that comes as a surprise. The vase, the open windows, the distant prolonged sound of a train, the paperweight on the desk acquire a significance that leads to an exhilarating burst of recognition.

Egon picks up the latest issue of *Treue*. So this is it. He leafs through it, skimming the text.

Gisela, as always anxious for his approval, comments on the cover: *Eigentlich ganz net. Nicht wahr?*

What is being presented is a picture of a flourishing German society. And what at this time—one may ask—could be more spontaneously joyous, more filled with expectations and promises? Even the foreign workers, even the Turkish sanitation men have come to express in their simple halting German *Heute sehr Gut, Morgen besser* their desire, their wish, their hope one day to participate in this miraculous rebirth of Germany. They, the Turks, the Yugoslavs, the Arabs may still live six to a room in their separate and certainly less attractive quarters, but nothing can prevent them from sharing the enthusiasm, the generosity, and the overwhelming brightness of Germany's future. Not that this single-minded concern with the future has, in any way, effaced the awareness of the past. For nothing can ever efface the voices, the grave but melodic German voices of Dietmar von Aist, Walther von der Vogelwide, Albrecht von Halberstadt. The classics are still being read: Gellert, Klopstock, Lessing, Herder, Göethe, Schiller, Heine, Hölderlin, Novalis, Fontane. All available in inexpensive paperback editions as well as in leatherbound sets suitable for the oak bookshelves of the doctors of jurisprudence and of philosophy and of medicine. The very backbone of Germany. Yes, there is still so much pleasure, so much gratification, so much insight to be derived from the works of Jean Paul, Friedrich Spielhagen, Stefan George, George Kaiser, Alfred Döblin, Ernst Jünger and Thomas Mann. And, after all, why not Mann? He remains *Echt Deutsch* despite his dubious decision to abandon his country at its greatest time of need. Can anyone deny or doubt the significance of these writers? Can anyone fail to recognize in them the attribute of a true German? Absolutely no irony intended. And, for that matter, a thorough reading of the classics should enable one to determine the degree to which anything, a house, a barren hill, a barn, a dog, a stein of beer, appears to be German and, accordingly, is slipping into something called *die Zukunft*, the future. As before, no irony intended.

Gisela and Egon.

They do not necessarily question the meaning of a thing. Why should they? They do not necessarily measure the degree to which it is authentic, or German. Or to what extent the one authenticates the other. The red carnations authenticate the graceful shape of the fluted vase. The large mirror in its heavy gilded frame objictifies the view of the interior space and nicely frames what is a certain attempt to achieve perfection.

Gisela and Egon.

Participants in an ongoing German drama. The interior of their house (their house in the country) presents to the brain a variety of alternatives: things that can be done, things that need be done, things that must be done. As such, each response, each decision, each action, whether it entails going to bed early, or sitting down to a leisurely breakfast, or watching the soccer game on TV, entails a certain involvement with one or with several of the objects, the carefully selected objects, in the house. After all, things are there to be used and not only viewed and admired. The German philosopher Brumhold had, in his book *Die Einzige Verfuhrung* published in 1927, raised the question pertaining to the meaning or *thingliness* of an object: 'Does the stated perfection of an object invite or activate a specific and appropriate response?'

   Gisela, in the bedroom, brushing her hair: One cannot lightly dismiss the pleasure that comes from seeing oneself on the cover of a popular German magazine that has an estimated one-and-a-half million readers.

Gisela and Egon.

Egon, in a double breasted white gabardine suit, leaning against the car. To be precise, he is casually (incidentally, this casualness cannot be overemphasized) leaning against the left front fender of his (their?) white Mercedes convertible. In the foreground what appears to be the photographer's shadow merges with the shadow of a clipped hedge. In the rear Egon and Gisela's country house. They call it a villa. The even row of French windows along its entire length are left invitingly ajar. The black and white vertically striped curtains billow slightly in the Spring or Summer breeze. In one of the rooms to the left of the entrance a section of a baby grand can be seen. Gisela in tight fitting leather trousers (black) and a long sleeved blouse (pale yellow silk) with ruffles around the throat is standing a few steps to the right of the stationary car. She is not standing, in the strict sense of the word, but bending at the waist—grace-

fully, to be sure—in order to adjust the collar on Dumas, their giant
Schnautzer. Dumas's alert dog face is turned inquiringly toward the
alien, the seeming intruder, the unseen photographer (Rita Tropf-
Ulmwehrt) who prompts: smile, smile, No. Now don't smile. But Gisela,
long accustomed to the intrusion of such individuals appears untroubled,
appears oblivious of the weaponlike camera aimed at her as she adjusts
the dog's collar. She is only doing this because the dog's collar requires
adjusting. It is a Saturday morning, and she was about to take a much
needed stroll in the nearby wood, or about to drive to town pick up a few
necessities, a few essentials, or was simply planning to relax with a good
book under a tree—don't believe it. The dog is trained for every eventuality. Like any guard dog trained to respond instantly to a variety of
urgent signals, he has grown accustomed to the uncertain existence—the
state of doubt—in that prolonged void between one signal and the next.
As for Egon: There is something to be said in favour of such a casual (that
word again) indifference to the distinct possibility that he might irrepara-
bly stain his white jacket or trousers with car grease. Not that there isn't
a plenitude of skilled Italian tailors in Germany who, given three days,
can replace his jacket or trousers; or that the car (gleaming in the sun)
hasn't been (lovingly?) cleaned, waxed and polished. In a sense, everything in the eight page article on Egon and Gisela in the magazine *Treue*
is already conveyed and analyzed on the front cover—albeit, in a far more
compressed manner. The meaning, the shades or layers of meaning are
to be found in the components: the ubiquitous gabardine suit, the paisley
scarf, the white silk handkerchief displayed in the breast pocket of his
jacket, the drooling Schnautzer, the black leather trousers, the high
heeled boots, Gisela's swept back blond hair, the hairdo emphasizing a
sleekness, a sexual sharpness, bringing her pale fine boned face into
greater prominence, the gleaming car with its red leather upholstery and,
finally, the partially opened French windows on the ground floor revealing vertical slivers of the interior life. All this to spell out the new German
competence and a sense of satisfaction and completion. It's all there
...the inate German upper and upper-middle class instinct to combine
what is essentially 'perfection' with 'the menacing'. All in all, it sums up
the new German restlessness as well as the general anticipation of the
greater German splendour yet to come. Are these not, also, the components of a German story? For ultimately, what may come about is a
matching of this finely developed sensibility, this heightened awareness
of perfection and its actual realization. It may be only a matter of time before everyone in Germany, including the guest workers, the Turks,
Greeks and Arabs, will develop an eye for the nuances of this German
perfection, an eye (seeing, after all, is linked to understanding) that will,
in time, facilitate the exchange, the reciprocity of perfections between the
authentic man and his perfect surroundings.

While at present...At present? Yes, this is the way it is at present.

Egon and Gisela

as presented and documented by Rita Tropf-Ulmwehrt. Here the words
at present are essential, since everything Egon and Gisela undertake to
carry out is not wedded to a profession, a specific outlook, the result of a
certain training, but to a dynamic impulse that derives what purpose and
energy it has from the dialectical concern with the tension and intensity of
life in Germany. At present Egon is the publisher of the Möglich Verlag:
six books in 1975, six in 1976, six in 1977, and five in 1978. A short description of the company follows. The usual story. Net investment, bank
loans, selection of manuscripts, near successes, abysmal failures, problems of distribution, problems with writers, future projects, and spinoffs
(an American term), that is to say: book clubs, movie rights, translations.
Accompanying the article is a shot of a somber Egon at his large desk,
signing a letter. Standing to one side, eyes downcast, is the young nameless secretary. From the window behind his desk a view of the old city,
the rebuilt courthouse, the cathedral, *Der Englischen Garten*, the narrow
winding streets. Everything made to look the way it was before the war.
On the wall to Egon's left a large photomural of a helmeted motorcyclist
racing his Harley or Honda along a wide stretch of dirt road, the magnifi-
cent landscape of Southern Bavaria is somewhat obscured by the cloud of
dust trailing the motorcyclist. It's difficult not to see the resemblance
between the motorcyclist and Egon. It is difficult not to see Egon's fond-
ness for his secretary in a number of the shots taken by Rita of the office.
But they have been omitted. What has not been omitted is a photograph
of Egon and Gisela at home. She, sprawled on their Breuer *Barcelona*
chair, wearing a silver T-shirt with the word PONY across the front,
spanning her small pointed breasts. Egon in a grey pinstriped suit, somewhat complacently (or smugly?) eyeing the camera. Yet, behind all the
apparent candour, the willingness to answer questions, the outpouring of
information—'We have always been overly fond of Thai food....', and the
matter of his having sniffed (the key word here is *sniffed*) coke when he
was younger—likes a deep heavy-lidded reticence, a reluctance to reveal
anything that is not on display. He did remark that his father had been a
pilot in the Luftwaffe, and that he, Egon, had briefly served in the diplomatic in—of all places—West Africa. This accounts for the capital D on
his licence plate. Since the text of the article is essentially an attempt to
package (this is the favoured American expression) the two of them or, for
that matter, an attempt to package Germany; the goods as seen on the
photographs deserve special attention. The strategically placed leather
couch, the glass topped chrome coffee table, the tall exotic plant from

Brazil, the other couple (presumably friends) dancing on the gleaming wood floor, while Egon watches with a bemused expression. Rita Tropf-Ulmwehrt also elicited from him a list of predictable preferences: car racing, tennis, sailing, mountain climbing, disco dancing.... In the article these preferences are given a weight, a significance they might not have otherwise, since they are made to indicate an individual commitment, and consequently bring into play the heavy responsibility that lies behind each individual choice.

Gisela and Egon.

He tall, blond, a rugged face struggling to dispel the suggestion of weakness in the petulant pout. The pale blue eyes, the strong jaw, the cheekbones, the nose twisted to one side, bent to the left (the result of an accident?) in sharp contrast to the weakness that is implied or conveyed by the protrusion of the lips, expressing a private resentment, a pique. And she, on the thin side. Sharp angular features, thin lips. A familiar—or so it seems to a spectator—an overwhelmingly familiar restlessness. *Hoch Gespannt*, the German for high pitched, or highly strung. A tendency to move quickly, also to overreact. A sudden high pitched laugh that has not yet entirely freed itself from its earlier association with hysteria. But that is only to be surmised. It may not be true. All in all, the photographs, the pictures in *Treue*, the German magazine, are an invitation—what else— to reinterpret Germany. A new Germany. Certainly not the Germany that was once firmly ensconced (the saddle, after all, is an appropriate metaphor) in the Prussian tradition of honour and obedience, old money and authority, the sabre, the uniform, the crumbling castle overlooking the Rhein.

Egon and Gisela.

A picture, really, of the new democratic Germany. This is made abundantly clear as they stand (posing for Rita?) in front of their villa with the bright red flowers demarcating the curve of the gravel path, the bright red also providing (on the magazine cover, anyhow) a necessary (?) counterpoint to the white Mercedes, the white suit and Gisela's black leather trousers. The viewer cannot remain unaware of the tasteful arrangement of all these possessions and of the combination of colours: the yellow villa, the red flowers, the black trousers and the black dog. Colours that are and always have been quintessentially German —*Schwartz, Rot, Gold*. Black was our past, red is the present, and gold is our future. Not that everything—colours aside—need be accepted at face value. Still, it is pleasant to contemplate this attractive setting, this attractive combination, this attractive couple, especially, knowing that there is no overwhelming reason to suspect their political motivation (they are *Echt Deutsch*), or fear—for instance—the possibility that they might be concealing in their attic or cellar one of the Einzige Gruppe, a group which has taken responsibility for the recent horrendous bombing of the post office in Würtenburg. Not that living in a villa or driving a Mercedes can automatically exclude one from such suspicion.

Egon and Gisela's schedule. A red leather bound appointment book next to the white telephone. It lists the occasional visit from her mother, now living in Italy. A daily record of luncheons, dentist appointments, tennis games, cocktail parties, birthdays, new acquisitions (shower curtains, a small house on the Costa Brava), weekends with friends in the country. In Egon's firm hand, under Thursday the 28th: Rita Tropf-Ulmwehrt 11.30 Lunch?

Something that is not shown is a shot of Gisela sulking. Gisela close to tears. Gisela crouching in a corner of her room. An atavistic return to the corner of her childhood? Mouth tightly clenched, body perspiring, tense. Eyes focused on some distant point in space.

Well, how long do you intend to crouch in that corner, Gisela? Egon asks amiably. I mean, and this is said reasonably, at some point you will have to go to the john, or to the mirror to comb your hair, or to the kitchen, or to answer the phone. You can't very well spend your life in a corner because you disagree with me.

I only disagree with your concern for other women, she says in a near whisper. Who is it now. Your secretary? Or Rita Tropf?

Tropf-Ulmwehrt, not Tropf.

Go away.

Why don't we drive to that Thai restaurant and have a leisurely dinner, then... .

I disagree with your head, she whispers. I disagree with the way you think.

Or how about a nice walk in the woods.

You are just waiting for me to inherit the money.

I can't possibly stay here all day and humour you.

Who is it now? She asks.

Egon.

Let me put it this way, Egon says to Rita Tropf-Ulmwehrt. Above all I fervently believe in an intrinsic harmony. A harmony that takes precedence over everything else. In other words, I believe in the harmony of my friendship to Gisela rather than in the binding force that the institution of marriage is said to represent. I believe in the fundamental harmony that permeates our house. It is a harmony that enables me to assess myself and my intentions in a fresh light. It is also, I might mention, the intrinsic harmony of our society that has enabled me to understand the dimensions, the full dimensions, of the terrorist threat to Germany. Clearly, the Einzige Gruppe intend to overthrow our system of government by destroying Germany's newly acquired harmony. For harmony spell democracy if you will, but democracy, alas, is a word that has been depleted of its meaning, its energy, its power. If anything can be said to represent the new Germany, it is the wish, the desire, no, the craving to attain a total harmony.

Let me put it this way, says Rita Tropf-Ulmwehrt with a tiny smile as she places her hand once again on that sensitive and by now to her familiar juncture between his legs. I'm so pleased, he says, without precisely stating what pleases him.

Another picture of Gisela and Egon that is not shown.

Spring or Summer. The fragrance of those red flowers in the garden below fills the bedroom with a sweet and somewhat cloying scent.

Egon in a white shirt, trouserless, selecting a necktie. A serious undertaking. Gisela in front of the mirror brushing her hair turns to him and asks breathlessly: Shall I wear the leather suit?
Egon: No.
I thought you liked it?
Must you always wear leather trousers?

Dumas is restlessly pacing back and forth in the garden. A silver clock on the bureau methodically shreds time. A wedding gift from her mother, it bears the inscription *Fur Jeder ein sich. Fur Dich kein Kummer.* For each one a self. For you no sorrow.

Gisela: Admit, you love the cover. Admit it.
Egon: For some reason you still seem to believe that black leather trousers are the latest thing. Everyone may be wearing them, but—
Gisela: Admit, admit, admit, admit, admit... .

The telephone rings downstairs. Someone answers it. If it is for him, whoever it is will call again. When Gisela wears her high heels, which she does frequently, she is three inches taller than Egon. She measures his moody face as he exazmines his neckties. In effect, his displeasure can be linked to their evening ahead. With a calculated thin lipped smile, she walks while still brushing her hair, to where he is sitting on their bed, inserting her upright body between his parted legs. Absentmindedly he embraces her, gripping her bare thighs, turning his face to the window.

Of course, there is always the unexpected.

One of these days I am going to build you a tiny, tiny house in the corner of this room. It will contain a blanket, and a little pillow, and maybe a miniature closet for your hairbrush, Egon says to Gisela tenderly.

If you promise to stop making love to Rita, she says, I promise to behave.

An hour later Egon leaves her crouching in the corner of her room. I'll tell them that you have a headache. I'll tell them that you will call up tomorrow. She embraces her legs, bringing her face closer and closer to her bony knees.

Egon.

At dinner the woman seated on his right asks him: do you ever regret having been too young to have fought in the war?

I don't know? He stares at her in wonder. I have never asked myself that question.

Later, in Rita's apartment, he repeats the question he had been asked.

You know when I first fell in love with you? She asks.

No.

Not when we first met. No. It was when I had the two of you standing next to the car, posing for me. I don't know why. But that's when it happened. It was so delightful.

Will you have dinner with us tomorrow night?

Dinner? With you and Gisela? Whatever for?

I don't know. I thought it might be fun.

Fun? Are you serious?

No. Of course not.

You know...sometimes you worry me.

Egon and Gisela.

I meant to tell you last night, says Egon, I really love the magazine cover.

Do you mean it?

Absolutely.

I'm so glad. I'm so glad. I'm so glad.

So am I. It's us.

Yes. It's us.

DAVID KATZ

The Wife

Ever notice the change that comes over
your gentle wife the minute she sets
foot in a grocery store? She pinches
the grapefruit. She squeezes the
bread. She looks for specials with an
eagle eye. For when it comes to spend-
ing your hard earned money, your wife
is a far tougher customer than you are.
This, believe it or not, is an expression
of love.

But to keep your wife, we must keep right
on pleasing her by constantly making
progress. If we ever stood still,
competition would wean her away. And that
would serve us right.
Your wife. She's made us what we are today, and we aim to keep her satisfied.
We never will be.

NORMAN BRYSON

City of Dis: The Fiction of Don DeLillo

FEELING ABOUT DON DELILLO currently runs high, and the word that probably characterizes the feeling best is 'imminent'. It has been his fate to be imminent for what is by now an unconscionably long time. When DeLillo's first novel, *Americana*, appeared in 1971, it was natural to bracket his name with the names of Barth and Pynchon—a bracketing which has, over time, acquired a certain mordancy. For while the Barth dissertations and the Pynchon theses have been piling high in the vaults, it hasn't always been easy to find editions of DeLillo, or Purdy, or many others who are beginning to look like a lost generation, left stranded by the decade's urge to pantheonize. It may turn out, of course, that DeLillo's work will remain always about to arrive and never arriving, for all time. But in case there is the chance that DeLillo's admirers are holding back because of difficulty in finding the right discourse to suit his production, it may be worth setting off in a definite direction, if only to find out later that there is a better route.

Perhaps the most striking feature in DeLillo's novels is the extra-ordinary nature and importance of their dialogue, evident not only in what is said by one character to another, but in the intricate, fluctuating *address* of speaker to speaker, the stances chosen by the speakers in rela-tion to each other and to the language they use. The stances prove to be as insistent upon the reader's attention as the primary or foregrounded topics the conversations move around. The world of DeLillo's fiction is essentially acoustic; the characters, though set within a notional mater-iality, are presented chiefly as voices in *fugato*. Within this acoustic, indi-vidual voices—vital, strident, ruthless—compete to be heard in an environment already deafened by an excess of human speech. To be heard at all, an individual must present an auditory profile which will be recognized at once as uniquely his: exaggerating his set of specific differences from the myriad other voices around him, and where this fails inventing further differences to supplement those he already possesses. And, throughout, DeLillo's characters behave as though aware in advance that even when they succeed in finding audience, the hearer is likely to reply in kind, with his own desperate idiolect, in dialogue but not in communication. DeLillo's domain is the voice: how it responds to those around it, how it is employed in strategies of self-protection and irony, of wilful survival and embattled self-expression, of aggression and parody. For DeLillo, humanity exists in so far as it speaks; but its speech is at every point threatened by forces which conspire to dehumanize it, by drowning it out or by supplying modes of discourse which take the speaker over—deforming his language, making him a verbal grotesque, a monster or plaything of the word.

DeLillo's early work charts routes of escape for those caught within a dehumanized or inhuman force-field of languages. *End Zone* (1971) and *Ratner's Star* (1972) claim that escape is still, on the whole, viable. *End Zone*'s subject is American football. Its characters are the not-too-talented team at Logos College (no comment), massacred in the big game by the gang from Centrex—terrifying Rollerball thugs who reduce them to pulp in minutes ('It's like taking on a major power'). Much of the book explores, with relish, the rich absurdity of the language of sport: coaches obsessed with *Führenprinzip*, foaming at the mouth at pep-talks; team warm-ups of primitive grunts and war-cries; 'jocks' communicating strategy in impenetrable dialect; mystical players of the Inner Game describing their epiphanies in the field; apprentice sportscasters glued to televized games and manically articulating their progress.

Each character is in his own way a word-grotesque, a language-creature deformed by specialized function into bizarre, idiotic, delightful misshapenness. At the same time the book includes a sufficient number of non-sportif characters, similarly deformed, to suggest the misshapenness as a generalized condition (at least in west Texas). If the characters are not crazed by the language of the game, they are crazed in other ways and by other discourses. These are various. Myna is addicted to sci-fi pulp and especially to the work of Tudev Nemkhu, a mad Mongolian whose trilogy on the Nautiloids occasions one of the book's funniest parodies. Zapalac, Logos College lecturer in what seems to be astro-chemistry, intercuts his visionary accounts of creation with paranoid disquisitions on the persistence of fascism. Anatole Bloomberg, the narrator's roommate, is trying to free himself of his Jewish 'Europicity' and to 'desemitize' his speech ('Some names possess a smell. I didn't like the way my name smelled. It was like a hallway in a tenement where a lot of Bulgarians live'). The text is periodically interrupted by lectures —addressed to the narrator—on the art of thermonuclear warfare.

DeLillo's sense of the absurd has a way of circling into territory where humour treads at its peril. Beneath the comic tone there are at least two sets of anxieties. One concerns violence and the other the nature of narrative. The novel is narrated by Gary Harkness, who, before arriving at Logos, has killed a player on the field; the eager recipient of the thermonuclear lectures, Harkness is obsessed with the language of holocaust: *firestorm, burn area, hostage cities, orbital attack*. Similarly his co-captain, Taft Robinson, is pre-occupied with the literature of genocide. Together, Harkness and Robinson provide the centre around which the novel develops its black comedy; but there is always a sense that both characters are going too far, doing more than what the novel can adequately and comically recuperate. DeLillo is a master of brinkmanship; we watch to see where the humour which bravely ventures into the terrain of the horrendous will cross that frontier beyond which things are no longer funny.

Humour of the grotesque presupposes an ideal or at least a norm against which deviation can be measured; yet DeLillo's work in this and other novels precisely questions the certainty of such measurement. *End Zone* is analogous to the engraving in Hogarth's *Line of Beauty* which shows a line of dancing couples of which the first is graceful, perfectly fashioned, ideal; behind stands a second pair, less Italianate, less fashioned, a sort of zero point on a scale which then slides into full deformity. To the back of the second couple is a third, as far behind the zero point as the first couple was ahead, and so on, through varying graduated degrees of unloveliness until at the end we come to the openly teratological, the prancing beasts. What is unsettling about the image is its relativization of the series: at any point on the scale there will be beauty above and ugliness below, at each and every point 'normality' is obtainable. For the viewer, the second couple are about neutral, a common donominator of humanity. But for the dancers absolute normality does not exist: it depends who your neighbours are; and, as a consequence, the viewer's selection of the zero point is dislocated, challenged as arbitrary. The analogy applies to DeLillo's posture as mediator of the deformed, misshapen idiolects that fill his pages. He does not, and it's a conspicuous feature of *End Zone*, contain the competing and specialized dialects of his speakers within a stabilizing master-discourse. The voice of the narrator is only *primus inter pares*, and for a number of reasons his vocalization seems as subject to implicit criticism as that of the more frankly grotesque minor figures.

The text is divided into three parts, the second of which is an extended description of the catastrophic game against Centrex. Since the

events there are set in spectacular, stadium space, one might expect the
writing at this point to move from idiolect to sociolect, to a communal or
choric style—which option the text entirely rejects and at the cost of
becoming nearly inaccessible to the reader unable to decode the arcane
terminology it brings to its descriptive task.

Each play must have a name. The naming of plays is important. All
teams run the same plays. But each team uses an entirely different
system of naming. Coaches stay up well into the night in order to
name plays. They heat and reheat coffee on an old burner. No play
begins until its name is called.
                    Middle-sift-W, alph-set, lemmy-2.

The vocabulary throughout the novel's central section becomes so
technical that it must perforce lose the majority of its readers. But the
effect is, I believe, very exactly calculated. At the precise point which
demands the narrator's mediation and his secession from the particu-
larized, out-of-shape discourses of the players, the novel withholds the
central median voice which could represent *the reader in the text*. To
return to the Hogarth illustration, it is the effect of losing the point of
insertion at which to place the normally and normatively human. The
novel provides no such absolute discursive centre, and this dislocation
renders highly uncertain the comedy of the grotesques. The misshapen
crew is mocked, but the question is by whom and by what standards. Not
by the characters, for they are all wierdly confined within their private
phatic zones. And not by the narrator, who when he steps forward to tell
us about the big game provides us with a recital from which it is impossible to reconstruct what he sees.
    The absence of a central, flexible, embracing voice crucially affects
how the reader *hears* the vocal lines. He knows that they are all deformed, ridiculous, radically incomplete; but he cannot say *from where* he
knows this, because no speech within the text provides the triangulation
points by which he can take his bearings. So far as each speaker is concerned, there may be *no* deformity; the discourses may be fully natura-
lized. By what right, then, are the words presented or taken as absurd?
Who sees the absurdity? It is around this point that the set of anxieties
centering on the issue of violence meets with the set which centres on discourse. Language can retrieve from the horrors, from the ovens and blast
zones, a certain measure of humour, because from the point of view of a
human norm—whose existence is attested to by the success of the
humour itself—the horrors are deviant, lapses out of humanity, dark mis-
haps and mishappenings of the human spirit. But beyond a certain point

the humour is incapacitated by our realization that the horrors are *us*. As DeLillo's humour crosses the frontier into what is no longer easily amusing, our habitual self-definitions and self-images begin to dissolve. A moment ago we were laughing: if we weren't exactly sure who we were, we were at least sure who we were not; we were not like the monsters, the satanic prancers. That the laughter has died suggests that it came from a false conception of ourselves which could not encompass the dark side of our history, our ritualized aggression. We know we are not like the idiolects, the idiom-lunatics, the speech-defectives. But we have no representative within the text to speak in our place, no norm against which to guage the consoling otherness of the manic crew.

Disoriented within a discourse, we are not, after all, so different from the caricatures within the novel. They too exist uncertainly in a background of voices where they must define their identity: they sense they are not like the rest, and they will not speak like the rest. Moreover—and more important—there is the sobering suggestion that the characters may have *voluntarily* entered their particular niche in the ecology of the voice. They may be cultivating not just a style, but Style: a wilful excess wherein they express a perverse mastery of the discourse by which, from another perspective, they seem so completely mastered. With most of the characters in this novel, DeLillo may be saying that a man's style is as much willed and controlled as his game. Just as on the field there is room for finesse—for a display that goes beyond the functional into excess, and in the excess the player's transcendence of the game appears, a glimmering of heroic stature; so it may be that in their cultivation of the unique acoustic profile, the odd ball speakers are expressing their rejection of standard, centrist, golden mean discourse. DeLillo presents their case ambiguously: they are heroic individualists, they are freaks. The narrator is responsible for the comedy, at their expense; or the characters are responsible, and the narrator is only a scribe. We are normal people and dissociate ourselves from the threat we witness; or we are formless, endlessly malleable creatures, our monstrosity hidden from us only as long as our fiction of a centre, of the norm, remains plausible.

Part of the fascination of *End Zone* comes from the way it manages to suggest these concerns in such a narrow compass, and without recourse to portentous shading or inflation of tone. This is a quality shared also by *Ratner's Star* (1972), a novel which takes as its linguistic provenance the language of science, and which at first sight seems to follow the same line of comedy as *End Zone*, depicting the absurdities of an enclosed, crazily specialized community of speakers. The characters are international scientists, gathered together at Field Experiment Number One, a research institute devoted, with demented energy, to the furtherance of human knowledge. Even more episodic in construction thatn *End Zone*, *Ratner's Star* takes the form of a conducted tour of the Experiment. Our guide is Billy Twillig, a fourteen year old mathematician from the Bronx called away from his work on zorgs and twilligons to decode a radio message picked up from a region in space near the star of the book's title. The verbal caricatures are now altogether wilder than *End Zone*'s teamsters—we have progressed much further down the line of beauty's or reason's dancers: Henrik Endor, Twillig's predecessor in the 'decoding', who having drawn some terrible and unnamed conclusion from the stellar transmission now lives in a hole; Shazar Lazarus Ratner, renowned astronomer and cabalist, whose work currently lies in a field somewhere between the *en-sof* and giant dwarfs; Orang Mohole, inventor of 'value-dark dimensions' and purveyor of sleazy erotica; Maurice Wu, historian turned speleologist whose 'contralogical' theory of cultural evolution is tested in remote, bat-infested caverns.

The satire works on two levels. On the first, we witness simple parody, accounts of scientific discourse shown in aberration: we are invited to relish the zaniness, accompanying our guide through the verbal menagerie where the curious beasts perform their tricks. The thumbnail sketches of the book's characters above illustrates the insistence and simplicity of the book's official satire: positions us safely on this side of the cage. On another level, *Ratner's Star* draws us within its own hysterical confines. The novel, like *End Zone*, never gives us a standard we can trust as reliable: our narrator's work on 'zorgs' sounds no less absurd than any other project we encounter. And the narrative voice—separable, in this text, from that of the narrating character—speaks without any apparent principle of organization. Here is a description of a helicopter descending:

> Free, unswerving, and independent of friction, the plunge was like a childhood sigh, devoid of obedience and rote, never evolving, nowhere close to the boned-out howl of those voices departed to the edge of the pure word, evident in the sequence of related sounds only as a timeless sigh—not of this woman in murmurous bliss or that man half leaping in her arms in the spangled blaze of bird-fish symmetry and delicate brute creation, but of a child, only that, a child is all, his sigh a knowing contemplation of time and place and all those darker energies that constitute his peril.

The syntactically dominant idea is that the plunge of the craft was like a child's sigh—a difficult image, but far less difficult than what follows it. No yoke of grammar detectably holds together the subsequent working out of its implications. Suggestions and connotations fly outward from the simile's centre, moving centrifugally into widening spirals, diffusing ideas and obfuscating their expression: only, in the end, to move, without apparent logic or coherence, back to the original image—'a child, only that, a child is all, his sigh'—and to an idea without reference: 'darker energies'. If this is the authority we find in the narrative, what is its effect on the text as a whole? How can this voice mediate among the discourses which the text presents?

Ratner's Star and *End Zone* do, as I suggested earlier, posit possibilities of escape from linguistic onstriction. In *End Zone,* speakers may *volunteer* for specialization, and by sheer virtuosity go beyond idiolect into bizarre, heroic Style. And while the possibility of this escape is questioned by what remains of the humour of the grotesque—inviting a perception of the characters as caricatures—it is also reinforced by the book's 'relativization' of speech, so striking in the arcane version of the Centrex football game. The removal of 'normal' speech—and thus the curtailment of a centralized policing of language—is essentially permissive, paralleling the anti-authoritarian, anarchic life-styles of the players. *Ratner's Star* suggests a different way out. With no central court of linguistic appeal to inhibit or manage the scientists' speech, each man is responsible only to himself: speak and let speak. There is, however, a new urgency, an anxiety not present in the earlier novel. The style of the narrative—and the sentence depicting the helicopter's descent is perfectly representative—seems to be engaged in a compulsive fight to deny priority in syntax and 'ideation' (a word unqiuely appropriate to this book). Despite affinities with free-association, sentences in this book seem to reach for a linguistic freedom accomplished by *untying* the bonds of association: the individual sentences seem to change direction the moment a set direction appears; as though fleeing their own shadow.

Ratner's Star is more complex than *End Zone,* its tone deeper, and is so, I am suggesting, because its style is informed by a paradox inseparable from the paradox of its subject: the tendency of language to create cages or prisons around the very speakers who use it. To describe that tendency, DeLillo must himself use language, language which at every point may be turning hard on him, crystallizing, blocking his mobility. The effort of the writing must then be directed towards disengagement from its own designs. We thus have to review our attitude towards the word-bound characters: they may simply be projections of the author's paranoia in language, phantoms at the edge of his freedom, and always closing in.

In *Players* (1977) and *Running Dog* (1978), DeLillo moves away from remote, eccentric communities of speakers to the language of the metropolis. At the same time, he shifts from narrative characterized by the episodic—and its particular sense of the improvized—to a narrative of intricate plots and classical unities, used (I am reminded of *Bajazet*) in a fashion that heightens the sense of confinement. It is an extraordinary change. *End Zone* and *Ratner's Star* were aerated, expansive texts, admitting into themselves all manner of vagary and digression. DeLillo's description in *Ratner's Star* of the work of Nobel prize-winning fictionalist Chester Dent can serve as an assesssment of his own achievement at that time: 'Piquant disquisitions on the philosophy of logic, the logic of games, the gamesmanship of fiction...handblocked in a style best characterized as *undiscourageably diffuse*' (my italics). The urban novels are claustrophobic, their characters hemmed in by the skyscrapers, locked in bolted apartments, prisoners of the discourse. They are also more aggressive: the city's middlemen, pushers, fixers, killers, moving in on their prey. They're still the basic DeLillo crew, frantically idiosyncratic voices caught up in manic plans. The difference is that they have now broken into the real world.

Players concerns an inner-city marriage gone dead. It opens with a scene which acts as proem to the whole action: passengers on a plane to New York are watching an in-flight movie whose subject is terrorism, opening with a game of golf and ending in carnage. And the passengers are unmoved throughout, sipping drinks and adjusting the headsets while a piano player provides a camp, silent-movie accompaniment: moral and sensory queasiness smoothly suppressed. The novel's couple are jaded, burnt out, anaesthetized and self-anaesthetizing. Pammy works (in the World Trade Center) for Grief Management, an organization devoted to helping the bereaved cope with their pain, to lessening, that is, the general awareness of death. Lyle likes to watch re-run pornography shows on T.V., to feel desire, it seems, not more but less intensely. Each realizes the marriage has died, and each has discovered a way of escape: for Pammy, it is escaping to the 'real' outside, to a cabin in Maine. For Lyle it is doubling his career on the Exchange with undercover, semi-official investigation of a group of urban terrorists, a secret life of danger and camouflage. DeLillo handles both plots in a hard, witty, deadpan style which offers few clues as to how we should view the couple's activities. Lyle's adventures inevitably prompt the reader to wonder how he can possibly think involvement with violence redemptive: it only extends the stage of numbness it seems meant to overcome. And we are given enough information about Pammy's solution to know in advance that she is likely to commit adultery with one of her friends, a bisexual. From what we see of the couple whose life she invades we can predict the outcome will be disastrous: given the book's pre-occupation with violence, the suicide of her partner comes as no surprise.

Absence of surprise is, however, very much part of the book's disquietingly deadpan method. And DeLillo's refusal to comment on or judge the actions of his characters is disturbing: we don't have to be Leavisite throwbacks to expect a novelist to be a more sensitive and observant version of ourselves; DeLillo's narrator—in a way analogous to the narrators of *Ratner's Star* and *End Zone*—is *continuous* with his morally amorphous characters. I don't think it fanciful to say that *Players* is spoken by the voice of the city itself. What that voice challenges is our expectation that the novel will somehow transcend the city, transcend itself, and provide some moral framework against which to see the behaviour of the characters as aberrant.

Players is full of figures on the make, out to extort from the world whatever it is they need—money, sex, attention, belief; and by repetition the book shows how the city dweller habitually copes with their perpetual solicitation. He reacts by deliberately lowering the threshold of what is acceptable, by deliberately violating his own innocence, and by engaging with the figures only as far as is necessary to prevent more violent forms of importunity. DeLillo's dialogue of the urban novels explores the vocal strategies of people forced to function in an environment becoming increasingly infernal. They seek languages which will contain the brutality, brutal dialects to match the brutal outside. They aid and abet each other in the general quest for speech commensurate with the horrors around them. They turn the quest into a formal, bantering game and above all by wrapping the dialects in an enveloping, unfocussed irony —by trying always to *seem* to be quoting from some base repertoire of speech—they try to maintain the genteel fiction that they remain, through everything and despite all the odds, uncontaminated.

What gives the dialogue in DeLillo's urban novels its edge is the absence of reciprocity: the speakers are not initiating speech or expressing what is unique within their subjectivity. Instead they *play* at shared monologue: they define their positions to each other obliquely, by agreeing to secede, together, from a discourse that is standardized, unintelligent, or exhausted. The style of floating irony offers them a position of safety always available; and when a speaker ventures too far—towards self-revelation and therefore vulnerability—he or she can return to the steady disengaged stage at once. The game of ironic cleansing from the taint of baser discourse acts as a kind of mutual grooming by which the speakers attain a bonding of a very limited sort: the essential and most intimate communication between one character and another is 'I know you are not the words you use.'

But what is DeLillo's position in all this? I have mentioned his reluctance or refusal to supply a moral framework by which we might 'place' the actions of his characters; at the same time I seem to have described a highly moralistic novel. It is this duplicity which, I think, provides the link between the two very different fictional styles DeLillo uses, the urban and the 'pastoral'. *Players* can be seen as a moralistic or crypto-moralistic novel; at the same time its narrative voice is deeply implicated in the corruption it describes. It is possible that the style in which the novel is cast—sophisticated, compassionless, amoral—is to be seen as the final product of the same process of self-violation and will anaesthesia which it has charted through its characters: an inverted *City of God,* an account of the journey by which the text's present condition of grace/depravity was reached. And it is equally possibly that the text omits the moral frame-work only because to supply that, under the present circumstances, would be too easy a solution: the reader must decide for himself what his atti-tude towards the novel's events shall be, unassisted by authorial guidance—a sort of *Lehrstück.*

Running Dog is even more difficult to 'locate'. The title refers us to the political co-ordinates from which the subject and *dramatic personae* of the novel might be quite confidently condemned. It is a narrative of the terminally decadent Western city, its characters drag queens, cops, pros-titutes, ex-Nazis, intelligence agents running private criminal baronies, senatorial disciples of the double life. All are joined together in quest for the allegedly ultimate fix, the original and only copy of a movie shot in Hitler's bunker during the final days of the Third Reich. The novel, however, despite its title and its subject, withholds the political/moral-istic discourse which might place the quest and the questers in the context of an overall explanation; far from condemning or even analyzing the events and the people it explores, the novel implies that the discourse of politics, if embraced, would add only one more derangedly vital, recruit-seeking world-view to those already represented. 'Capitalist lackeys and running dogs'—the style of *that* discourse is not so different from the other styles used to define the characters' verbal grotesqueness, their capitulation to the urban paranoia. The mark of madness in DeLillo is to surrender before discursive pressure, to embrace *without irony* a dialect—any dialect—that promises to pattern the chaos of city and world: the placarding crank in *Players*, the Logicon projectors in *Ratner's Star*, the crazies swarming the sidewalk in DeLillo's play *The Engineer of Moonlight*:

They're in the libraries.
They're in the subways...
They like to talk. They talk out to people. This is their way. They talk from inside out. They don't gather data. It's what's inside them. They use themselves.

Sanity might reside in refusing the solace of the totalitarian vocabulary; yet DeLillo's prognosis for the sanity of refusal is far from sanguine. The reluctance or the inability to place the self within discourse has already been seen in *Players* as symptomatic of urban alienation: systematic irony, though a useful survival strategy, is experienced finally as part of the general numbness, the inability to feel horror or love. *Running Dog* organizes its plot around an object which promises to lower the threshold of tolerance to its nadir. Those chasing Hitler's film are shown as fugitives from experience, scurrying around the last curves of descent until they finally reach the lake of ice where there will be no more pain. If the metaphor seems too Dantesque or archaic to apply to DeLillo's updated City of Dis, consider the following:

The man sitting on the step near the toilets hadn't stopped talking about the FBI. He was able to see cameras and listening devices. They were installed everywhere he went. If he went to another bar around the corner, they would be there. If he took a bus uptown, he'd see the little bugging devices, the little cameras under the seats and along the metal edges of the windows. People kept telling him that he had DTs. But the DTs were when you saw rats and birds and insects. It was little cameras he saw. Tiny transmitters. And they were everywhere.

DeLillo conceives of the urban régime as one of perpetual surveillance and intrusion, and in *Running Dog* the bugging devices and tapes are everywhere: in his version of the *città dolente* there is no escape from those who watch, listen, film. The metaphor at the heart of the novel is that of celluloid: the 'empty' substance which by its very emptiness instates a spectacular distance between self and world. That distance is what the characters most desire—a distance continuous with, and indistinguishable from, the ironic interval across which they address and perceive the world. The greater the interval, the greater their release; the greater the interval, the greater their alienation.

DeLillo is certainly offering diagnosis: what he sees is deformity in the social organism, a perversion of growth. At the same time his own position in relation to the deformity is far from clear. Like Warhol, he is unusually sensitive to the hidden beauty to be reclaimed from the urban waste. And *Running Dog's* unnerving neutrality can perhaps be attributed to the paralyzing encounter between a moral sense which seeks to denounce the American Babylon and an aesthetic sense which seeks to celebrate and make sacred the weirdest Babylonic phenomena. The book as a whole can be placed within the aesthetic Warhol provides, in that it defines itself by its relation to the twin poles of the trivial and the sensational—of boringness and freakishness. At times reading *Running Dog* I had the feeling that in DeLillo's New York almost any crime could be

absolved if executed with sufficient *élan*, and that the lament about de-
sensitization and self-administered anaesthesia was merely dutiful. At
other times, the books's neutrality seemed to emanate from a sensibility
appalled by the degree to which it had become unable to feel, genuinely
afraid that some part of it had died. In this concern for what happens to
'sensibility' in the decadent or decaying inner city, Warhol and DeLillo
part company. The cultivated blandness with which Warhol protects
himself from the freaky isn't at all like the tormented and disquieting
neutralism by which DeLillo seeks to contain his particular vision of Dis.

For DeLillo, as for the photographer Diane Arbus, urban monstrosity is less interesting in itself than the way in which it is viewed. The
Arbus people are the freaks and pariahs of New York, the inmates of the
welfare hotels, the competitors at the drag contests, the addicts, the jokes
of nature and of culture (recall, for example, her photograph entitled 'A
Jewish giant at home with his parents in the Bronx, NY, 1970'). But what
is unnerving about the Arbus images isn't their content but their address
to the viewer. The subjects are not caught at unguarded moments. They
have posed for the camera, and they have composed themselves. They
don't seem to be suffering at all; they are in certain ways just like us.
DeLillo's crew are the same people, talking. Arbus saw the flaws. ('You
see someone on the street and essentially what you notice about them is
the flaw'); DeLillo hears them. And to hear so accurately he must to some
degree have engaged with these voices as an equal, mixed his own voice
with theirs, entered into confidences, just as Arbus must have become
intimate with her sitters to have persuaded them to display their flaws to
her camera so ingenuously. DeLillo has gone out into the underworld and
mingled with the grotesques, and in this he is, of course, in a hallowed
tradition that included Baudelaire and Manet and Dreiser. But the
questions of association and dissociation are much more difficult for
DeLillo to solve than for his predecessors. To go out so far towards monstrosity and to engage with it in parity is either to become monstrous
oneself, or—what is more disturbing—to lose the category of 'the monstrous'. And in a sense, that category is the most important in any cogni-
tive taxonomy: against it the world acquires its intelligibility. To lose the
right to label what doesn't fit the taxonomy as the grotesque or as madness or as the dehumanized is to dissolve the system by which beauty,
sanity, and humanity are defined. On the other hand, to recoil from aberration into a sophisticated, inscrutable cool is to enter a realm of increas-
ing numbness: the self begins to go dead, and the only way to keep it alive
is to feed in ever more intense sensations, wilfully violating and traumati-
zing the organism. The perfect statement of this process is the snuff-flick,
the ruling metaphor of *Running Dog*: the terminal cases can go to it to feel
they are still alive, just; but in so far as they *are* alive and refuse to iden-

tify with what is being displayed, they widen the interval between self and world so far that almost nothing more can reach them. One step further and the world is ice. Penultimate man.

ROBERT BOYERS
The Weightless Characters
of William Styron

THE BELIEF IN free will is necessary to most good fiction. Without it, characters must be made to drift indifferently from one prospect to another. Human decisions will seem either not to matter or to be unconvincingly portrayed. It is not essential that the novelist himself fully believe in free will, only that he conduct the business of his novel as if he had not altogether decided against it. In practice this is something that has little to do with deliberate deception or the mastery of familiar confidence tricks. Writers need to believe they are getting at the truth if they are to remain exercised about matters that are by nature demanding and serious. To subscribe to free will in a novel is to determine that characters will be permitted to develop in accordance with their natures, and that their susceptibilities will be plausibly various; also, that they will seem to us, as they develop, to be substanitally accountable for what they do or fail to do. The novelist need not pass explicit judgements for himself in order to make us feel that judgements are possible. And we, in turn, will want to feel that we have been given leave to care for this character or that without being asked to renounce the possibility of judgement. Nothing more, or less, is involved in the novelistic 'illusion' of free will.

In his new novel, *Sophie's Choice*, William Styron has created a character who develops quite as variously and as plausibly as one could wish. But she is made to develop in such a way that, though we care very much for her and are moved to grief and rage over what she has had to suffer, we are never invited to think of her as a responsible human agent. Responsive, yes; responsible—to herself, to us, even to Styron—no. If, more than ten years ago, Styron gave us in Nat Turner a character virtuo-

sic in assigning responsibility and in positioning himself deliberately at
the bar of justice, he has here given us just the reverse. Nor is the portrait
of Sophie a special instance in a novel that concerns itself almost equally
with two or three other characters. Styron is here in the grip of a very
simple and important idea, namely, that to counter evil, one must learn to
love and to express love. In intellectual terms this is to say that understanding and judgement are separable activities and ought not to be confused with one another. In literary terms Styron's idea comes across as
affection for characters who do not have to earn our loyalty. Having suffered or opened themselves to the suffering of others, they assume the
status of victims, and those of us who feel with them are thereby enabled
to believe that we have borne witness to the central truth of our time: that
'absolute evil is never extinguished from the world. ' This is a truth we can
acknowledge without tracing out corresponding insights or making large
and unreasonable demands upon ourselves or upon those we have come
to love.

   Styron's novel has taken the United States by storm, and it is no
secret that, as he earlier sought to get inside the experience of slavery, he
has now attempted to come to terms with Auschwitz. This he does by
drawing upon the memories of a Polish survivor—not à Jew—who tells
her story in bits and pieces to a young Southern writer immediately recognizable as the young Styron himself. In so organizing his novel, Styron
can play off Sophie Zawistowska's memories against his own reflections,
measuring the general validity of her account against the accounts of
other concentration camp survivors and writers like Hannah Arendt, Elie
Wiesel, and George Steiner. From the point of view of earnest, dispas-
sionate inquiry, Styron makes the best of his opportunity. He tries out
first one idea, then another, always curious and eager to improve his
grasp of the relevant facts. His respect for the historical truth and his love
of ideas for their own sake together make him a careful though never
slavish exploiter of other men's theories and opinions. And Sophie's
account is subjected to the kind of tender scrutiny that makes us feel we
have understood why she takes so long to get it out and to correct what
had been a succession of earlier falsehoods.
   The problem with all of this is that Styron nowhere feels compelled
to tell what we are to make of the presented material. The refusal to
fashion a perspective from which Sophie may be judged is part of a larger
refusal to see people we like as anything but victims: of history, of the
zeitgeist, of their own innocence of idiosyncrasy. This may be preferable
to a fiction in which characters either do or do not measure up to an
abstract standard of goodness or competency and are summarily dismis-
sed or congratulated on that basis alone. But there is only so far that a

novelist can go with characters for whom he feels so much affection that he cannot make us feel they are accountable for themselves in the way that others are supposed to be. No one expects the novelist to resolve every uncertainty, and the taking of positions—on persons as on ideas—has so often become a substitute for thought that the writer frequently does well to avoid it. But we do expect the novelist to follow up the issues he has set in motion, to try out the ideas that fasscinate him not only on figures for whom he has no feeling but on the characters that most occupy him. To fail in this is to create confusion about what ultimately the novel intends. An ambitious writer like Styron cannot be thought to be satisfied with the evocation of terror and suffering as if these might tell us all we need to know. If Sophie, or her lover Nathan, or the narrator Stingo, are to stand, permanently, in the degree that enduring characters persist for us in memory, they must be more than the pathos or frailty with which they are invested.

Styron's Sophie is, in several respects, a powerfully realized character. What is unrealized in the novel are the ideas that are made to circulate without being allowed to settle on her fair shoulders. The title of the book tells us that Sophie had a choice, though really she is confronted by more than one. Why Styron did not call his novel 'Sophie's Choices' we cannot say for sure. Apparently he felt that, having gone through Auschwitz, she had but one actual choice left her: to live or to die. But to read the character and her situation in this way is to reduce her human stature and to conclude more or less in advance that all other, less ultimate questions are of no real consequence. In this sense, it might be said that Sophie is free ot live or to die, but not to live as others live, in the shadow of a succession of choices to which she is or is not equal. Nor is Styron's character a victim merely of Auschwitz, and on that account alone exempted from considerations that obtain for others who have suffered less. Even as a young woman, before the onset of war and Hitler's invasion of her native Poland, Sophie was a helpless creature, unable to do what she would intuitively have liked to do, and no less exempt from the kinds of judgement we ordinarily direct at one another. Confronted by unreasonable demands, she has a desire to run away and to save her self-respect. But she fails to move, to resist what others would make of her. Though she is revolted by a wretched anti-semitic pamphlet prepared by her father for distribution at his university, she can do nothing but yield to his demand that she help in the distribution. 'I knew that I *would* be there ...,' she recalls for Stingo,

> passing out these sheets just like I done everything he told me to do since I was a little girl, running these errands, bringing him things, learning to use the typewriter and knowing shorthand just so he could use me whenever he wanted. And this terrible emptiness come over me when I

realize just then there was nothing I could do about it, no way
of saying no, no way possible to say, 'Papa, I'm not going to
help you spread this thing.'

Was this not one of the choices Sophie failed to acknowledge and to
act upon? Styron's reader may wonder why Sophie found it impossible to
say no to her father, but the reader is urged again and again to move on to
the 'larger' issues and to concern himself with absolute evil; the failings
of Sophie Zawistowska are too small and pitiful to think about in any extended way. The fact that she was revolted by the anti-semitic pamphlet
and allowed herself to feel a measure of hatred for the man who wrote it
ought to be enough for us. She may not have acted well, but her heart
could be counted upon most of the time to be in the right place.

It never occurs to Styron to ask why Sophie gives in so easily, why
she feels she has no choice though, for example, her friend Wanda is busy
choosing frantically even when most of the better options have been taken
away. He speculates bravely about less prominent characters, but is
determined to love Sophie as she is, and feels this will be hard to do if he
presses too hard. For all he tells us about Sophie, for all she is made to tell
Stingo about herself, she remains something less than the representative
human being she is meant to be. Though we feel her presence, we do not
understand her: a major flaw in a novel that seeks to understand the Nazi
period by examining the experience of this character especially. Is it the
case that Styron would have had to face the same dilemma no matter what
the name or particular background of the representative human being he
decided to install at the centre of his novel? Our answer necessarily
depends upon our sense of Styron's options. And one of his options would
have been to handle Sophie very differently. Clearly he could have tried to
account for her failings and in so doing made her a responsible agent. He
would then have had on his hands, say, the product of a particular ethos
or milieu or social class. And he would have had to indicate what chance
such a person would have had to break free of inherited constraints and
inadequacies. Was Sophie a typical young woman of her time and situation? This the novel does not say. Though she had a very unusual father to
grow up with, she is in no way represented as a product of that relationship alone. It is surely possible that Sophie, as presented, might well have
been the same kind of person had her father been a cleric or a customs
official. So far as Styron is concerned, Sophie is an acceptably representative human being in the sense that she cannot bring herself to do what she
likes, and suffers because there is evil in the world. To shape her nature
as the product of cultural or social conditions is to become involved in
something else, to distract us from what is central.

Styron also had the option, of course, of making Sophie a very different sort of person, someone more like her friend Wanda, a resistance

fighter and Polish patriot whose political zeal and fervent rationality are the most attractive things in the novel. To have done this, of course, would have been not only to write a different book, but to aim at a very different statement, namely that absolute evil may be extinguished by the collective efforts of persons who do whatever they can to resist what it would make of them. That is the sort of 'up-beat' affirmation that tends to embarrass modern readers—and writers—who have been taught to feel superior to affirmations of any kind. Styron is not afraid of words that, in his own account, 'have the quality of a strapping homily,' but he is apparently no more ready than the rest of us to embrace causes and movements.

To have made Sophie a victim who struggled bravely would have been to assign her a range of viable choices on the basis of which we might have judged her. But Styron is not interested in performance, and Sophie seems to him most definitively a victim in the sense that she cannot bring herself to choose or to act. Though, in the most terrible moment in the novel, she is asked to decide which of her two children must be taken to the ovens, she cannot be said even there to have made a choice and to have assumed responsibility. Though she 'chooses' her daughter she does so without conviction or anger or sense of purpose. Nor does she seek to hold back the officer who takes the child, or follow the child's departure with her eyes. No one can say, at this point in the novel, what he would have done in Sophie's place, and the last thing one would think to do is to feel that there Sophie betrayed her humanity. What, after all, could she have done that would have been effectual? But this terrifying encounter is emblematic for us of what Sophie has all along failed to be and to do. In her suffering and dumb acquiescence she stands for some part of the human possibility. But there is something missing, and we excuse her—and her creator—too easily if we conclude that she fails only to be heroic and to transcend her ordinariness.

Our objection to Sophie as a character is not in itself a moral objection but an objection to a kind of characterization that puts unnecessary restrictions on moral reflection. In *Sophie's Choice* Styron is less interested in moral issues than in a peculiar metaphysics of suffering, and he has prompted even his more tolerant reviewers to complain that he has no gift for psychological analysis or sustained ethical reflection. As if to disprove the charge by anticipation, Styron indulges here and there a flourish of virtuosic psychologizing in a Dostoyevskian mode. Not only Rudolph Höss but a much less important Nazi officer becomes the occasion for Styron's display for psychological depth-analysis. 'His strivings were essentially religious,' he tells us of a Dr Jemand von Niemand, who makes Sophie decide which of her two children is to die. Why must the man have been religious? Because it seems likely that a fellow who would do something so extravagantly monstrous—and something, moreover, quite unusual

even among the atrocities committed by his kind—would have had to act
in the service of an overmastering impulse. He must have seen that his
boredom and revulsion were in part the consequence of an inability to
commit a sin, and 'that the absence of sin and the absence of God were
inseparably intertwined....All of his depravity had been enacted in a
vacuum of sinless and businesslike godlessness, while his soul thirsted
for beatitude.' What he determines to do is, of course, in Styron's version, 'to affirm his human capacity for evil, by committing the most intol-
erable sin....Goodness could come later. But first a great sin.' This analysis is accompanied by details of von Nieman's general anxiety and drunk-
enness, and some very close attention to the dynamics of the transaction
between Sophie and her tormentor.

Though it is painful to read of Sophie's ordeal, the reader retains
sufficient presence of mind to be put off by the gratuitous analysis of von
Niemand. The business about his religious mania is much more inventive
than anything lavished on Sophie. We're expected, no doubt, to applaud
the performance, to brood on the enigma of human perversity. But von
Niemand's mania is in no way related to the ambitions of other characters
in the novel. It may suggest to some that radical evil is by nature extreme
and unpredictable, but in that case, why should Styron make so much of
efforts to understand evil, to see it as an expresssion of our common
humanity? The analysis of von Niemand would seem useful only if it were
commensurate with efforts to come to terms with what is most peculiar
about Sophie. Since Styron accepts Sophie as she is, he should be less
ready to work up the elements of von Niemand's unpardonable sin.

And what, after all, do the von Niemand passages contribute in the
way of moral insight? Dostoyevski would no doubt have had something
memorable to say of the man, and of Sophie, confronted by the doctor's
thirst for beatitude. Styron seems to believe that he does enough simply
by invoking the syndrome. The reader will know what to make of it all by
referring it to the tradition in which it belongs. But this is a dangerous
assumption. Von Niemand is after all incapable of reflecting upon the
origins of his sin. He may or may not actually suffer agonies of repentence
once the sin has been committed. And Styron, of course, is not interested
enough to make us stay around and find out. If the analysis of von
Niemand were more than gratuitous we should be made to regard him as
a more important character, or we should have impressed upon us the
contrast between the man and his victim. But Sophie is no more capable
of extended moral reflection than von Niemand. The complex unconscious
motives assigned him do not serve as a basis for understanding anyone
else, and so come across as a form of novelistic exhibitionism. In an isolated passage Styron shows what he can do without bothering to consider what he has refused to do for other characters.

Some connection between Sophie and von Niemand might have been indicated. Like him, she appears to act in part out of unconscious motives that are more complex than anything Styron will allow. Even in Brooklyn, two years after her liberation from the concentration camp, she has not learned to defend herself or to do what is best for her. She seems to be playing out a drama she has no hand in directing. Styron might have made something of this, might have asked questions about her needs or had something to say about her perverse indifference to things most of us cannot be casual about. To do so, however, would necessarily have been to see her as finally responsible for herself, no matter what the burden of unconscious motivation. Is it a sin to hold responsible one who has had to bear so much? May the victim of a radical evil never be held responsible, never have her deeds or omissions subjected to overt moral scrutiny? What of the aftermath of her ordeal, when the conditions of terror have been removed and circumstances are more genial?

At a New York beach, Sophie and Stingo-Styron become sexually 'involved' quite as Stingo hoped and fantasized they would. Though Sophie is still very much attached to her lover Nathan, still feels she owes her recovery to him, she advances lecherously upon the younger Stingo and concludes their session by rubbing his semen all over her face. In a moment Stingo observes that his companion is 'seemingly no more touched by our prodigious intimacy than if we had done a two-step together'. What to make of this? Nothing, apparently, for Styron is content to leave the narrator's observation at that. The reader is free to wonder whether Sophie's indifference has something to do with Auschwitz, with other impinging preoccupations, or with the person she has always been. Styron himself will have no part in such speculations, and will insist simply that Sophie is Sophie and nothing more need be said about it. The kind of analytic pressure applied to von Niemand is somehow inappropriate to her.

Our grasp of the narrator is no better. Is he in fact the novelist himself? Are we to take everything he says as coming from Styron? Our uncertainty is bound to cause considerable—and unnecessary—discomfort, since much that he says is either puerile or insupportable. He is a decent enough fellow, and he covers himself here and there by admitting to stray prejudices and to a young man's staggering 'inexperience'. But it is this same Stingo who earnestly studies the holocaust literature and brings back vivid samples for our edification. It is Stingo who addresses us at novel's end in solemn accents and describes quite plausibly the vision of evil the novel is to convey. To say that he is capable of regarding himself with tolerant irony and amusement—particularly as he recalls his departed youth—is in no way to conclude that he shows an instinct for self-parody in the novel as a whole. He appears, for better or worse, to speak for Styron. We are confused by the occasional puerile observations and by much that seems arbitrary in the book because, again Styron also fails to make Stingo a responsible agent. 'All my life I have retained a strain of uncontrolled didacticism,' says Stingo. But where is this didacticism in a novel that cries out for the application of free-floating ideas to the central characters? To discuss theories and formulate ideas is not to to be didactic, after all, but to raise the possibility of at least provisional resolutions. These we never get, not in a sustained or serious way, and that is an element of the major flaw in this overheated work. Stingo ought to be able to reflect more satisfactorily on the material he presents, and Styron ought to indicate what we are to make of Stingo's reflections. When Stingo fails to do justice to a train of thought he has set in motion or to make adequate sense of a detail, Styron should either fill the gap or acknowledge, at least, that there is a gap; also, that there are reasons—characterological reasons—for Stingo's represented incapacity.

It is one thing to project Sophie as an absolute victim who may not be called to a strenuous accounting. To some of us this may not seem legitimate, but we can entertain the idea in a serious way. But Stingo is in no comparable way a victim, and it is his experience that dominates much of the novel. In fact, only one quarter of so of the book is devoted to Sophie's memories of Warsaw and Auschwitz. Stingo's world—his father's American South and his own adopted post-war Brooklyn—is not on the face of it terrible and intimidating. Once or twice we are reminded of violence Southern-style: racial conflict, lynchings, and so on. And there is a good deal of domestic violence perpetrated by Nathan in the Brooklyn rooming house they occupy. But for the most part this is menace on a different scale, and always it is cast into diminished perspective by the persistent dredging up of incidents from Auschwitz. Stingo is a free man. He can write his novels, fantasize all he likes about carnal transport, and pursue friendships with some hope that they will not turn sour. Styron's failure to hold him accountable for gross lapses of taste and insight is a reflection not of the novelist's self-pity but of his conviction that he is after bigger game. Why be severe with Stingo when there are graver things to deplore?

There is some truth in this view, of course. Stingo, as indicated, is not a bad fellow, and he is generously candid about his more obvious deficiencies. And there *are* larger matters for Styron to contend with. But Styron does not understand that the character ceases to matter to us as he should in the degree that his creator seems not to take him seriously. It is not enough for the novelist to show an interest in the character's ideas or to dwell to the point of tedium on his sexual adventures. To take him seriously is to invest him with the capacity to make choices and discriminations. A book that means to address the holocaust cannot afford to project weightless characters, as if the gravity of the issues might be communicated simply by insisting that people suffered and that philosophers have debated the matter passionately. Weightless characters typically move about from one option to another without feeling pressed to distinguish for themselves between good and bad, normal and abnormal, significant and trivial. Their creator treats them as illustrations of this tendency or that and does his best to make us care about them while refusing to allow for the prospect that they might have done better. They are susceptible only to irrational guilt, never to the sense that they have actually transgressed against some presiding cultural presence or violated a commandment. To be healthy means, for them, to be flexible, to be tolerant of their own failings, and to generate signs of a capacity to respond to others. Love objects are to be relentlessly supported. Their stray gestures may seem offensive or momentarily disturbing, but nothing enacted by one of them may be thought to be wrong or genuinely symptomatic of malevolent intention. Crime, if it exists at all, is 'radical' and belongs to others. Cruelty may not be ignored, but it is easy to forgive in one who shows signs of madness or contrition.

To speak of Styron's characters as weightless is to say that in some essential way they are made up, that they have no moral centre. They may have a past, a parentage, a repertoire of characteristics, but they lack, in any defining sense, *character*. Sophie is what happens to her and what Stingo can learn from her. She is not a character who makes her fate. She suffers it as, in the novelist's conception of things, each of us must suffer the fate to which circumstance assigns us. For a man who wanted to write a book about choice and about the intersection of personal and political experience, Styron made a terrible decision. He allowed himself to fall in love with characters—including Stingo—who have not the stature required to bear witness to the treacheries of modern experience in a persuasive and instructive way. Alongside of remembrance and lamentation we should have preferred an evocation of inwardnesss. Styron is too committed to the advantages of confessional self-expression to write a book about good and evil.

Prose Feature: John Barth

JOHN BARTH IS among a group of American authors devoted to developing a fiction-tradition that has its antecedents among the dominant figures of modernism. The issues raised by Joyce or Kafka or Proust are not, for a writer like Barth, issues which can be overlooked, and for any serious, contemporary author to write as if they could be demonstrates shallowness and aesthetic irresponsibility. 'I deplore,' Barth says in an article just published in *Atlantic Magazine,* 'the artistic and critical cast of mind that repudiates the whole modernist enterprise as an aberration, and sets to work as if it hadn't happened; that rushes back into the arms of nineteenth century middle-class realism as if the first half of the twentieth century hadn't happened.'

Thirteen years ago John Barth wrote 'The Literature of Exhaustion', an article which served almost as a manifesto for a number of writers in the sixties and early seventies who faced, in Barth's words, 'the real technical question' of 'how to succeed not even Joyce and Kafka, but those who've *succeeded* Joyce and Kafka.' The *Exhaustion* of the article's title refers to the exhaustion or 'used-upness' of the forms and possibilities of fiction. The victory of the writer of 'exhaustion' is that he can confront an apparent intellectual dead end, and employ it against itself to accomplish new work. Barth is not glibly dismissing the novel as dead; rather, he is celebrating those writers like Beckett, Nabokov, Borges and more recently Italo Calvino and Gabriel Garcia Marquez who can use the occasion of that *perceived* death as the occasion, or at least the starting point, for artistic invention. Borges is, in this respect, exemplary, as he can, for Barth, 'paradoxically turn the felt ultimacies of our time into material and means for his work — paradoxically because by doing so he transcends what had appeared to be his refutation.'

Like the *ficciones* of Borges, Barth's novels are remarkable and remarkably vital for their determination to use established conventions for the purpose of transcending them. *The Sot Weed Factor*, written in 1960, is formally based on the eighteenth century picaresque novel, but, with a mad, modern crowding of sub-plots, digressions, and exhilarating pastiche, the novel does far more within that form than the form would seem able to admit, using its structure to change our perceptions of not just it but all conventions. *Giles Goat Boy* — an assemblage of letters, forewords, and disclaimers which enclose the main narrative in equivocal frames — is informed by an insistent succession of literary references — to figures as diverse as Moses, Odysseus, and Don Quixote — all apparently distributed through the text by an out-of-control computer which, Barth hints, may be the true author of the book. *Chimera* reuses and newly develops elements from Greek mythology and its assumptions of heroism. Much of *Lost in the Funhouse* is likewise an extended improvisation on classical themes. Barth's greatest, or at least most complete, achievement, however, is his most recent. *LETTERS* employs not only a past available through ostensibly exhausted conventions — it is, for instance, written in the style of the epistolary novel — but a past which is explicitly the product of the mind which invented it: *LETTERS* depicts the developing relationship of a set of characters already created by Barth — most are from his previous novels — writing letters to Barth, their author.

Barth is the comedian of forms, the controlled anarchist who deals realities, roles and fictions like playing cards, inventing — as in a game — an endless succession of names for the world. 'A certain kind of sensibility,' Barth observed several years ago, 'can be made very uncomfortable by the recognition of the arbitrariness of physical facts and the inability to accept their finality.' The material for Barth's fiction is the fictions we occupy; his aspiration is to transcend — to encourage us to transcend — the limiting confines we create for ourselves: 'Ontology and cosmology are funny subjects to improvise. But if you are a novelist of a certain type of temperament, then what you really want to do is re-invent the world. God wasn't too bad a novelist, except he was a realist.'

The following interview was conducted by Heide Ziegler on three different occasions: the short, first part is excerpted from a very long interview which took place on the ninth and sixteenth of November in 1976, and the second part, devoted almost entirely to John Barth's new novel — a long extract from which we include in this issue — took place last September, shortly before the book first appeared in the States.

HEIDE ZIEGLER
An Interterview with
John Barth

*Heide Ziegler: Perhaps the most striking feature of your writing is the
importance you give to the past. In* The Sot Weed Factor *you are concerned with the historical past; in* Lost in the Funhouse *and* Chimera *with
the mythic past. But it is the twentieth century mind that is at work in all
of your novels. In which way do you believe that the past relates to the
present in your fiction?*

John Barth: The Latin motto of one of the characters in the work in progress [*LETTERS*]—he is an industrialist borrowed from my first novel,
The Floating Opera, who has expanded his pickle business into chemical
fertilizers and freeze-drying—*Praeteritas futuras stercorat:* The past shits
up the present. His PR man changed that to *Praeteritas futuras fecundat*:
the past *fertilizes* the present, a proper motto for a chemical fertilizer
firm, I suppose. But in *LETTERS*—and I think this applies to the other
novels as well—any historical or mythic past that haunts, craps up fertilizes the present is an emblem of our personal past. The theme, certainly
of the Perseus story, certainly of the Bellerophon story [two of the three
novellas in *Chimera*], and most certainly of *LETTERS*, is the comic,
tragic, or paradoxical re-enactment of the past in the present.

Bellerophon is a good example: he attempts to become a mythic
hero by perfectly imitating the 'programme' for mythic heroes. Of course,
that doesn't work, and he finds that by perfectly imitating the model of
mythic heroism, what he becomes is a perfect imitation of a mythic hero.
My characters in the new novel, *LETTERS*, will act out, whether they
know it or not, Marx's notion that historical events and personages recur,

the first time as tragedy and the second time as farce. This is also what happens to Perseus in *Chimera:* his attempts to re-enact his heroic past become farcical, a fiasco. It is only when he reassesses his situation (with the help of Calyxa and eventually Medusa) that he is able to elevate his re-enactment into something greater: which, if not heroic, is at least more personally successful.

HZ: That implies, then, that it is important that the hero character overcomes his past in the end, doesn't it?

JB: Indeed, it does.

Try to imagine a chambered nautilus whose prior chambers are accessible: a creature who carries its past on its back but isn't confined strictly to the present room of that past. He can move freely into past rooms, using what's there to energize and inform the present.

That's the optimistic view. I am reminded, though, of a statement by D'Arcey Thompson, the English biologist who attempted to describe organic growth and form mathematically. He points out that it is only the very lip of the shell of marine mollusks that is alive and generative; the rest of it is dead material. He also remarks that it is not the snail that shapes the shell, but the shell that shapes the snail. I think that applies in an obvious way to ourselves: our thirties are a product of what we were in our twenties and what we were in our teens. But we are not *just* product. Our past lives a more or less active half-life in us, let's say, but we're continuously reshaping and reinterpreting it, restructuring it: re-orchestrating it, if you like.

HZ: Does this mean that we approach the past as something like a game?

JB: Oh, indeed so! Somebody in *The Sot Weed Factor*—Burlingame, I think—says that the past is a clay that, willy-nilly, we must sculpt. And sculpting is play as well as work.

Heide Ziegler: The most astonishing trait, to me, in your recent novel LETTERS *is what I would like to call your new flirt with realism. A realism, however, which, although it refers to recognizable times and places, even to strictly autobiographical details, is, at the same time, less past-oriented than it is 'mildly prophetic'. Does this 'realism', then, define a special relationship—a dialectic—between the fictional and the factual?*

JOHN BARTH: It's been a while since I wrote any fiction that has to do with the here and the now, with recognizable places, and with characters characterized in the fashion of traditional bourgeois realism. The other thing, the dialectic—the contamination of the real by the fictitious and of the fictitious by the real—is one of the main lines of the plot. Do you remember, Heide, Borges's remark that among the four characteristics of the fabulous in fiction is the contamination of reality by dream? We just have to change the terms: the contamination of reality by fiction. But Borges himself, I think, sometimes includes in that notion the contamination of exterior reality by the imagined, by fiction, and, as witness the story 'Tlön, Uqbar, Orbis Tertius', the reverse process, where the fictitious begins to contaminate the real. Yes: if that convention is not the backbone of the novel, it's certainly part of the armature of the theme and of the action. But, as you have seen, the whole mode of operation of that novel is the reorchestration of old conventions, beginning with the convention of the epistolary novel. The dialectic between the fictitious and the real is a convention that goes way back past the modernists; it's at the heart of *Don Quixote*. When you said earlier that you found an element of the prophetic in the novel, I wondered what you meant.

HZ: I thought it meant that, once written, fiction can, in a sense, influence the subsequent life of its author. In this sense, couldn't we say that the relationship between the fiction an author writes and his own life is a precarious version of 'life following art'?

JB: Precarious but real. And while that prophetic aspect is not at the heart of the novel, it certainly spooks around the corners and margins. The theme of *LETTERS* is reenactment; and reenactment is a phenomenon at least as full of hazards and perils as of opportunities.

HZ: One of the most interesting aspects, I find, in your re-use of characters from previous novels is that the characters seem to constitute the author. In a way, he exists for them, as the centre for their lives and the information they impart. What struck me, though—and what must strike

most of your readers—is the question of your relationship to these charac-
ters, whom you have, over the years, created, and who, over the years,
seem to be influencing you—the greatest manifestation of which is
LETTERS *itself.*

JB: Obviously the things we do, either as artists or as human beings,
change and affect us. The dreams we dream as novels, novels that occupy
years of our imaginative energy, obviously work changes in us. That old
convention of earlier modernism—of the dialogue between the author and
his characters, the assumption of an independent life by those characters,
even the mutiny of the characters against the author—that's simply a
metaphor for the way things actually are. I'm not very romantic about
writing, and it always makes me uncomfortable when I hear an old-
fashioned writer talk about the way his or her characters assume a life of
their own: 'I wanted this character to be such and such. But, no, she
insisted on...'.This is the kind of hogwash you hear from a certain kind of
writer who talks in a romantic way about art. But on the level of simple
fact, I think it's undeniable that the work we do changes us; the dreams
we dream change us. Everything we do in art is likely to turn out to be
either prophecy or exorcism, whatever its other intentions.

HZ: But I think it should be stressed that you make use of this fact in a
particular way. I assume that every author knows that his own characters
will influence him and that he has to live with them after he has created
them. But, in LETTERS, *the characters literally constitute their own*
author: he exists on the fictitious level for his other characters in the same
way that they seem to exist on a kind of 'real' level for him.

JB: Is that a reversal of Flaubert's famous remark about *Madame
Bovary*: 'C'est moi?' Not only is Madame Bovary Flaubert, but Flaubert
is Madame Bovary. That's certainly true in the case of my characters.
      You will find, and I think you have probably found already, that the
author of the letters from the author in *LETTERS* is the least characterized character. Not only does the author very properly not engage in the
action—he doesn't affect the plot or become at all involved in it. But also
he is the one who, if you were trying to draw little character sketches, you
would have the least handle on, I believe. No doubt that's because, for
the purposes of the novel at least (and it's not just a modernist game
that's being played), his character is simply a kind of emptying-out—a
kénosis, as the theologians say.

In a mild way, every author who's involved, especially in realistic fictions, in drawing characters absolutely from the whole cloth, as these characters are drawn—who have no counterparts in real life—is doing just that. No future Ph.D. investigator is ever going to find anybody now living who could be said to be the real-life models for Lady Amherst or Ambrose Mensch or Todd Andrews. That amuses me because most actual realistic writers have not historically worked in that fashion. They do draw from life; and, of course, people from the period of Germaine de Staël boasted of the fact that their novels were drawn literally from their lives and that they were all romans à clef. These are not, and I think that this emptying-out of the characteristics of the author into the characteristics of his characters is most likely to happen when you try to write something that will pass for verisimilitude in characterization, but is, in fact, not drawn from life.

Hazlitt made a wonderful remark about Richardson that I came across when I was doing a little homework on Richardson. He said that, for all of Richardson's much touted realism, he, Hazlitt, suspected that Richardson's characters weren't drawn from life at all. Hazlitt's phrase was that Richardson simply spun them out of his own head. I'm sure that's true. Hazlitt meant it as a criticism, but I regard it as a marvellous truth. And I'm sure that, as soon as you have heard that remark, you cannot read through any of *Pamela* or *Clarissa* and for a moment believe in the reality of those characters in the sense that Mr B. is carefully modelled after so and so, etc. They are as absolutely make-believe characters as ever came down the pages of literature, I'm sure. I would regard it as a tribute if somebody made that Hazlitt kind of remark about *LETTERS*. I would be delighted.

HZ: My next question takes up what we have been talking about on the level of form. In LETTERS *as well as in* Chimera, *Jerome Bray is trying to create the perfect novel with the aid of the computer Lilyvac II. He wants to create a novel that will of necessity 'contain nothing original whatever, but be the quintessence, the absolute type, as it were the Platonic Form expressed.'*

JB: I'm sure *LETTERS* doesn't so much aspire to as stumble towards it. It's certainly not 'the Platonic Form expressed', but it certainly participates in the Platonic idea that Bray is speaking of. Clearly this is a novel in which, on one level, there is nothing original whatsoever; that is, it is a novel which is conspicuously assembled out of old literary conventions. On the other hand, I regard it is a very original novel. Bray's serious role in the novel is to be a kind of mad, limiting case of preoccupations which are also my preoccupations. The difference is that Bray takes them dead seriously and, of course, he is going to refine and escalate his aspirations as he goes along until, finally, not even literature will do. No novel made out of mere words, mere language could ever arrive at Bray's notions of formal perfection and purity.

I look at the activities of the old and new formalists with a kind of fascination: there *is* a kind of madness in the speculations of Propp and Klebnikhov. But they are perfectly fascinating as limiting cases. However, you are not to regard *LETTERS* as a kind of *Remembrance of Things Past*, where at the end you realize that you are holding in your hand the artifact which demonstrates the author's preoccupations about time: I mean that wonderful climax where Marcel is going to sit down to write the novel, and when he sits down to write the novel, you have finished the novel, and time, literally, is defeated. At the end of *LETTERS*, you are holding in your hand not hte novel that Jerome Bray aspires to compose, not the mad limiting case or the pure form, but something that has fallen from Plato, although it participates in Bray's idea.

HZ: The Platonic idea is, in the end, a static idea, and, moreover, because it presupposes substance, can't really serve as an analogue for post-modern literature. Your concept of history in the novel, however, is more useful, as it suggests that documents constitute history while being, at the same time, interpretations of it. Substance—or fact—doesn't really exist then. Nevertheless, doesn't this suggest the possibility of a sort of dialectic at work in your writing which, although it does away with the notion of substance, can nevertheless, through sheer continuance—the sheer length of the novel, for instance—create something like a substitute for the Platonic idea, a substitute for substance?

JB: I hope so. I like the idea. Our friend John Hawkes, in the conversation which we had in Cincinnati that was later published in the *New York Times*, made a remark which touched me much at the time and seemed, to me, to look deep into my preoccupations as a writer. Jack said that he had the feeling about my novels, especially the long ones, that they were spun out against a kind of nothingness, almost as a shield against a kind of nothingness. I guess, leaving Plato aside for the moment, that there is an impulse, if not in all long novels, certainly in my long novels, that somehow they will assume a kind of substance, or pseudosubstance, or similitude of substance by their mere persistence. I think that's an exorcism of nothingness, of the vacuum that one fears might exist if one stops to look at the void. It's a long exorcism of silence, too. As for the quality of this persistence: I believe it takes seven years for every cell in the human body to replace itself. One should write a novel that would take just that long to read—maybe this one will—so that the reader, at the end, is literally not the reader who began the novel. Not just in a mild Heraclitean sense, but literally. No material cell that was in the reader's body on page 1 is still there on page 772. I would love that.

HZ: So LETTERS *reconstitutes itself just as the reader's body?*

JB: Also the writer's.

HZ: I think that what you just said can be related to one of the characters in your novel. In The Floating Opera *Todd Andrews held that* nothing *had intrinsic value; in* LETTERS *he has changed his concept and has come to believe that* nothing has *intrinsic value, which I understand to mean that* nothing *contains intrinsic value or may lay* sole *claim to intrinsic value. Therefore, 'everything has intrinsic value'. I wanted to ask what it means when Todd Andrews speaks of value in this way. Does it mean that* nothing *contains intrinsic value or may lay* sole *claim to intrinsic value. Therefore, 'everything has intrinsic value.' I wanted to ask relating, in your novel, so very many facts which really are connected by coincidence (I am thinking, for example, of the long catalogues of dates and lists of persons born on one or the other particular date or of things that happened on that date) do you intend to give intrinsic value to every word?*

JB: Mind you, Heide, I regard both of Todd Andrews's propositions as strictly unintelligible. The two fates that await all of the principal characters in the novel are either (a) that they will literally reenact crises from earlier on in their lives or their careers, or (b) that they will realize an opposite notion or be driven by a notion that is exactly the reverse of the notion that drove them previously.

Todd Andrews's notions are his and not mine, and they were in the original case, too. I have never been a nihilist in the complete and naive way that Todd Andrews was in *The Floating Opera.* But Andrews's notion, which he fears himself and admits to himself that he doesn't quite understand, is that perhaps his earlier nihilism is the reverse of the truth. If that is extended to other aspects of the novel, it would lead, of course, to the absolute chaos and anarchy of indiscrimination that threatens the novel, that threatens all lists, catalogues, anatomies and the rest. But against which, in fact, I hope novels like *LETTERS* are shores or buttresses. I might add, too, that, by the rules of dramaturgy, it's fatal to come to the kind of conclusion that Todd Andrews comes to. He is risking death in the same way that you risk moral chaos and paralysis by flirting with the notion that everything has intrinsic value. When Todd Andrews says that nothing *has* intrinsic value, that's as much as saying that everything has intrinsic value—just by the old rule of logic that whatever is true

of everything in general is true of nothing in particular. That's fatal intel-
lectually and morally. And because we are writing novels and not talking
philosophy, it's also fatal in the other sense: a character must die if he
comes to the realization that Todd Andrews did. Or at least he risks
death.

*HZ: That's what I thought his notion of taking the tragic view of the tragic
view of life implies. It's true that Todd Andrews is only one character in
the novel. On the other hand, he is very self-conscious, very self-
reflective, and he knows, himself, that whatever opinion he holds he risks
being wrong.*

JB: That's right. This does not paralyze him for action, though it always
threatens to, and I will say, unabashedly, that I am more sympathetic to
Andrews's character and ideas than to those of any other character in the
novel. It's not a case of Todd Andrews *c'est moi* at all, but it is a case of
there, but for the grace of God, go I. When Todd Andrews is talking about
the tragic view, he is certainly echoing ideas close to my own thought
—especially when he wonders if he must take the tragic view even as the
tragic view, because it doesn't always work. I feel that way, too.

*HZ: Would it, then, make sense to say that you take the tragic view of
character in LETTERS? Drawing a line from, let's say, Ambrose
Mensch's realistic description of his East Dorset family to the letters
which Todd Andrews is writing to his dead father, or which A.B.Cook IV
is writing to his unborn son or daughter, to eventually the author's own
fictitious but elusive personality within the novel, one could say that the
concept of character gradually seems to disintegrate. On the other hand,
if one understands Ambrose Mensch as the* alter ego *of the author, then
this would become a re-affirmation of characterization or—because
Ambrose but not the author dissolves—character.*

JB: I would subscribe to that—with an amendment which acknowledges
that the characterization which they and I realize is completed by the end
of the novel, but what they have become are completed fictional characters. The tragic—or skeptical view—of characterization, I suppose, would
be the recognition that, even in the hands of a great psychological realist
(which I am not), even in the hands of a Tolstoy, let's say, the characters
that are achieved are finally fictitious characters. The tragic view of
characterization is that we cannot, no matter how hard we try, make real
people by language. We can only make verisimilitudinous people. That
view itself is on the minds of the characters themselves in a novel like
LETTERS, and it's very much on the author's mind in a novel like

LETTERS.

But as to the countermotions that you mentioned: those characters who don't actually dissolve by the end do come indeed through as characters should in a plot—if not to an affirmation of themselves, then to a kind of integration of themselves. But what is integrated is not a person, but a fictitious character. I want the reader to be left with the feeling—it has just the right flavour—that these are remarkably lifelike puppets going back into the box. I want them to act like real people in the reader's imagination for a time, but I want them to begin by seeming made up and to end by seeming made up. I take the tragic view of the tragic view of character.

JOHN BARTH
Letters from LETTERS

A: Lady Amherst to the Author. *Inviting him to
accept an honorary doctorate of letters from Marshyhope
State University. An account of the history of that
institution*

Office of the Provost
Faculty of Letters
Marshyhope State University
Redmans Neck, Maryland 21612

8 March 1969

Mr John Barth, Esq., Author

Dear sir:
    At the end of the current semester, Marshyhope State University
will complete the seventh academic year since its founding in 1962 as
Tidewater Technical College. In that brief time we have grown from a
private vocational-training school with an initial enrollment of thirteen
students, through annexation as a four-year college in the state university
system, to our present status (effective a month hence, at the beginning
of the next fiscal year) as a full-fledged university centre with a projected
population of 50,000 by 1976.

To mark this new elevation, at our June commencement ceremonies we shall exercise for the first time one of its perquisites, the awarding of honorary degrees. Specifically, we shall confer one honorary doctorate in each of Law, Letters, and Science. It is my privilege, on behalf of the faculty, (Acting) President Schott, and the board of regents of the state university, to invite you to be with us 10 A.M. Saturday, 21 June 1969, in order that we may confer upon you the degree of Doctor of Letters, *Honoris Causa*. Sincerely hopeful that you will honour us by accepting the highest distinction that Marshyhope can confer, and looking forward to a favourable reply, I am,

Yours sincerely,

Germaine G. Pitt (Amherst)
Acting Provost

GGP(A)/ss

P.S.: A red-letter day on my personal calendar, this—the first in too long, dear Mr B., but never mind *that!*—and do forgive both this presumptuous postscriptum and my penmanship: some things I cannot entrust to my 'good right hand' of a secretary (a hand dependent, I have reason to suspect, more from the arm of our esteemed acting president than from my arm, on which she'd like nothing better, if I have your American slang aright, than to 'put the finger') and so must pen as it were with my left, quite as I've been obliged by Fate and History—my own, England's, Western Culture's—to swallow pride and

But see how in the initial sequence (*my* initial sequence) I transgress my vow not to go on about myself, like those dotty women 'of a certain age' who burden the patience of novelists and doctors—their circumstantial ramblings all reducible, I daresay, to one cry: 'Help! Love me! I grow old!' Already you cluck your tongue, dear Mr-B.-whom-I-do-not-know (if indeed you've read me even so far): life is too short, you say, to suffer fools and frustrates, especially of the prolix variety. Yet it is you, sir, who, all innocent, provoke this stammering postscript: for nothing else than the report of your impatience with just this sort of letters conceived my vow to make known my business to you *tout de suite*, and nothing other than that vow effected so to speak its own miscarriage. So perverse, so helpless the human heart!

And yet bear on, I pray. I am...what I am (rather, what I find to my own dismay I am become; I was not always so...): old schoolmarm rendered fatuous by lonliness, indignified by stillborn dreams, I prate like a 'coed' on her first 'date'—and this to a man not merely my junior, but... No matter.

I *will* be brief! I *will* be frank! Mr B.: but for the opening paragraphs

of your recentest, which lies before me, I know your writings only at
second hand, a lacuna in my own life story which the present happy circumstances gives occasion for me to amend. Take no offence at this
remissness: for one thing, I came to your country, as did your novels to
mine, not very long since, and neither visitor sojourns heart-on-sleeve. A
late good friend of mine (himself a Nobel laureate in literature) once
declared to me, when I asked him why he would not read his contem-
poraries—

But Germaine, Germaine, this is not germane! as my ancestor and
namesake Mme de Staël must often have cried to herself. I can do no
better than to rebegin with one of her own (or was it Pascal's?) charming
openers: 'Forgive me this too long letter; I had not time to write a short.'
And you yourself—so I infer from the heft of your *oeuvre*, stacked here
upon my 'early American' writing desk, to which, straight upon the close
of this postscript, I will address me, commencing with your earliest and
never ceasing till I shall have overtaken as it were the present point of
your pen—you yourself are not, of contemporary authors, the most
sparing...

To business! *Cher Monsieur* (is it French or German-Swiss, your
name? From the lieutenant who led against the Bastille in *Great-
great-great-great-grand-mère's* day, or the late theologian of our own?
Either way, sir, we are half-countrymen, for all you came to light in Maryland's Dorset and I in England's: may this hors d'oeuvre keep your
appetite for the entrée whilst I make short work of soup and salad!)...

Salad of laurels, sir! Sibyl-greens, Daphne's death-leaves, honorific
if worn lightly, fatal if swallowed! I seriously pray you will take it, this
'highest honour that Marshyhope can bestow'; I pray you will not take it
seriously! O this sink, this slough, this Eastern Shore of Maryland, this
marshy County Dorchester—whence, to be sure, *you* sprang, mallow
from the marsh, as *inter faeces* etc. we are born all. Do please forgive—
whom? How should you have heard of me, who have not read you and yet
nominated you for the M.U.Litt D.? I have exposed myself already; then
let me introduce me: Germaine Pitt I, née Gordon, Lady Amherst, late of
that *other* Dorset (I mean Hardy's) and sweeter Cambridge, now 'Distinguished Visiting Lecturer in English' (to my ear, the *only* resident
speaker of that tongue) and Acting (!) Provost of Make-Believe University's Factory of Letters, as another late friend of mine might have put it:
a university not so much pretentious as pretending, a toadstool blown
overnight from this ordurous swamp to broadcast doctorates like spores,
before the stationer can amend our letterhead!

I shall not tire you with the procession of misfortunes which, since
the end of the Second War, has fetched me from the ancestral seats of the
Gordons and the Amhersts—where three hundred years ago is reckoned
as but the day before yesterday, and the 17th-Century Earls of Dorset are

gossipped of as if still living—to this misnamed shire (try to explain, to
your stout 'down-countian,' that *-chester⟨castra* = camp, and that thus
Dorchester, etymologically as well as by historical precendent, ought to
name the seat rather than the county! As well try to teach Miss Sneak my
secretary why *Mr* and *Dr* need no stops after), which sets about the celebration this July of its tercentenary as if 1669 were classical antiquity. Nor
shall I with my passage from the friendship—more than friendship!—of
several of the greatest novelists of our century, to the supervisal of their
desecration in Modern Novel 101-102: a decline the sadder for its paral-
lelling that of the genre itself; perhaps (God forfend) of Literature as a
whole; perhaps even (the prospect blears in the eyes of these...yes...
colonials!) of the precious Word. These adversities I bear with what
courage I can draw from the example of my favourite forebear, who,
harassed by Napoleon, abused by her lovers, ill-served by friends who
owed their fortunes to her good offices, nevertheless maintained to the
end that animation, generosity of spirit, and brilliance of wit which make
her letters my solace and inspiration. But in the matter of the honorary
doctorate and my—blind—insistence upon your nomination therefor, I
shall speak to you with a candour which, between a Master of Arts and
their lifelong Mistress, I must trust not to miscarry; for I cannot imagine
your regarding a distinction so wretched on the face of it otherwise than
with amused contempt, and yet upon your decision to accept or decline
ride matters of some (and, it may be, more than local) consequence.

Briefly, briefly. A tiny history of 'Redneck Tech' has been a seven-
year battle between the most conservative elements in the state—
principally local, for, as you know, Mason and Dixon's line may be said to
run north and south in Maryland, up Chesapeake Bay, and the Eastern
Shore is more Southern than Virginia—and most 'liberal' (mainly not
native, as the natives do not fail to remark), who in higher latitudes would
be adjudged cautious moderates at best. The original college was
endowed by a local philanthropist, now deceased: an excellent gentleman
whose fortune, marvellous to tell, derived from *pickles*...and whose
politics were so Tory that, going quite crackers in his final years, the dear
fellow fancied himself to be, not Napoleon but *George III*, still fighting the
American Revolution as his 'saner' neighbours still refight your Civil
War. His Majesty's board of trustees was composed exclusively of his
relatives, friends and business associates—several of whom, however,
were of more progressive tendencies, and sufficiently influential in this
Border State to have some effect on the affairs of the institution even after
it joined the state university complex. Indeed, it was they who pressed
most vigorously, against much opposition, to bring the college under
state administration in the first place, hoping thereby to rescue it from
parochial reaction; and the president of the college during these first
stages of its history was a man of respectable academic credentials and
reasonably liberal opinions, their appointee: the historian Joseph

Morgan.

To console the Tories, however, one John Schott—formerly head of a nearby teachers college and a locally famous right-winger—was appointed provost of the Faculty of Letters and vice-president of (what now was awkwardly denominated) Marshyhope State University College. A power struggle ensued at once, for Dr Schott is as politically ambitious as he is ideologically conservative, and had readily accepted what might seem a less prestigious post because he foresaw, correctly, that MSUC was destined for gigantic expansion, and he sensed, again correctly, opportunity in the local resentment against its 'liberal' administration.

In the years thereafter, every forward-looking proposal of President Morgan's, from extending visitation privileges in the residence halls to defending a professor's right to lecture upon the history of revolution, was opposed not only be conservative faculty and directors of the Tidewater Foundation (as the original college's board of trustees renamed itself) but by the regional press, state legislators, and county officials, all of whom cited Schott in support of their position. The wonder is that Morgan survived for even a few semesters in the face of such harassment, especially when his critics found their Sweet Singer in the person of one A.B. Cook VI, self-styled Laureate of Maryland, of whom alas more later—I daresay you know of that formidable charlatan and his mind-abrading doggerel, e.g.:

Fight, Marylanders, nail and tooth,
For John Schott and his Tow'r of Truth, etc.

Which same tower, presently under construction, was the gentle Morgan's undoing. He had-aided by the reasonable T.F. trustees, more enlightened state legislators, and that saving remant of civilised folk tied by family history and personal sentiment to the shire of their birth—managed after all to weather storms of criticism and effect some modest improvements in the quality of instruction at Marshyhope. Moreover, despite grave misgivings about academic gigantism, Morgan believed that the only hope for real education in such surroundings was to make the college the largest institutional and economic entity in the area, and so had led the successful negotiation to make Marshyhope a university centre: not a replica of the state university's vast campus on the mainland, but a smaller, well-funded research centre for outstanding undergraduate and postgraduate students from throughout the university system: academically rigorous, but loosely structured and cross-disciplinary. So evident were the economic blessings of this coup to nearly everyone in the area, Morgan's critics were reduced to grumbling about the radical effects that an influx of some seven thousand 'outsiders' was bound to have on the Dorset Way of Life—and Schott & Co were obliged to seek fresh ground for their attack.

They found it in the Tower of Truth. If the old isolation of Dorchester was to be sacrificed any road on the altar of economic progress (so their argument ran), why stop at seven thousand students—a kind of academic elite at that, more than likely long-haired radicals from Baltimore or even farther north? Why not open the doors to *all* our tidewater sons and daughters, up to the number of, say, seven times seven thousand? Fill in sevenfold more marshy acreage; make seven times over the fortunes of wetland realtors and building contractors; septuple the jobs available to Dorchester's labour force; build on Redman's Neck a veritable City of Learning, more populous (and prosperous) by far than any of the peninsula's actual municipalities! And from its centre let there rise, as a symbol (and advertisement) of the whole, Marshyhope's beacon to the world: a great white tower, the Tower of Truth! By day the university's main library, perhaps, and (certainly) the seat of its administration, let it be by night floodlit and visible from clear across the Chesapeake—from (in Schott's own pregnant phrase) 'Annapolis at least, maybe even Washington!'

In vain Morgan's protests that seven thousand dedicated students, housed in tasteful, low-profile buildings on the seven hundred acres of farmland already annexed by MSUC, represented the maximum reasonable burden on the ecology and sociology of the county, and the optimal balance of economic benefits and academic manageability; that Schott's 'Tower of Truth', like the projected diploma mill it represented, would violate the natural terrain; that the drainage of so much marsh would be an ecological disaster, the influx of so huge a population not a stimulus to the Dorset Way of Life but a cataclysmic shock; that both skyscrapers and ivory towers were obsolete ideals; that even if they weren't, no sane contractor would attempt such a structure on the spongy ground of a fresh filled fen, et cetera. In veritable transports of bad faith, the Schott/Cook party rhapsodised that Homo sapiens himself—especially in his rational, civilised, university-founding aspect—was the very embodiment of 'anti-naturalness': towering erect instead of creeping on all fours, opposing reason to brute instinct, aspiring ever to what was deemed beyond his grasp, raising from the swamp primordial great cities, lofty cathedrals, towers of learning. How were the fenny origins invoked of Rome! How *learning* was rhymed with *yearning, Tow'r of Truth* with *Flow'r of Youth!* How was excoriated, in editorial and Rotary Club speech, 'the Morgan theory' (which he never held) that the university should be a little model of the actual world rather than a lofty counterexample: lighthouse to the future, ivory tower to the present, castle keep of the past!

Cook's rhetoric, all this, sweetly resounding in our Chambers of Commerce, where too there were whispered libels against the luckless Morgan: that his late wife had died a dozen years past in circumstances never satisfactorily explained, which however had led to Morgan's 'resignation' from his first teaching post, at Wicomico Teachers College; that his absence from the academic scene between that dismissal (by Schott himself, as ill-chance would have it, who damningly refused to comment on the matter, declaring only that 'every man deserves a second chance') and his surprise appointment by Harrison Mack II as first president of Tidewater Tech was not unrelated to that dark affair. By 1967, when Morgan acquiesced to the Tower of Truth in hopes of saving his plan for a manageable, high-quality research centre, the damage to his reputation had been done, by locker-room couplets of unacknowledged but unmistakeable authorship:

> Here is the late Mrs Morgan interred,
> Whose *ménage à trois* is reduced by one-third
> Her husband and lover survive her, both fired:
> *Requiescat in pacem* the child they both sired, etc.

In July of last he resigned, ostensibly to return to teaching and research, and in fact is a visiting professor of American History this year at the college in Massachusetts named after my late husband's famous ancestor—or was until his disappearance some weeks ago. John Schott became acting president—and what a vulgar act is his!—and yours truly, who has no taste for administrative service even under decent chiefs like Morgan, but could not bear to see MSUC's governance altogether in Boeotian hands, was prevailed upon to act as provost of the Faculty of Letters.

How came Schott to choose me, you ask, who am through these hopeless marshes but (I hope) the briefest of sojourners? Surely because he rightly distrusts all his ordinary faculty, and wrongly supposes that, visitor and woman to boot, I can be counted upon passively to abet his accession to the actual presidency of MSU—from which base (read 'tow'r' and weep for Marshyhope, for Maryland!) he will turn his calculating eyes to Annapolis, 'maybe even Washington'! Yet he does me honour by enough distrusting my gullibility after all to leave behind as mine his faithful secretary-at-least: Miss Shirley Stickles, sharp of eye and pencil if not of mind, to escape whose surveillance I am brought to penning by hand this sorry history of your nomination.

Whereto, patient Mr B., we are come! For scarce had I aired against my tenancy the provostial chamber (can you name another university president who smokes cigars?) when there was conveyed to me, via his minatory and becorseted *derrière-garde*, my predecessor's expectation, not only that I would appoint at once a nominating committee for the proposed Litt.D. (that is, a third member, myself being already on the committee *ex officio* and Schott having appointed, by some dim prerogative, a second: one Harry Carter, former psychologist, present nonentity and academic vice-president, Schott's creature), but that, after a show of nomination weighing, we would present to the board of regents as our candidate the 'Maryland Laureate' himself, Mr Andrew Cook!

Schott's strategy is clear: to achieve some 'national visibility,' as they say, with his eyesore of a Tower; a degree of leverage (in *honoris causa!*) in the state legislature with his honorary doctorates (the LL.D., of course, will go to the governor, or the local congressman); and the applause of the regional right with his laurelling of the hardy rhymer of 'marsh mallow' and 'beach swallow'—a man one could indeed simply laugh at, were there no sinister side to his right-winged wrongheadedness and his rape of Mother English.

Counterstrategy I had none; nor motive, at first, beyond mere literary principle. Unacquainted with your work (and that of most of your countrymen), my first candidates were writers most honoured already in my own heart: Mrs Lessing perhaps, even Miss Murdoch; or the Anthony Powell or Burgess. To the argument (advanced at once by Dr Carter) that none of these has connexion with MSUC, I replied that 'connexions' should have no connexion with honours. Yet I acceded to the gentler suasion of my friend, colleague, and committee appointee Mr Ambrose Mensch (whom I believe you know?): Marshyhope being not even a national, far less an international, institution, it were presumptuous of us to think to honour as it were beyond our means (literally so, in the matter of transatlantic air fares). He then suggested such Americans as one Mr Styron, who has roots in Virginia, and a Mr Updike, formerly of Pennsylvania. But I replied, cordially, that once the criterion of mere merit was put by, to honour a writer for springing from a neighbouring state made no more sense that to do so for his springing from a neighbouring shire, or civilisation. Indeed the principle of 'appropriateness', on which we now agreed if on little else, was really Carter's 'connexion' in more palatable guise: as we were in fact a college of the state university and so far specifically regional, perhaps we could after all do honour without presumption only to a writer, scholar, or journalist with connexion to the Old Line State, preferably to the Eastern Shore thereof?

On these friendly deliberations between Mr Mensch and myself, Dr Carter merely smiled, prepared in any case to vote negatively on all nominations except A.B. Cook's, which he had put before us in the opening minutes of our opening session. I should add that, there being in the bylaws of the college and of the faculty as yet no provision for the nomination of candidates for honorary degrees, our procedure was *ad hoc* as our committee; but I was given to understand, by Sticklish insinuation, that if our nomination were not unanimous and soon forthcoming, Schott would empower his academic vice-president to form a new committee; further, that if our choice proved displeasing to the administration, the Faculty of Letters could expect no budgetary blessings next fiscal. Schott himself, with more than customary tact, merely declared to me his satisfaction, at this point in our discussions, that we had decided to honour a native son...

'*I.e.*, the Fair-Land Muse himself,' Mr Mensch dryly supposed on hearing this news (the epithet from Cook's own rhyme for Maryland, in its local two-syllable pronunciation). I then conveyed to him, and do now to you, in both instances begging leave not to reveal my source, that I had good reason to believe that beneath his boorish, even ludicrous, public posturing, Andrew Burlingame Cook VI (his full denomination!) is a dark political power, in 'Mair'land' and beyond: not a kingmaker, but a maker and unmaker of kingmakers: a man behind the men behind the scenes, with whose support it was, alas, not unimaginable after all that John Schott might one day cross the Bay to 'Annapolis, maybe even Washington.' To thwart Cook's nomination, then, and haply thereby to provoke his displeasure with our acting president, might be to strike a blow, at least a tap, for decent government!

I speak lightly, sir (as did Germaine de Staël even in well-founded fear of her life), but the matter is not without gravity. This Cook is a menace to more than the art of poetry, and any diminution of his public 'cover', even by denying him an honour he doubtless has his reasons for desiring, is a move in the public weal.

And now I believe, what I would not have done a fortnight past, that with your help—*i.e.*, your 'aye'—he may be denied. 'Of course,' Mr Mensch remarked to me one evening, 'there's always my old friend B....' I asked (excuse me) whom that name might name, and was told: not only that you were born and raised hereabouts, made good your escape, and from a fit northern distance set your first novels in this area, but that my friend himself—*our* friend— was at that moment under contract to write a screenplay of your newest book, to be filmed on location in the county. How would your name strike Carter, Schott, and company? It just might work, good Ambrose thought, clearly now warming to his inspiration and wondering aloud why he hadn't hit on it before—especially since, though he'd not corresponded with you for years, he was immersed in your fiction; is indeed on leave from teaching this semester to draft that screenplay.

In sum, it came (and comes) to this: John Schott's appointment to the presidency of MSU is quietly opposed, in our opinion, by moderate elements on the board of regents and the Tidewater Foundation, and it can be imagined that, among the more knowledgeable of these elements, this opposition extends to the trumpeting false laureate as well. Their support comes from the radical right and, perversely, the radical left (that minority of two or three bent on destroying universities altogether as perpetuators of bourgeois values). A dark-horse nominee of the right colouration might just slip between this Scylla and this Charybdis.

Very casually we tried your name on Harry Carter, and were

pleased to observe in his reaction more suspicious curiosity than actual opposition. This curiosity, moreover, turned into guarded interest when Ambrose pointed out (as if the thought had just occurred to him) that the 'tie-in' at our June commencement of the filming of your book and the county's Tercentennial (itself to involve some sort of feature on 'Dorchester in Art and Literature') would no doubt occasion publicity for Marshyhope U. and the Tower of Truth. He, Ambrose—he added with the straightest of faces—might even be able to work into the film itself some footage of the ceremonies, and the Tower...

This was last week. Our meeting ended with a sort of vote: two-nothing in favour of your nomination, Dr Carter abstaining. To my surprise, the acting president's reaction, relayed through both Dr Carter and Miss Stickles, is cautious nondisapproval, and today I am authorised to make the invitation.

You are, then, sir, by way of being a compromise candidate, who will, I hope, so far from feeling therein compromised, come to the aid of your friend, your native county, and its 'largest single economic [and *only* cultural] entity' by accepting this curious invitation. Moreover, by accepting it promptly, before the opposition (some degree of which is to be expected) has time to rally. That Schott even tentatively permits this letter implies that A.B. Cook VI has been sounded out and, for whatever mysterious reasons, chooses not to exercise his veto out of hand. But Ambrose informs me, grimly, that there is a 'Dr Schott' in some novel of yours, too closely resembling ours for coincidence, and not flatteringly drawn: should he get wind of this fact (Can it be true? Too delicious!) before your acceptance has been made public.

Au revoir, then, friend of my friend! I hold your first novel in my hand, eager to embark upon it; in your own hand you may hold some measure of our future here (think what salubrious effect a few well-chosen public jibes at the 'Tow'r of Truth' and its tidewater laureate might have, televised live from Redmans Neck on Commencement Day!). Do therefore respond at your earliest to this passing odd epistle, whose tail like the spermatozoon's far outmeasures its body, the better to accomplish its single urgent end, and—like Molly Bloom at the close of *her* great soliloquy (whose author was, yes, a friend of your friend's friend)—say to us *yes*, to the Litt.D. *yes* to MSU *yes*, and *yes* Dorchester, *yes* Tidewater, Maryland *yes yes yes!*

Yours,
GGP(A)

G: The Author to the Reader. LETTERS *is 'now'*
begun.

'March 2, 1969'

Dear Reader, and
    Gentles all: *LETTERS* is now begun, its correspondents introduced
and their stories commencing to entwine. Like those films whose credits
appear after the action has started, it will now pause.
    If 'now' were the date above, I should be writing this from Buffalo,
New York, on a partly sunny Sunday mild for that area in that season,
when Lake Erie is still frozen and the winter's heaviest snowfall yet
ahead. On the 61st day of the 70th year of the 20th century of the Chris-
tian calendar, the human world and its American neighborhood, having
survived, in the main, the shocks of '1968' and its predecessors, stood
such-a-way: Clay Shaw was acquitted on a charge of involvement in the
assassination of President John Kennedy, Sirhan Sirhan was pleading in
vain to be executed for assassinating Senator Robert Kennedy, and
James Earl Ray was about to be convicted of assassinating the Reverend
Martin Luther King, Jr. Ex-President Dwight Eisenhower was weakening
toward death after abdominal surgery in February; ex-President Lyndon
Johnson, brought down by the Viet Nam War, had retired to Texas; his
newly inaugurated successor, Richard M. Nixon, was in Paris conferring
with French President de Gaulle and considering the Pentagon's new
antiballistic missile program. The North Vietnamese were pressing a
successful offensive toward Saigon while the Paris peace conference
—finally begun in January after the long dispute over seating arrange-
ments—entered Week Six of its four-year history. Everywhere university
students were rioting: the Red Guard was winding up Mao's Cultural
Revolution in China; the University of Rome was closed; martial law had
been imposed here and there in Spain, tear gas and bayonets in Berkeley
and Madison; in Prague students were burning themselves alive to protest Soviet occupation of their country. Hostility between the Russians
and the Chinese was on the verge of open warfare at the border of Sink-
iang Province; along Israel's borders with Egypt, Syria, and Jordan,
things once again had crossed that verge. The U.S.S. *Pueblo* inquiry,
souvenir of one war ago, was still in progress. The Apollo-9 spacecraft
was counting down for launch toward its moon-orbiting mission, the
French-British *Concorde* for the first supersonic transport flight, both to
be accomplished on the following day. Ribonuclease, the 'key to life,' had
just been synthesized for the first time in a chemical laboratory; in
another, also for the first time, a human egg was successfully fertilized
outside the human body. The economy of the United States was inflating

at a slightly higher annual rate than the 4.7% of 1968, which had been the highest in seventeen years; the divorce rate was the highest since 1945. Having affirmed the legality of student protest 'within limits,' our Supreme Court was deciding on the other hand to permit much broader use of electronic surveillance devices by law-enforcement agencies. Every fourth day of the year, on the average, an airliner had been hijacked: fifteen so far. Before the month expired, so would Mr. Eisenhower; and before the year, Senator Everett Dirksen, Levi Eshkol, Ho Chi Minh, and Mary Jo Kopechne, with difficult consequences for Senator Edward Kennedy. Tom Mboya would be assassinated in Nairobi, Sharon Tate and her friends massacred in California, large numbers of Southeast Asians in Southeast Asia. Sirhan Sirhan would be sentenced to death, James Earl Ray to 99 years' imprisonment; Charles Manson and Family would be arrested and charged with the Tate killings, but the Green Beret murder trails would be dropped when the C.I.A. forbade its implicated agents to testify. Ave Fortas would resign from the U.S. Supreme Court and be replaced by Warren Burger, whose court (in opposition to President Nixon) would order immediate desegragation of Southern schools and soften the penalties for possession of marijuana; the U.S. Court of Appeals would reverse the 1968 conviction of Dr. Benjamin Spock and his alleged coconspirators; and Judge Julius Hoffman would begin the trial of the Chicago Seven for inciting riot at the 1968 Democratic National Convention. The Russian-Chinese border fighting would be 'resolved' by talks between Aleksei Kosygin and Chou En-lai, and Chairman Mao would declare the Cultural Revolution accomplished. While the Paris peace talks reached an impasse, the cost to the United States of the Viet-Nam War would reach 100 billion dollars, fresh U.S. atrocities would be reported, the draft lottery would begin, the first contingent of American troops would be withdrawn from South Viet Nam, the Defense Department would deny, untruthfully, the presence and activity of U.S. forces in Laos, the student riots, strikes, and building seizures would spread to every major campus in the nation, and a quarter-million demonstrators, the largest such crowd in the 193 years of the Republic, would march in Washington on the occasion of the 'Moratorium.' U.S. forces in Spain would practice putting down a hypothetical anti-Franco uprising; U Thant would declare the Mideast to be in a state of war; the British Army would take over the policing of Northern Ireland after a resurgence of warfare between Catholics and Protestants; China would explode thermonuclear test weapons in the atmosphere; the U.S. and Russia would reply with underground thermonuclear explosions of their own, in the Aleutians and Siberia, and begin arms-limitation conferences in Helsinki. President Ayub would resign in Pakistan, Georges Pompidou would succeed Charles de Gaulle in France, Golda Meir the late Levi Eshkol in Israel, and a military junta the deposed president of Bolivia. Nixon would lift the ban on arms sales to Peru (and meet with President Thieu on Midway, and exercise his broader 'bugging' rights against political dissenters, and postpone the fall desegregation deadline for Southern schools, and close the Job Corps camps, and visit South Viet Nam, and greet the returning Apollo-11 astronauts aboard the U.S.S. *Hornet*). Those latter, and their successors in Apollo-12, would have left the first human footprints on the moon and fetched home a number of its rocks to prove it, despite which evidence a great many Americans would half-believe the whole exploit to have been faked by their government and the television networks; the Mariner spacecrafts 6 and 7 would photograph canalless, lifeless Mars; Russia's Venus 5 and 6 would reach their namesake planet and reveal it also to be devoid of life. The New York State legislature would defeat a liberalized abortion bill. Complete eyes would join hearts and kidneys on the growing list of successfully transplanted human parts. The Department of Health, Education, and Welfare would recommend an absolute ban on the use of DDT. Unemployment, inflation, prime-interest, and first-class-postage rates would rise in the United States, the stock market plunge; 900 heroin deaths, mostly of young people, would be reported in New York City; the Netherlands would temporarily shut off public water when U.S. nerve gas accidentally poisoned the Rhine. Dorchester County, Maryland, would celebrate its Tercentenary; fire would melt a wax museum at Niagara Falls, and the American Falls itself would be turned off for engineering surveys. At least six more airliners would be hijacked; Thor Heyerdahl in *Ra I* would embark upon the Atlantic, along with tropical storms Anna, Blanche, Carol, Debbie, Eve, Francelia, Gerda, *et al.*; in East Pakistan a child would be swallowed by a python; the National Committee on Violence would describe the 1960's as one of the most violent decades in United States history, but the French wine-growers association would declare '69 a vintage year.

But every letter has two times, that of its writing and that of its reading, which may be so separated, even when the post office does its job, that very little of what obtained when the writer wrote will still when the reader reads. And to the units of epistolary fictions yet a third time is added: the actual date of composition, which will not likely correspond to the letterhead date, a function more of plot or form than of history. It is *not* March 2, 1969: when I began this letter it was October 30, 1973: an inclement Tuesday morning in Baltimore, Maryland. The Viet Nam War was 'over'; its peacemakers were honoured with the Nobel Prize; the latest Arab-Israeli war, likewise 'over,' had preempted our attention, even more so the 'energy crisis' it occasioned, and the Watergate scandals and presidential-impeachment moves—from which neither of those other crises perfectly diverted us. The campuses were quiet; the peacetime draft had ended; détente had been declared with Russia and proposed with China—unthinkable in 1969!—but the American defense budget was more enormous than ever. In Northern Ireland the terrorism continued; the generals had taken over in Greece and Chile, and Juan Perón was back in Argentina; Sirhan Sirhan and James Earl Ray were still in jail, joined by Charles Manson and Lieutenant Calley of the My Lai massacre. The Apollo space program was finished; there would not likely be another human being on the moon in this century. We were anticipating the arrival of the newly discovered comet Kohoutek, which promised to be the most spectacular sight in the sky for many decades. Meanwhile the U.S. Supreme Court had struck down all antiabortion laws but retreated from its liberal position on pornography, and the retrials of the Chicago Seven had begun. The prime interest rate was up to 10%, the Dow-Jones Industrial Average, after a bad year, up to 980, first-class postage up to eight cents an ounce. Airport security measures had virtually eliminated skyjacking except by Palestinian terrorists; the 'fuel shortage,' in turn, was occasioning the elimination of many airline flights. Plans for the 1976 U.S. Bicentennial were floundering.

Now it's not 10/30/73 any longer, either. In the time between my first setting down 'March 2, 1969' and now, 'now' has become January 1974. Nixon won't go away; neither will the 'energy crisis' or inflation-plus-recession or the dreadfulnesses of nations and their ongoing history. The other astronomical flop, Kohoutek, will return in 75,000 years, as may we all. By the time I reach *Yours Truly*....

The plan of *LETTERS* calls for a second Letter to the Reader at the end of the manuscript, by when what I've 'now' recorded will seem already as remote as 'March 2, 1969.' By the time *LETTERS* is in print, ditto for what shall be recorded in that final letter. And—to come at last to the last of a letter's times—by the time *your* eyes, Reader, review these epistolary fictive *a*'s-to-*z*'s, the 'United States of America' may be setting about its Tri- or Quadricentennial, or be still floundering through its Bi-, or be a mere memory (may it have become again, in that case, like the first half of one's life, at least a pleasant memory). Its citizens and the planet's, not excepting yourself and me, may all be mainly just a few years older. Or perhaps you're yet to have been conceived, and by the 'now' your eyes read *now*, every person now alive upon the earth will be no longer, most certainly not excepting.

Yours truly,

N: The Author to Lady Amherst. *Politely declining her invitation.*

Department of English Annex B
State University of New York at Buffalo
Buffalo, New York 14214

March 16, 1969

Prof. Germaine G. Pitt (Amherst)
Acting Provost, Faculty of Letters
Marshyhope State University
Redmans Neck, Maryland 21612

Dear Professor Pitt (Amherst?):

Not many invitations could please me more, ordinarily, than yours of March 8. Much obliged, indeed.

By coincidence, however, I accepted in February a similar invitation from the main campus of the State University at College Park (it seems to be my year down there), and I feel that two degrees in the same June from the same Border State would border upon redundancy. So I decline, with thanks, and trust that the ominous matters you allude to in your remarkable postscript can be forestalled in some other wise.

Why not award the thing to our mutual acquaintance Ambrose Mensch? He's an honorable, deserving oddball and a bona fide avant-gardist, whose 'career' I've followed with interest and sympathy. A true 'doctor of letters' (in the Johns Hopkins Medical School sense), he is a tinkerer, an experimenter, a slightly astigmatic visionary, perhaps even a revolutionizer of cures—and patient Literature, as your letter acknowledges, if not terminal, is not as young as she used to be either.

Cordially,

P.S.: 'I have made this longer only because I did not have the leisure to make it shorter': Pascal, *Letters provinciales,* XVI. Perhaps Mme de Staël was paraphrasing Pascal?

P.P.S.: Do the French not customarily serve the salad *after* the entrée?

E: The Author to Lady Amherst. *A counterinvitation.*

Department of English, Annex B
State University of New York at Buffalo
Buffalo, New York 14214

March 23, 1969

Prof. Germaine G. Pitt (Amherst)
Acting Provost, Faculty of Letters
Marshyhope State University
Redmans Neck, Maryland 21612

Dear Professor Pitt (Amherst):

Ever since your letter of March 8, I have been bemused by two coincidences (if that is the word) embodied in it, of a more vertiginous order than the simple coincidence of the College Park invitation, which I had already accepted, and yours from Marshyhope, which I felt obliged therefore to decline in my letter to you of last Sunday.

The first coincidence is that, some months before the *earlier* invitation—last year, in fact, when I began making notes toward a new novel—I had envisioned just such an invitation to one of its principal characters. Indeed, an early note for the project (undated, but from mid-1968) reads as follows:

A man (A—?) is writing letters to a woman (Z—?). A is 'a little past the middle of the road,' but feels that 'the story of his life is just beginning,' *in medias res.* Z is (*a*) Nymph, (*b*) Bride, and (*c*) Crone; also Muse: i.e., *Belles Lettres.* A is a 'Doctor of Letters' (honorary Litt. D.): degree awarded for 'contribution to life of literature.' Others allege he's hastening its demise; would even charge him with malpractice. Etc.

Then arrived in the post the College Park invitation in February and yours in March. I was spooked more by the second than the first, since it came not only from another Maryland university, but from—well, consider this other notebook entry, under the heading 'Plot A: Lady _____ & the Litt. D.':

A (British?) belletrist 'of a certain age,' she has been the Great Good Friend of sundry distinguished authors, perhaps even the original of certain of their heroines and the inspiration of their novels. Sometimes intimates that *she* invented their best conceptions, her famous lovers merely transcribing as it were her conceits, fleshing out her ideas—and not always faithfully (i.e., 'doctoring' her letters to them). Etc.

This circa September 1968. Then, two weeks ago, your letter, with its extraordinary postscript....

Hence my bemusement. For autobiographical 'fiction' I have only disdain; but what's involved here strikes me less as autobiography than as a muddling of the distinction between Art and Life, a boundary as historically notorious as Mason and Dixon's line. That life sometimes imitates art is a mere Oscar Wilde-ish curiosity; that it should set about to do so in such unseemly haste that between notes and novel (not to mention between the drafted and the printed page) what had been fiction becomes idle fact, invention history—disconcerting! Especially to a fictionist who, like yours truly, had long since turned his professional back on literary realism in favor of the fabulous irreal, and only in this latest enterprise had projected, not without misgiving a détente with the realistic tradition. It is as if Reality, a mistress too long ignored, must now settle scores with her errant lover.

So, my dear Lady Amherst: this letter—my second to you, ninth in the old *New England Primer*—is an *In-vi-ta-ti-on* which, whether or not you see fit to accept it, I pray you will entertain as considerately as I hope I entertained yours of the 8th instant: Will you consent to be A Character in My Novel? That is, may I—in the manner of novelists back in the heroic period of the genre—make use of my imagination of you (and whatever information about yourself it may suit your discretion to provide in response to certain questions I have in mind to ask you) to 'flesh out' that character aforenoted? Just as you, from *my* side of this funhouse mirror, seem to have plagiarized my imagination in your actual life story...

The request is irregular. For me it is unprecedented —though for all I know it may be routine to an erstwhile friend of Wells, Joyce, Huxley. What I'd like to know is more about your history; your connection with those eminent folk; that 'fall' you allude to in your postscript, from such connection to your present circumstances at MSUC; even (as a 'lifelong mistress of the arts' you will surely understand) more delicate matters. If I'm going to break another lance with Realism, I mean to go the whole way.

I am tempted to make your acquaintance directly, prevailing upon our mutual friend to do the honors; I'd meant to pay a visit to Dorchester anyhow in June, from College Park. But I recall and understand Henry James's disinclination to hear *too much* of an anecdote the heart of which he recognized as a potential story. Moreover, in keeping with my (still vague) notion of the project, I should prefer that our connection be not only strictly verbal, but epistolary. Cf. James's notebook exclamation: 'The correspondences! The correspondences!'

Here's what I can tell you of that project. For as long as I can remember I've been enamored of the old tale-cycles, especially of the frame tale sort: *The Ocean of Story, The Thousand and One Nights*, the *Pent-*,

Hept-, and *Decamerons*. With the help of a research assistant I recently reviewed the corpus of frame-tale literature to see what I could learn from it, and started making notes toward a frame-tale novel. By 1968 I'd decided to use documents instead of told stories: texts-within-texts instead of tales-within-tales. Rereading the early English novelists, I was impressed with their characteristic awareness that they're *writing*—that their fictions exist in the form, not of sounds in the ear, but of signs on the page, imitative not of life 'directly,' but of its documents—and I considered marrying one venerable narrative tradition to another: the frame-tale and the 'documentary' novel. By this time last year I had in mind 'an open (love) letter to Whom It May Concern, from Yours Truly.' By April, as grist for what final mill I was still by no means certain, I had half a workbookful of specific formal notes and 'incidental felicities': e.g., 'Bit 46,' from Canto XVIII of Dante's *Paradiso*: the choirs of the blessed, like sailors in formation of an aircraft-carrier deck or bandsmen at halftime in an American football match, spell out with themselves on the billboard of Heaven DILIGITE IUSTITIAM QUI IUDICATIS TERRAM ('love justice, [ye] who judge [on] *earth'; or 47, an old English hornbook riddle in the* Kabbalistic tradition of the Holy Unspeakable Name of God: 'AEIOU His Great Name doth Spell;/Here it is known, but is not known in Hell.'

I could go on, and won't. 'The correspondences!' I was ready to begin. All I lacked were—well, characters, theme, plot, action, diction, scene, and format; in short, a story, a way to tell it, and a voice to tell it in!

Now I have a story, at least in rough prospectus, precipitated by this pair of queer coincidences. Or if not a story in Henry James's sense, at least a narrative method in Scheherazade's.

But it is unwise to speak much of plans still tentative. Will you be my 'Lady A,' my heroine, my creation?

And permit *me* the honor of being, as in better-lettered times gone by, your faithful

Author

LETTERS: *an old time epistolary novel by seven fictitious drolls & dreamers, each of which imagines himself actual.* They will write always in this order: Lady Amherst, Todd Andrews, Jacob Horner, A.B. Cook, Jerome Bray, Ambrose Mensch, the Author. Their letters will total 88 (this is the eighth), divided unequally into seven sections according to a certain scheme: see Ambrose Mensch's model, postscript to Letter 86 (Part S, p.770). Their several narratives will become one; like waves of a rising tide, the plot will surge forward, recede, surge farther forward, recede less far, et cetera to its climax and dénouement.

On with the story.

Don David Guttenplan

On the Death of Elizabeth Bishop

Elizabeth Bishop, poet, born and reared in Maine, died this November at the age of sixty-eight. Awarded the Pulitzer Prize in 1955 for a combined edition of *North and South* and *A Cold Spring*, and in 1969 the National Book Award for *The Complete Poems*, Elizabeth Bishop was one of the finest poets of this century.

Robert Lowell said of Elizabeth Bishop:

> She is too sure of herself for empty mastery and breezy plagiarism, too interested for confession...., too powerful for mismanaged fire, and too civilized for idiosyncratic incoherence.

In England, however, her death went largely unnoticed—even *The Times* on its return failed to include her name in its huge obituary sections—and the neglect is, once again, a sad testimony to Britain's insularity. It's sadder—and more sadly ironic—because at the time of her death, Elizabeth Bishop was finally achieving the recognition she deserved, and Britain's seemed finally beginning to recognize not just the existence of her poetry but its value.

Her grace, acuity, and easy command of language make Elizabeth Bishop's writing a delight to both the mind and the ear. The beauty of her line and the dexterity of her rhyme fill the reader who comes to her work with not just pleasure but quiet astonishment. 'I admire compassion, lightness, and agility, all rare in this loose world,' she wrote. Bishop's verse gives short shrift to the national vices of laceration and lamentation. Its chief virtue is justice: accuracy is its most remarkable quality. This should not be taken to suggest that she limits her emotional range. On the

contrary, her ability to combine form and feeling is often breathtaking.
'A Miracle for Breakfast' begins:

> At six o'clock we were waiting for coffee,
> waiting for coffee and the charitable crumb
> that was going to be served from a certain balcony,
>   —like kings of old, or like a miracle.
> It was still dark. One foot of the sun
> steadied itself on a long ripple in the river.
>
> The first ferry of the day has just crossed the river.
> It was so cold we hoped that the coffee
> would be very hot, seeing that the sun
> was not going to warm us; and that the crumb
> would be a loaf each, buttered, by a miracle.

And a nursery rhyme about Ezra Pound entitled 'Visits to St. Elizabeth's'
begins—

> This is the house of Bedlam.
>
> This is the man
> that lies in the house of Bedlam.

—and ends:

> This is the soldier home from the war.
> These are the years and the walls and the door
> that shut on a boy that pats the floor
> to see if the world is round or flat.
> This is the Jew in a newspaper hat
> that dances carefully down the ward,
> walking the plank of a coffin board
> with the crazy sailor
> that shows his watch
> that tells the time
> of the wretched man
> that lies in the house of Bedlam.

Elizabeth Bishop's poetry gives a sense of people, objects, places,
and climate, deeply felt and scrupulously noted. This, for instance, is the
lover in the city:

I hear the day-springs of the morning strike
from stony walls and halls and iron beds,
   scattered or grouped cascades,
   alarms for the expected:

queer cupids of all persons getting up,
whose evening meal they will prepare all day,
   you will dine well
   on his heart, on his, and his,

so send them about your business affectionately,
dragging in the streets their unique loves.
   Scourge them with roses only,
   be light as helium,

for always to one, or several, morning comes,
whose head has fallen over the edge of his bed,
   whose face is turned
   so that the image of

the city grows down into his open eyes
inverted and distorted. No. I mean
   distorted and revealed,
   if he sees it at all.

In 'The Colder the Air', a poem which both reminds one of Emily
Dickinson and weathers the comparison, Bishop describes winter in terms
equally applicable to her own abilities:

The target-center in her eye
is equally her aims and will.

With the death of Elizabeth Bishop, the English language moves
further from the miraculous to the mundane. This is not kindness; it is
simple justice. For posterity to deal justly with Elizabeth Bishop,
it will have to be very generous indeed.

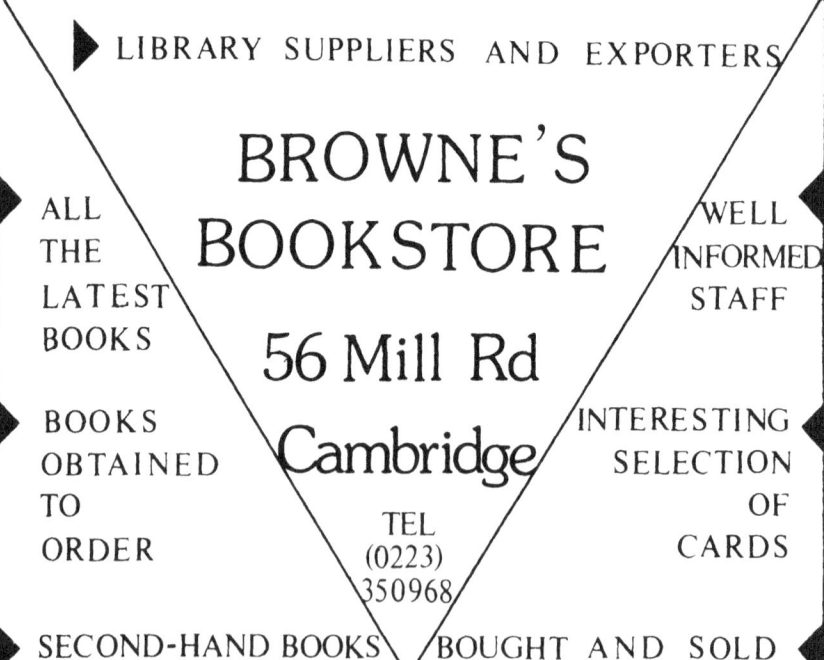

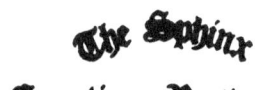

Among the Books Received

I. FICTION.

J.G. Ballard, *The Unlimited Dream Company* (Jonathan Cape, £4.95): Ballard's most optimistic and vividly written book in years.

Donald Barthelme, *Great Days* (Routledge & Kegan Paul, £4.50): sixteen short stories including seven formally related dialogues, one of which, 'The New Music', appeared in Granta's *New American Writing*.

David Black, *Like Father* (Red Dembner Enterprises Corp., New York, $8.95): A moving depiction of the relationship between a son and his father and grandfather.

George Dennison, *Oilers and Sweepers, and Other Stories* (Random House, New York, $7.95): Dennison's first book of fiction which includes three short stories (originally published in *New American Review*), a novella, and a vaudeville play.

Stanley Elkin, *The Living End* (Jonathan Cape, £4.95): In which God, an important character, reveals many things: where He gets His ideas, the name of Kennedy's assassin, the reason children suffer, and how to do the latest disco steps.

Jacob Epstein, *Wild Oats* (The Alison Press, @Secker & Warburg, £5.90): Highly over-rated novel about tough times in college, remarkable for forty pages of reasonable writing.

Barry Hannah, *Airships* (Alfred A. Knopf, New York, $8.95): Winner of the Arnold Gingrich Short Fiction Award, *Airships* is a collection of twenth controversial stories, strongly grounded in the Mississippi idiom and society of the author's upbringing.

Ron Hansen, *Desperadoes* (Alfred A. Knopf, $8.95): Hansen's first novel is the story of the notorious gang, the Daltons, from their beginnings to the final morning when all but one are shot down in the fatal raid on Coffeyville, Kansas. A well-written and serious Western. Really.

Desmond Hogan, *The Ikon Maker* (Writers and Readers Publishing Cooperative, £3.95): A middle-aged woman from Galway sets out to chase down her son, self-exiled in England.

Desmond Hogan, *The Diamonds at the Bottom of the Sea* (Hamish Hamilton, £5.95): A collection of seventeen stories, some lyrical and strongly imaginative, and some over-written to a point verging on indulgence. All show tremendous promise.

Neil Jordan, *Night in Tunisia* (Writers and Readers Publishing Cooperative, £3.95): A re-issue of one of the best short story collections published in quite a while. Winner of the Guardian Fiction Prize.

Charles Simmons, *Wrinkles* (Alison Press, Secker and Warburg, £4.95): A novel consisting of forty-odd biographical sketches, each from one to four pages in length, of an unnamed middle-aged man, and each successively moving from childhood through maturity to old age.

Peter Taylor *In the Miro District* (Alfred A. Knopf, $7.95): First collection in eight years by one of America's best story writers; still without a British publisher.

John Updike, *Problems and Other Stories* (Andre Deutsch, £5.95): New collection of stories, most of which appeared in the *New Yorker*, and all written between 1971 and 1978. Available May 22.

Kurt Vonnegut, *Jailbird* (Jonathan Cape, £5.50): The story of Walter F. Starbuck—the oldest and least-celebrated of the Watergate conspirators—and the strange relationship he renews with Mary Kathleen O'Looney, the ancient remains of the first girl he ever slept with, whose personal effects are carried in six tattered shopping bags and her astronomically large will in her over-sized basketball shoes.

II. NON-FICTION.

Harold Bloom, ed., *Deconstruction and Criticism* (Routledge & Kegan Paul, £8.95): Five essays from the 'Yale School'—De Man, Derrida, Hartman, Hillis Miller, and Bloom—demonstrating the variety and differences in their individual approaches to literature and criticism.

Paul De Man, *Allegories of Reading* (Yale University Press, £12.35): A collection of essays written since the publication of De Man's *Blindness and Insight*, organized around the general theme of figural language. Essays on Nietzsche, Proust, Rilke and Rousseau.

Jacques Derrida, *Spurs, Nietzsche's Styles* (Chicago University Press, £5.40): Derrida's playful essay on his logical precursor. Parallel French text.

Gerald Graff, *A Literature Against Itself* (Chicago University Press, £10.50): A controversial collection of essays, providing a critique of the leading assumptions in recent criticism and fiction, arguing that today's literary 'radicals' are greatly influenced by—and in turn extend—the ethos of a consumer society.

Daniel Hoffman, ed., *Harvard Guide to Contemporary American Writing* (Harvard University Press, £12.95): Twelve essays provide an introduction to, and synopsis of, many aspects of contemporary American writing: experimental, naturalist, Southern and Jewish fiction; black literature; women's literature; drama; poetry; and literary criticism.

Tillie Olsen, *Silences* (Delacorte Press/Seymour Lawrence, $10.95): Essays from the last two decades exploring the problem of literary 'silences' in the careers of both the acknowledged great and those who ceased to write; to be published, along with Tillie Olsen's other work, by Virago in the autumn.

Leonard Michaels and Christopher Ricks, eds., *The State of the Language* (University of California Press, £6.95): Large but quite inexpensively priced collection of essays registering observations about the state of the English language.

III. POETRY AND COLLECTIONS.

Len Fulton and Ellen Ferber, eds., *International Directory of Little Magazines and Small Presses,* 15th Edition, 1979-80 (Dustbooks, PO Box 1056, Paradise, California 95969, $11.95).

Robert Hass, John Matthias, James McMichael, John Peck, Robert Pinsky, *Five American Poets, An Anthology* (Cancanet, £3.25): Important British introduction of above five poets, unified by their voice and their background experience at Stanford in the sixties, working with Yvor Winters.

Michael Horovitz, *Growing Up: Selected Poems and Pictures 1951-1979* (Allison & Busby, £2.50): A collection representing Horovitz's development, enlivened by his drawing, paintings, snapshots, collages, and calligraphic 'picture-poems'.

Emma Tennant, ed., *Saturday Night Reader: Tales of Horror, Travellers' Tales, Tales of Adventure* (W.H. Allen, £5.95): A fascinatingly eclectic collection of stories, poems and 'conversations', including Ted Hughes' 'The Head' and J.G. Ballard's 'Having a Wonderful Time', an interview of 'Marcus Gutteridge at 80' by John Mortimer, and work from Angela Carter, Elaine Feinstein, and John Sladek.

John Gardner, *On Moral Fiction* (Basic Books, New York, $8.95): Idiosyncratic, often irritating critique of virtually every interesting American writer.

Elaine Feinstein, *The Silent Areas* (Hutchinson, £5.95): An impressive first collection of short stories, many of which are sensitive depictions of private, quite emotional suffering. Also an imaginative new rendering of the Hansel and Gretel tale.

NOTE: That books are listed here does not necessarily mean that they will not be discussed or reviewed in later issues.

Notes on Contributors

TONY TANNER is a Fellow of King's College, Cambridge, and the author of a number of books including *The Reign of Wonder, Naïvety and Reality in American Literature* and *City of Words, A Study of American Fiction in the Mid-Twentieth Century.* Johns Hopkins University Press has just published his latest book, *Adultery in the Novel: Contract and Transgression.*

GEORGE STEINER is Extraordinary Fellow of Churchill College, Cambridge, and Professor of English and comparative literature at the University of Geneva. He has also taught at Stanford, Princeton, Harvard and Yale, and has been the Albert Schweitzer Visiting Professor in the Humanities at New York University. His many books include *Tolstoy or Dostoevsky, The Death of Tragedy, In Bluebeard's Castle, Extraterritorial, After Babel, Language and Silence,* and most recently *On Difficulty.* He has also published a volume of short fiction to be re-issued shortly in America.

RICHARD GODDEN's poetry has been published in a number of journals and magazines. He teaches in the American Studies Department of Keele University.

JEREMY LANE received his M.A. from the University of Sussex, where he now lectures. His previously published short story 'Flight' was included in the *South East Arts Review.*

JEROME KLINKOWITZ is a Professor of English at the University of Northern Iowa. He is co-editor of *The Vonnegut Statement* and author of *Literary Disruptions, The Practice of Fiction in America,* and *The American 1960's.*

THOMAS REMINGTON lectures at the University of Northern Iowa, and has written a number of articles on science fiction. He is on the editorial board of *Extrapolation.*

DAVID MILLER teaches English and comparative literature at the University of California, Berkeley.

PETER ROBINSON lives with his wife in Cambridge. He has published three books of poetry, the latest of which is *A Part of Rosemary*. Forthcoming publications include *Overdrawn Account* (poetry), a translation of the poems of Pierra Reverdy, and an edition of Adrian Stokes poetry to be published by Carcanet Press.

ROBERT COOVER's novels include *The Origin of the Brunists*, *The Universal Baseball Association, Inc., J. Henry Waugh, Prop.*, *The Water Tower*, and *The Public Burning*. He has also published a collection of plays and *Pricksongs and Descants*, a collection of short stories. With his wife and three children, he has lived in England until this year, during which he has been teaching at Brown University in Rhode Island.

DAVID BLACK was educated at Amherst College and Columbia University. *Like Father*, his second novel, was published in 1978 by Red Dembner Enterprises in New York.

M.J. FITZGERALD was educated in Italy and England, where she received her B.A. from Sussex University and her B.Phil. in Medieval Studies from York. She is working in London, writing her first novel; 'Bachelor Life' is her first published story.

WALTER ABISH has published a volume of poetry and three books of fiction, *Alphabetical Africa, Minds Meet*, and *In the Future Perfect*. He received an Ingram Merril Fellowship for his novel *Sweet Truth*, to be published later this year by New Directions; he is also a recent recipient of a grant from the National Endowment of the Arts. He lives in New York City and teaches at Columbia University.

DAVID KATZ received his B.A. from the University of California, Berkeley. He now lives in New York working as an editor.

NORMAN BRYSON received his Ph.D. from Cambridge University, and is presently a Fellow of King's College. He has just completed a book on eighteenth-century French painting.

ROBERT BOYERS is the editor of the quarterly *Salmagundi* and Professor of English at Skidmore College. He is the author of recent books on Lionel Trilling and F.R. Leavis.

HEIDE ZIEGLER lectures at the University of Würzburg in West Germany. With Christopher Bigsby, she is compiling interviews of American and British authors, to be published eventually as a book.

JOHN BARTH was educated at the Juilliard School of Music in New York and at Johns Hopkins University, Baltimore, where he now teaches in The Writing Seminars. He is the author of several novels including *The Floating Opera*, *The Sot-Weed Factor*, *Giles Goat-Boy; or The Revised New Syllabus*. *Chimera*, a collection of three novellas, won the National Book Award in 1972. *LETTERS*, his first published fiction in seven years, will be published in England by Secker and Warburg at the end of May.

DON DAVID GUTTENPLAN is a graduate of Columbia University and a Kellett Fellow now studying at Clare College, Cambridge.

New American Writing. £1.50 including postage.
Individuals: £5.50 for one year, £12.50 for three.
Institutions: £7.00 for one year, £18.00 for three.

All prices include postage.

Name _____

Address _____

_____

Postal Code _____

For foreign subscriptions, add £2.00 per year for postage.

GRANTA

Box 666, King's College, Cambridge CB2 1ST

Granta is edited by William Buford, Pete de Bolla, Cathryn Gwynn, Jonathan Levi, and Michael Hoffman. Granta, Box 666, King's College, Cambridge CB2 1ST and 25 Claremont Avenue, New York, New York 10027